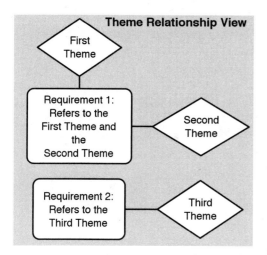

Theme Relationship View

First Theme

Requirement 1: Refers to the First Theme and the Second Theme

Second Theme

Requirement 2: Refers to the Third Theme

Third Theme

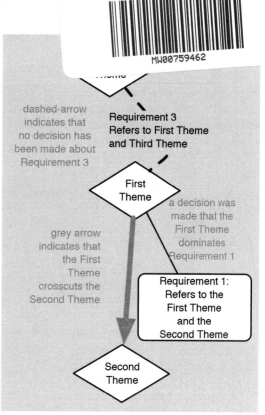

dashed-arrow indicates that no decision has been made about Requirement 3

Requirement 3 Refers to First Theme and Third Theme

First Theme

a decision was made that the First Theme dominates Requirement 1

grey arrow indicates that the First Theme crosscuts the Second Theme

Requirement 1: Refers to the First Theme and the Second Theme

Second Theme

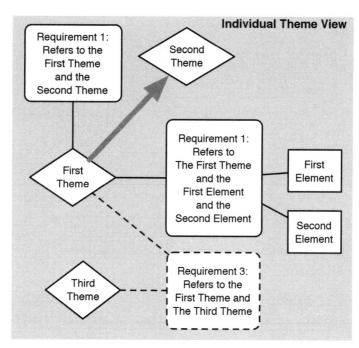

Individual Theme View

Requirement 1: Refers to the First Theme and the Second Theme

Second Theme

First Theme

Requirement 1: Refers to The First Theme and the First Element and the Second Element

First Element

Second Element

Third Theme

Requirement 3: Refers to the First Theme and The Third Theme

Praise for *Aspect-Oriented Analysis and Design*

"Developers who are using aspect-oriented programming will appreciate this contribution to aspect-oriented analysis and design. The authors are pioneers in this area and have elaborated on past research to produce a detailed methodology and notation for early aspects."

—RON BODKIN, CHIEF TECHNOLOGY OFFICER
New Aspects of Software

"Aspect-orientation is a powerful approach for programming complex systems. There is a lot to be gained from applying this approach during modeling and designing, as well. The Theme approach in this book represents an important advancement in AOP adoption by providing practitioners means to apply aspect-orientation early on."

—RAMNIVAS LADDAD
Author of Aspect J in Action

"Clarke & Baniassad have written an interesting book that shows how to use aspects to solve a difficult problem: composing independent program fragments with overlapping functionality. The included case studies well illustrate the principles. I recommend the book."

—CHARLES B. HALEY
Research Fellow, The Open University

"This book presents a very useful set of techniques for helping software developers to identify the aspects. I am sure that this book will rapidly become a landmark reference for the software community!"

—JOÃO M. FERNANDES
Ph.D., Universidade do Minho

Aspect-Oriented Analysis and Design

The Addison-Wesley Object Technology Series

Grady Booch, Ivar Jacobson, and James Rumbaugh, Series Editors
For more information, check out the series web site at www.awprofessional.com/otseries.

The Component Software Series

Clemens Szyperski, Series Editor
For more information, check out the series web site at www.awprofessional.com/csseries.

Aspect-Oriented Analysis and Design

The Theme Approach

Siobhán Clarke

Elisa Baniassad

✦✦Addison-Wesley

Upper Saddle River, NJ • Boston• Indianapolis • San Francisco
New York • Toronto • Montreal • London • Munich • Paris • Madrid
Capetown • Sydney • Tokyo • Singapore • Mexico City

The publisher offers excellent discounts on this book when ordered in quantity for bulk purchases or special sales, which may include electronic versions and/or custom covers and content particular to your business, training goals, marketing focus, and branding interests. For more information, please contact:

U. S. Corporate and Government Sales
(800) 382-3419
corpsales@pearsontechgroup.com

For sales outside the U. S., please contact:
International Sales
international@pearsoned.com

Visit us on the Web: www.awprofessional.com

Library of Congress Number: 2004117135

ISBN 0-321-24674-8

Text printed in the United States on recycled paper at R. R. Donnelley in Crawfordsville, Indiana.

First printing, March 2005.

Contents

Preface

Aspects are a natural evolution of the object-oriented paradigm. They provide a solution to some difficulties you may have encountered with modularizing your object-oriented code: sometimes functionality just doesn't fit! You've probably found yourself repeating the same lines of code in lots of different object-oriented classes because those classes each need that functionality, and so you can't easily wrap it up in a single place. Good examples of this kind of code are audit trails, transaction handling, concurrency management, and so on. You can now modularize such code with aspects.

We've seen similar levels of enthusiasm with adopting aspects as there were with adopting objects—an enthusiasm we share; but starting out with aspects can be a tricky business. Making the shift to aspect-oriented thinking may not be as tough as many people found the shift to object-oriented thinking, but aspects still might take a little getting used to. The big question that springs to mind when trying out aspect-orientation for the first time is "What are my aspects?" and early adopters have taken various approaches to try to address it.

We've heard of practitioners trying to apply aspects, but who can't think of any except those typical, and somewhat trivial ones. The usual examples are out there to be tried: logging, debugging, coordination. But to make fluent use of aspects, you also want to be able to use them for concerns that are specific to your own code.

We've heard of others who have made so many tiny aspects that the classes in their core system have no functionality whatsoever! They achieved so much "separation of concerns" that they could hardly work out the control-flow of their programs.

Another typical approach to answering the "what are my aspects" question is to just program vanilla OO code, and then try to spot the functionality that doesn't quite fit in. That approach has some serious disadvantages. In particular, it keeps you from being able to reason about aspects until you start to code. After all, you probably don't wait until you start to write code before figuring out what your classes should be (even if they're only a starting point). It's the same deal with aspects.

Besides being somewhat confusing, early adoption of a paradigm has some risks. Aspect-orientation is in an exciting phase of growth, but that means that new languages and new possibilities are coming out frequently, and that the basic notions of an "aspect" shifts subtly as new philosophies are revealed. There are different styles of decomposition, even within aspect-orientation. Which should you choose?

In this book we describe the Theme approach for identifying aspects in requirements, and modeling them at design. A major strength of the Theme approach is that it allows you to identify and model aspects regardless of the aspect-oriented programming language you choose. Our intention in developing the Theme approach was to enable it to withstand these shifts by keeping it separate from any particular programming language and by offering a general-purpose way to identify and describe aspects, regardless of their definition at the code level.

In addition to talking about the Theme approach and how to apply it, we also describe the different "worlds" of aspect-orientation, and how the Theme approach fits into them. You will come away from reading this book with not just tools for analysis and design, but also with an understanding of the general field of AO as it stands today. That knowledge will help you make more informed choices when picking an aspect-oriented implementation language, and decomposition paradigm.

Audience

For a wide range of situations, AOSD improves the software development process. This book offers a high-level introduction to the aspect-oriented approach, and gives instruction on a useful approach for identifying aspects in requirements, and for designing them in an aspect-oriented way using UML with a small number of extensions.

We have written this book for practitioners and early adopters of aspect-orientation. This book will be particularly helpful for those who are trying to answer the common questions of "What is an aspect?" and "Which aspects should I be coding?" This book gives you a starting point for thinking about aspects, and accounting for them in your requirements and design.

Even if you've been using aspect-oriented languages for a while, you can read this book to learn more about identifying aspect functionality in requirements documentation and how to plan for aspect-design and implementation. The Theme approach gives a flexible way to identify aspect-functionality, and a UML-based design modeling language that can describe aspects independently of programming language. Whatever your aspect-oriented programming language, the analysis and design approach and principles described in this book will be helpful and informative.

Of course, this book would also be helpful to academics or students wishing to learn more about the aspect-oriented paradigm.

For all readers, we assume that you are familiar with the object-oriented paradigm, and are comfortable with the UML notation.

History of Aspect-Oriented Analysis and Design and The Theme Approach

Analysis and design approaches for software engineering paradigms have traditionally emerged after people have explored the ideas at the programming level for a while. From there, application of the ideas tends to move backwards through the software lifecycle. This is true of aspect-oriented analysis and design and so before we look at the origins of Theme, we'll first take a quick look at what was happening at the code level from the early 1990s.

It's hard to choose where to begin a history of aspect-oriented programming, as a lot of the work we talk about as AOP emerged from the creators' previous work in the general area. We could also take a broader view in the larger context of software engineering, as many researchers have been working on improving software modularization for decades in work that is not viewed under the "Aspect" umbrella. We'll take the easy way out here, and simply mention the four main approaches to improved modularization that are popularly regarded as being the origins of aspect-oriented software development.

The most well known approach is the one popularized by the AspectJ language, which was first developed by a team from Xerox PARC in 1997, led by Gregor Kiczales. Previously, the team had worked on metaobject protocols and reflection, with ideas evolving to the modularisation of "crosscutting" concerns. Meanwhile, in 1993, a team from IBM T.J. Watson Research Center, led by William Harrison and Harold Ossher, published work on "subject-oriented programming". Subject-oriented programming (and its later incarnations as multi-dimensional separation of concerns co-led by Peri Tarr) looks at flexible decomposition and composition of software modules based on different dimensions of concern. The academic community was also hard at work; the next two approaches emerged from university research. At the University of Twente in The Netherlands, Mehmet Aksit and his team had been working on Composition Filters since the early 1990s. With this approach, behavior is modularized in "filters" that can be used to capture and enhance the execution of object behavior. Karl Lieberherr at Northeastern University in the US defined the Demeter Method in the mid 1990s that provides abstractions of the class structure and navigation to support better separation of this knowledge from an operation's behavior. Crista Lopes worked with both Karl Liberherr and Gregor Kiczales in developing D-Java, and the first official set of "Aspect languages" in 1997. Fast-forward to 2004 and aspect-oriented programming languages are coming out of the woodwork! Notably, though, each of the new ones is rooted in principles that originated from one or more of the original four.

Back to analysis and design. In those early years of aspect-oriented programming, there was little to no work being published on supporting aspect-like principles at earlier stages in the development lifecycle. The Theme approach to aspect-oriented design was the first approach to incorporate aspects into the UML, with Siobhán giving some early ideas their first "outing" at an OOPSLA workshop in 1997. Its further formulation was worked on in collaboration with IBM Research, in particular with Peri Tarr, Harold Ossher and William Harrison, and also with Robert Walker from (at the time) the University of British Columbia. The design model benefited considerably from subject-oriented programming principles to the extent that it was labeled "subject-oriented design" for a few years. However, as you'll see reading this book, we see the Theme approach as encompassing different aspect schools of thought, and so Siobhán re-labeled the work on "subject-oriented design" to "Theme/UML" in 2001.

Identifying and visualizing concerns in documentation was initially explored by Elisa with Gail Murphy of University of British Columbia, and Christa Schwanninger of Siemens AG. That work motivated Theme/Doc's emergence in 2003 as the aspect-oriented analysis part of the Theme approach. Theme/Doc is intended as a complement to your existing analysis process, and is the missing link between having a set of requirements, and knowing what aspects should be designed using Theme/UML.

In forming the Theme approach, we kept in mind the real goals of the programmer: to understand the problem space (the requirements), and design appropriately. Our goal was to create an approach that allows the developer to map requirements to design to code. Theme/Doc and Theme/UML provide this mechanism. Theme/Doc helps you find the aspects in your requirements. Theme/UML helps you design them. Together, they form the Theme approach.

How to Read This Book

Of course, the most straightforward way to read this book is from start to finish. The book follows the basic structure of introduction and motivation (Chapters 1 and 2), overview and illustration of the approach (Chapters 3-6), guidance on mapping your designs to some AOP languages in Chapter 7 and examples of its application (Chapters 8 and 9).

However, different parts of the book may be of more interest than others, depending on your perspective. If you're not sure what an aspect even is, then Chapters 1, 3 and 4 will be of lots of help. They go over the basic concepts and walk you through finding aspects in a set of requirements.

If you're not convinced aspects are all that great, and are asking the question "Why do we need them anyway?" then Chapter 2 will be for you. Chapters 8 and 9 will also provide you with examples of how aspects can be applied in different kinds of systems.

If you'd like instruction on capturing aspects in design, then Chapters 5 and 6, which provide details of Theme/UML will walk you through designing the aspects and the core of your system, and on capturing the specification of their composition.

Acknowledgments

We very gratefully acknowledge the assistance of many people in the writing of this book.

Several people contributed to the technical content. Mary Lee worked on applying the Theme approach in the early stages. Andrew Jackson contributed most of the code samples in the book. Harold Ossher and William Harrison contributed the CME code. Alan Gray, David McKitterick, Tonya McMorrow, Karl Quinn, and Conor Ryan were on the development team of the original Crystal Game on which the book's example is based. Christa Schwanninger and Ivana Dusparic advised and contributed the case studies. We had interesting discussions with Vinny Cahill on developing peer-to-peer systems.

We also thank those who reviewed copies of the manuscript throughout its creation: Ron Bodkin, Adrian Colver, Yvonne Coady, João M. Fernandes, Charles Haley, Paul Holser, Wes Isberg, Gregor Kiczales, Ramnivas Laddad, Awais Rashid, Ryan van Roode, Michael J. Ward, and Tim Walsh.

Throughout the history of the Theme approach, William Harrison, Stuart Kent, Michael Kircher, Gail Murphy, John Murphy, Harold Ossher, Christa Schwanninger, Peri Tarr, and Robert Walker were invaluable influencers and contributors, for which we are indebted.

Finally, we thank all at Addison-Wesley for making this possible: Kristy Hart, Brenda Mulligan, Mary O'Brien, Kerry Reardon, and Chris Zahn.

About the Authors

Siobhán Clarke

Siobhán Clarke is a lecturer at Trinity College, Dublin. She holds BS (1986) and PhD (2000) degrees from Dublin City University. Siobhán worked for IBM Ireland Ltd. in various leading software engineering roles from 1986 to 1997. In 1997, she started her PhD, which was based on extending the modularization and composition capabilities of UML. This work evolved into Theme/UML.

Siobhán's current research focus is on design and programming models for mobile, context-aware systems. The complexities associated with developing such systems require advanced software engineering techniques. In particular, she is investigating and extending aspect-oriented software development (AOSD) techniques as a means to address these complexities.

Siobhán has served on the program committees of AOSD and UML conferences, and on the organizing committees for AOSD, and MoDELS. She has co-organized and/or been on the program committee for multiple workshops at conferences such as OOPSLA, ECOOP, ICSE, AOSD, and UML in the area of design and programming models and context-aware computing. She is on the editorial boards of IEEE Internet Computing and the Springer Transactions on AOSD.

Elisa Baniassad

Elisa Baniassad is a professor at the Chinese University of Hong Kong. She received her PhD in 2002 from the University of British Columbia, Canada, where she worked with Gail Murphy. Elisa then carried out a postdoctoral fellowship, funded by the National Science and Engineering Council of Canada and held at Trinity College, Dublin.

Elisa first became intrigued by the AO world during a visit to Xerox PARC in 1997 while involved in some of the earliest empirical work on AOP. She then began looking at concerns in documentation with her PhD work on Design Pattern Rationale Graphs: finding concerns in design patterns text and tracing them through design to code. This work included broader research into how programmers relate to both their code and to the documentation upon which they rely. Her main group of victims were gathered by Christa Schwanninger of Siemens AG.

She then turned to investigating how to bridge from requirements to aspect-oriented design and started research on Theme/Doc. That work is currently ongoing, involving empirical studies of programmers and tool development.

Elisa is involved in several software engineering conferences and has served on the organizing and/or program committees of OOPSLA, ECOOP, and AOSD. She has also published papers at these conferences as well as at ICSE. Elisa is an organizer of the Early Aspects workshop that is typically held at AOSD and OOPSLA.

1

Introduction

You've probably picked up this book because you've heard that aspects will solve difficulties you're having with writing your object-oriented software. You've heard that aspects offer a new way to modularize your code, but you're here because you have questions like, *What are aspects? Why do I need them? Are objects obsolete?* Or perhaps you've picked up this book because you've tried programming with an aspect-oriented language and are interested in delving more deeply into the paradigm. You may have questions like, *How do I plan for aspects before design and implementation?* and *How do I design aspects so that I can better plan for implementation?* This book answers these questions and also guides you through the process of identifying and designing your aspects.

Software Development and the Object-Oriented Paradigm

Few would disagree that the object-oriented paradigm is one of the most important contributions to software development in its history. Those of us who remember developing software without objects most keenly appreciate their value. Everything to do with a "thing" is all in one place! When we want a "thing" we already have in one application to be used in another application, we can just pick it up and use it! And there are many more benefits besides.

To this day, we both remain big fans of objects. But of all the benefits associated with object-oriented development, the two of encapsulation and reuse that we hinted at above were not selected lightly. Can we really always put everything to do with a thing all in one place? Have you ever found that there was some piece of processing that did not seem to fit in any one particular class, and yet it did not feel as if it belonged in a class in its own right either? This is probably because it was too tightly coupled to behaviors in many other classes.

Think about, for example, objects that require some transaction management. It is difficult, if not impossible, to modularize all setup, communication with a transaction manager, and rolling back that may be needed to handle transactions. This is because all objects (or methods in objects) that require transaction management need to be aware that their operation is impacted by a transaction context and must behave accordingly. In other words, transaction-handling code must be placed in every object that needs it. Take a look at the code you've written in the past, and you will probably find many examples of similar (if not the same) pieces of code repeated in different places. The common, though compromised, solution to a problem like transaction management is to copy the code into the different places that need it. Code copying then results in poor modularization for much of your code and leaves you with considerable maintenance and evolution headaches. This phenomenon is also known as *scattering*, as code for a concern is scattered across multiple parts of the system.

In addition, from a reuse perspective, modules that contain code relating to many concerns are likely to be less generally useful in different situations. The phenomenon where multiple concerns are intermixed in the code is known as *tangling*.

Of course, good use of design patterns will help you encapsulate in many situations, but you will find the repetition and concern-mixing phenomena even where design patterns are well used. Ultimately, you will always encounter processing that relates to and impacts upon many portions of a system.

The Case for Aspects

> *We know that a program must be correct and we can study it from that viewpoint only; we also know that it should be efficient and we can study its efficiency on another day. . . . But nothing is gained—on the contrary—by tackling these various aspects simultaneously. It is what I sometimes have called "the separation of concerns."*

—EDSGER DIJKSTRA[1]

Aspect-oriented programming (AOP)[2] was introduced to provide a solution to the scattering and tangling described above. It is often described as liberating developers from the *hegemony of the dominant decomposition*.[3] Simply put, this means that whichever modularity you choose (objects, functions, etc.) will at some point impose unwanted constraints on your design. In the object-oriented case, the dominant decomposition is the modularity of classes, and methods. The hegemony refers to the fact that when pinned to object-orientation, developers are forced to make design decisions that lead to scattering and tangling. In some cases, developers must be able to break out of that modularity and design code that *crosscuts* an object model.

AOP allows a developer to program those crosscutting portions of a system separately from any of these structural entities. Even though in its infancy, AOP has proven to be of great use in modularizing source code and has provided a wide spectrum of benefits, from performance enhancement to more evolvable code. Aspect-oriented languages provide support for programming such crosscutting concerns, or *aspects*, in one place and then automatically propagating the behavior to the many appropriate points of execution in the code. In this way, aspects allow a developer to specify behavior that overlays an existing class model.

---

[1] "On the role of scientific thought," *EWD*. 477, 30 August 1974, Neuen, The Netherlands.

[2] G. Kiczales, J. Lamping, A. Mendhekar, C. Maeda, C. Lopes, J.-M. Loingtier, and J. Irwin. "Aspect-Oriented Programming." In *ECOOP'97—Object-Oriented Programming*, 11th European Conference, LNCS 1241, pp. 220–242, 1997.

[3] P. Tarr, H. Ossher, W. Harrison, and S. M. Sutton, Jr., "N Degrees of Separation: Multidimensional Separation of Concerns," *Proc. ICSE 99*, IEEE, Los Angeles, May 1999, ACM press, pp. 107–119.

However, aspects certainly should not be used as the hammer for every nail. Just as considering when to use inheritance, it is important to consider when an aspect is an appropriate choice for some functionality. Nonetheless, aspect-orientation has been shown, when used properly and appropriately, to transform necessarily hairy code into something manageable and reasonable.

What Is an Aspect?

Simply put, an aspect is a particular kind of concern. A concern is any code related to a goal, feature, concept, or "kind" of functionality. An aspect is a concern whose functionality is triggered by other concerns, and in multiple situations. If the concern was not separated into an aspect, its functionality would have to be triggered explicitly within the code related to the other concern and so would tangle the two concerns together. Additionally, because the triggering is in multiple places, the triggers would be scattered throughout the system.

There are many examples of behavior like this—indeed, any functionality that has policies that need to be carried out in different modules of an object-oriented code base are likely candidates.

We've already described transaction management as an example of such code. Another typical example is logging or tracing code, since to add tracing code to a system, many locations must be modified, and every time the tracing scheme is changed, all those locations have to be altered. Another example is synchronization code, which is painful to implement, since it requires a developer to visit each method to be synchronized and add the necessary locking and unlocking functionality. Any code that may be needed in multiple places has the potential to be problematic. Having a programming model that means such code only needs to be written once and is in only one place when it requires change or deletion provides an obvious gain for the developer.

Aspects are not just a neat trick for adding logging or synchronization or other simple functionality. Such an assumption would be analogous to thinking of object-orientation as simply a means of organizing source code files. Aspects are a programmatic construct in and of themselves. Aspects provide active support, not just textual code manipulation, for separating concerns in source code. Aspects have been applied to far more complex crosscutting concerns than synchronization, logging, and tracing. For example, they have been applied in operating systems as a way to encapsulate and improve their performance.[4]

Let's look at a small example. In any banking system, almost all changes to the balance of an account affect more than one place—for example, transferring funds requires debiting one account and crediting another; interest to be credited to a customer account implies a liability to the bank's ledger (its own account); charges on a customer account imply a corresponding bonanza to the bank's ledger. These are classic examples of transactions that must complete in entirety to be valid. Figure 1–1 illustrates simplified code for these examples.

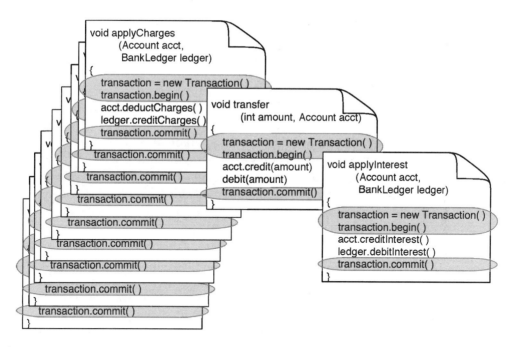

Figure 1–1 *Transaction handling occurring in multiple places.*

---

[4] "Back to the Future: A Retroactive Study of Aspect Evolution in Operating System Code." Yvonne Coady and Gregor Kiczales. In *Proceedings of the International Conference on Aspect-Oriented Software Development 2003.*

In Figure 1–1, each of the places where transaction handling occurs in each sequence of actions is circled. As you can see, transaction functionality is present in multiple places in the code. Because transaction handling is triggered in different situations by other concerns (such as money transfer, account updating, interest charging), transaction handling should, for this system, be implemented as an aspect.

Aspects can also be evident at earlier phases of the development lifecycle. Aspects manifest in requirements as behavior that is *described* as being triggered by many other behaviors. Requirements that described the banking system, for instance, would have mentioned that transaction handling was required for a range of activities, including managing interest, transferring money, and so on. Aspects manifest in UML designs as behavioral design elements that are triggered by other behavioral design elements in the UML models. Designs that describe the banking system would have transaction behavior tangled in the behavioral models for the banking activities.

Why Consider Aspects in Analysis and Design?

As with systems in any programming paradigm, aspect-oriented systems need to be designed with good software engineering practices in mind. The analysis and design of a system are at least as important as the implementation itself, and many professionals consider these phases to be more significant in their contribution to the success of a project as a whole.

In any development effort, it is helpful for a developer to be able to consider the structure of the final implementation at all stages of the software lifecycle. Otherwise, the developer would have to make a mental leap to get from a particular way of encoding design to another way of coding the software. In other words, developers must be able to easily map their designs to the code in order for the design to continue to make sense during the development lifecycle.

In addition to seamless traceability between the design and code, we also consider the benefits of separating aspects in the design for the design's own sake. The same benefits derived at the code level through applying aspect orientation can be derived at the design level. In the infancy of aspect orientation, developers simply used object-oriented methods and languages (such as standard UML) for designing their aspects. This proved difficult, as standard UML was not designed to provide constructs to describe aspects: Trying to design aspects using object-oriented modeling techniques proved as problematic as trying to implement aspects using objects. Without the design constructs to separate crosscutting functionality, similar difficulties in modularizing the designs occur, with similar maintenance and evolution headaches. We need special support for designing aspects, as we can then improve the design process and provide better traceability to aspect-oriented code.

A similar set of problems arises when analyzing requirements documentation to determine how to design a system. Approaches for decomposing requirements from an object-oriented perspective simply don't go far enough when trying to plan for aspect orientation. Heuristics and tools to support such an examination are helpful to the developer.

Aspects and Other Concerns

In the world of aspect-oriented language development, aspects have taken on different forms. Two are most prominent: the *asymmetric* and the *symmetric* approaches.

Asymmetric Separation

In the *asymmetric* school of thought, aspects are separate from the core functionality of a program. Aspects are encoded as events that are triggered before, after, or as a replacement for certain other events, or in certain situations are located in the core. They describe additional dynamic behavior of a system that will have an effect on the core functionality. In a distributed system, for instance, there may be a collection of domain-specific objects that need to be managed in terms of distribution, synchronization, and transaction management.

The core contains the structure and behavior relevant to the domain functionality of the system. Separate from that core are aspects like the distribution of the objects in the system, the synchronization scheme associated with the methods belonging to those objects, and the wrapping of a set of operations into a single transaction. These are described in a separate module (each in its own aspect) and are invoked at certain strategic points in the execution of the core of the program. For instance, before certain methods are executed, the synchronization aspect may be used. Or, transaction-handling processing is initiated before and after the set of operations that make up a single transaction. In our banking example, as illustrated in Figure 1–2, the *core* is the set of banking-specific classes, and the *aspect* is a separate transaction handling entity.

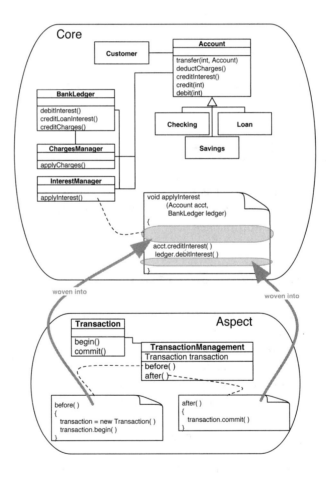

Figure 1–2   *Aspects and core in the asymmetric paradigm.*

At a conceptual level, aspects have two important properties in this scheme. First, the aspect will only be triggered because of some execution in the core—for example, transaction handling is required only when changes are made to the balances of accounts. Second, the aspect is highly likely to be triggered in many parts of the system—it really is not generally all that useful to separate design/code into an aspect if it is executed in only one part of a system.

Table 1–1 provides definitions of the terms as typically used in this paradigm.

Table 1–1 *Definition of Terms in the Asymmetric Separation Paradigm*

Term	Description
Crosscutting	Concern behavior that is triggered in multiple situations.
Advice	The triggered behavior.
Aspect	The encapsulation of the advice and the specification of where the advice is triggered.
Core	The traditional object-oriented part of the system to which aspects are applied.
Joinpoint	A possible execution point that triggers advice.
Pointcut	A predicate that can determine, for a given joinpoint, whether it is matched by the predicate
Weaving	Applying the advice to the core at the joinpoints that match the pointcut statements in the aspects.

Symmetric Separation

In the symmetric separation model, in addition to the modularization of aspects, the core as described above is also analyzed for further modularization. Consider the core banking system from Figure 1–1. This example illustrates a small amount of real banking functionality with three basic features or concerns: transferring funds between two accounts, applying charges to an account, and applying interest to an account. In a real banking system, not only are there many other features, but these three features are subject to a significant number of banking rules. These rules depend on many different properties, such as the type of account, type of customer, legal and tax concerns (national/EU or state/federal, etc.), and so on. Figure 1–3 illustrates how it is possible that each feature is likely to result in many other methods that are likely to have an impact across the core set of banking classes.

Figure 1–3 necessarily depicts just a small proportion of the possible impact of each of these three features on the classes. As you can see, there are multiple methods in the account classes that handle the business rules. The Checking, Savings, and Loan classes all have many methods related to checking charges and checking interest. It may appear as if those could just be swept into the Account superclass. Unfortunately, that's not the case. Each of the accounts handles those rules very differently, and so the functionality has to be present in each of them.

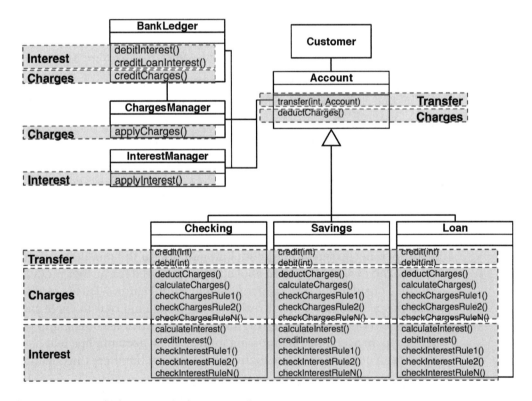

Figure 1–3   *Multiple concerns in the asymmetric core.*

We hope you can visualize the potential real impact of including the full behavior not just of these three features, but also of all banking features on the core system. In the symmetric paradigm, different features of the system can be modularized into separate programs, as illustrated at the design level in Figure 1–4.

An entire system is therefore made up of bits of separate functionality that could be thought of as features or concerns. These can then be recombined in various ways to form a functioning whole. With this approach, a set of distributed objects would be formed by composing bits of basic object functionality together with bits of distribution functionality and synchronization functionality and transaction functionality.

At first glance, the duplication present in the symmetric approach looks as if it actually worsens scattering. For instance, all of the concerns except for the Transaction Management concern in Figure 1–4 have an `Account` class as well as a `Checking` class, a `Savings` class, and a `Loan` class. This duplication is required in the symmetric approach in order to provide a complete *view* of the system from the perspective of a particular concern. The completeness of the view enhances separate understandability of a particular concern in the system.[5] This understandability is achieved through increases in *locality*: Only and all relevant functionality for a concern is present within the concern module. Concern maintainability is also considered enhanced because of this functional locality. It is true that altering every method belonging to a class would require visiting many concerns, but since maintenance efforts are often performed to address particular concerns, the locality of all concern functionality within an identifiable group of modules is actually a help to system maintainability.

Of course, the symmetric approach can be applied on a continuum. It is unnecessary to keep minute concerns separate, just as it is unnecessary to bundle all the core concerns together. This spectrum is one that the developer is encouraged to explore, as each extreme has its own trade-offs and advantages.

---

[5] *Asymmetrically vs. Symmetrically Organized Paradigms for Software Composition.* W. H. Harrison, H. L. Ossher, P. L. Tarr, IBM Research Division, Thomas J. Watson Research Center. RC22685 (W0212-147) December 30, 2002.

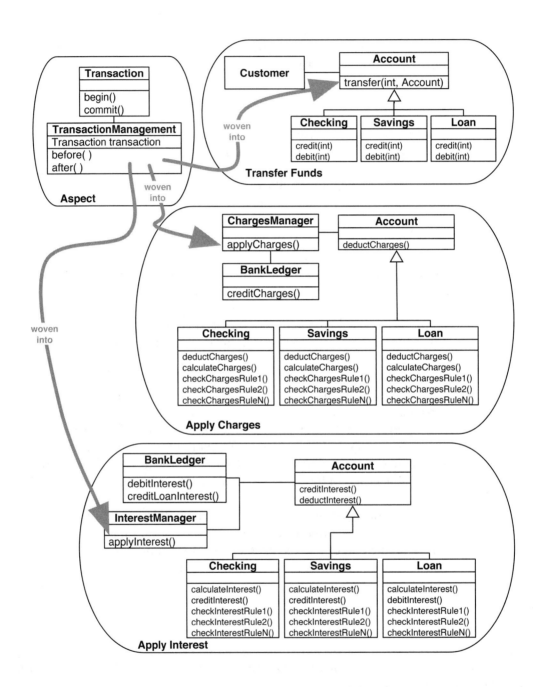

Figure 1–4 *Separation of different features in the symmetric paradigm.*

The terms for the symmetric approach are given in Table 1–2. Notice that the terminology for this approach is different from the asymmetrical approach described above. Crosscutting, for instance, takes a wider stance: that it is widely triggered functionality, but also that structure and behavior (concepts) related to a particular concern are scattered throughout the system.

Table 1–2 *Definition of Terms in the Symmetric Separation Paradigm*

Term	Definition
Concern	Some "kind" of functionality in your system. This could be a feature or a type of processing.
Crosscutting	A concern triggered in multiple situations or whose structure and behavior are scattered across the code base and tangled with code related to other concerns.
Composition	Combining the separately implemented concerns to form a functioning system.

The Theme Approach

In this book, we cover how to identify aspects in a set of requirements and how to model them in UML style designs. The methodology we introduce here is the *Theme* approach to analysis and design. The terminology we use is a hybrid of the symmetrical and asymmetrical paradigms. The terminology is described in Table 1–3. Grayed-out cells in the table indicate that the term is not used in the particular paradigm.

What Is a Theme?

The word *theme* should not be considered a synonym for *aspect*. Themes are more general than aspects and more closely encompass concerns as described above for the symmetric approach. We view each piece of functionality or aspect or concern a developer might have as a separate theme to be catered to in the system. You can see in Table 1–3 that a concern is described as "Some 'kind' of functionality in your system. This could be a feature or a type of processing," and a theme is described as "An encapsulation of a concern."

Table 1–3 *Definition of Terms as Used in This Book*

Term	Theme Approach Definition	Asymmetric Separation Definition	Symmetric Separation Definition
Concern	Some "kind" of functionality in your system. This could be a feature or a type of processing.		
Theme	An encapsulation of a concern.		
Crosscutting	Triggered in multiple situations.		Triggered or located in multiple places.
Concern Scattering	When the behavior related to a concern is found in more than one class		One kind of crosscutting.
Crosscutting theme	A theme that has some behavior triggered by other themes in multiple situations.		
Concept sharing theme	A theme that describes domain concepts also described in another theme, though from its own perspective. Solves difficulties associated with concern scattering.		One kind of concern.
Aspect	A crosscutting theme parameterized to handle the triggers for its behavior. Solves crosscutting.		A concern, whether triggered or not.
Base	Base theme: the theme that triggers any aspect's behavior The base: themes that trigger a particular aspect's behavior and themes that are not aspects.	The core: traditional OO design into which aspects are woven.	
Composition	Combining themes based on a composition relationship.	Weaving an aspect into the core.	Combining concerns based on a composition relationship
Merging	Merging themes that share concepts and composing base and aspect themes.		One kind of composition.
Binding	Specifying the triggers of the aspect from the base.	Weaving an aspect into the core.	

For example, the three banking-related features and the transaction-handling component in Figure 1–4 are four separate themes. Themes can encapsulate aspect behavior (behavior that is triggered in multiple situations), but can also encapsulate non-aspect concern functionality.

At the requirements level, a theme is a subset of the responsibilities described in a set of requirements. At the design level, themes include the structure and behavior needed to carry out their requirements-level responsibilities.

Relationships Between Themes

Themes may be related to each other in the same way as requirements or features or aspects are related to other parts of the system. Such relationships may cause overlaps in the themes. There are two ways in which themes can relate: by sharing concepts and by crosscutting.

Concept Sharing

The first category of relationship is *concept sharing*, where different themes have design elements that represent the same core concepts in the domain (see Figure 1–5). Take, for example, the **transfer funds**, **apply charges,** and **apply interest** features in Figure 1–4. Each of these three features works with `Account`—all three work with `Checking` and `Savings` accounts, while two

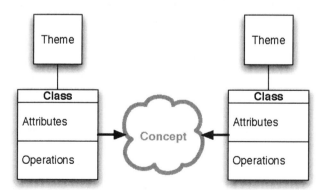

Figure 1–5 *Themes related by concept sharing.*

of them also work with Loan accounts. Each theme contains specifications for those same concepts designed from the perspective of the theme. Another way of looking at concept sharing is to think of it, at some level, as "structure" sharing. Strictly speaking, though, we don't consider that themes actually "share" structure because each theme will have its own version as appropriate to the feature under design. Encapsulation in this manner has the benefit of locality, where only and all relevant functionality for a concern is present in a theme.

Concept sharing is one category of crosscutting in the symmetric separation paradigm, as is shown in Table 1–3. Concept sharing is not discussed in the asymmetric separation paradigm. Encapsulation in this manner has the benefit of locality, where only and all relevant functionality for a concern is present in a theme.

Crosscutting

The second category of relationship is the asymmetrical *crosscutting*, where behavior in one theme is triggered by behavior in other themes. Transaction handling from Figure 1–4 is an example of such a theme. Table 1–3 shows that this definition is shared with the asymmetrical separation approach and is considered "one kind of crosscutting" in the symmetrical separation approach.

Throughout the book, we use the terms *base theme, crosscutting theme,* and *aspect theme*. Aspect and crosscutting themes are used synonymously and are always themes that have behavior triggered in tandem with behavior in other themes. Aspects in the Theme approach are the same as aspects in the asymmetric separation approach.

Base themes are the themes that trigger aspect themes. They might be themes that share concepts with other themes, and they might be aspects themselves and have their own base. We also sometimes talk about a base that is the result of a composition of other themes to which we then apply an aspect (see Figure 1–6).

As seen in Table 1–3, we don't use the term *core* in relation to themes, since we consider a core, in the sense of the asymmetric separation paradigm, to be made up of multiple bases. In this we adhere to the symmetrical approach.

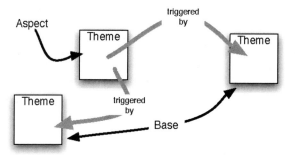

Figure 1–6 *Themes related by crosscutting: The base theme triggers the aspect theme.*

Applying the Theme Approach

The Theme approach is made up of two portions: Theme/Doc, which is a set of heuristics for analysis of software requirements documentation, and Theme/UML, which is a way to write themes (both aspects and base) as UML. In this section, we present a high-level overview of the activities involved in applying the Theme approach. These activities are depicted in Figure 1–7.

Analyzing Requirements with Theme/Doc

At the requirements level, themes are "responsible" for certain functionality described in the requirements document. Themes at this point are, essentially, named subsets of requirements.[6]

Theme/Doc (which stands for Themes in Documentation) is the part of the Theme approach that assists in identifying themes in requirements documents. It also provides heuristics for identifying which of those themes are crosscutting, or aspects.

---

[6] Requirements can take any form as long as they contain text. For instance, they can be entire use cases or sentences within use cases. In this book, we talk about them as though they're individual sentences in an informally written document.

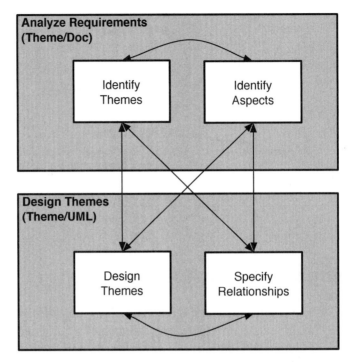

Figure 1-7 *High-level view of the Theme approach activities.*

The Theme/Doc analysis process has two main activities: (1) identifying the main themes in your system, and (2) determining whether the responsibilities of a certain theme mean that it should be modeled as an aspect. You interleave these two activities (theme identification and aspect identification) to plan for design or accommodate changes as your system evolves.

Starting Out

The process begins with determining an initial set of themes. These might be just a set of concerns you think seem important at first glance. Or, if you've already applied a requirements analysis approach and have a set of features or concerns readily in mind, then using those might make sense.

The Theme/Doc tool provides graphical depictions of relationships between requirements and themes. Figure 1–8 shows a stylized Theme/Doc view. You can see in the figure that diamonds represent themes and rounded boxes show the text of a requirement. If a requirement's text mentions a theme's name (or any term considered its synonym), it is linked to that theme. Unless at some point later in the process you sever the link, the theme is responsible for that requirement. For instance, both requirements attached to the transfer theme in Figure 1–8 mention transfer, so they are linked to it in the view.

Theme Identification

The *theme identification* activity involves iterating over the themes until you have a set you think makes sense. This process involves looking at the responsibilities of each theme to see whether, together, they represent a coherent set of behavior.

Aspect Identification

To identify aspects using the Theme approach, you look for tangling in the requirements. Two themes are tangled if they *share a requirement*. You can see an example of a shared requirement in Figure 1–8. The shared requirement mentions both **transaction handling** and **transfers**.

If two concerns are described together in a requirement, their responsibilities may be tangled. However, identifying tangling alone is not enough to

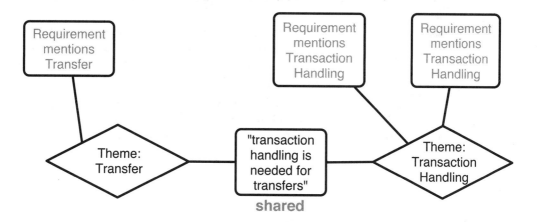

Figure 1–8 *Stylized Theme/Doc relationship view.*

identify an aspect. To locate an aspect, you ask several *aspect identification questions* about the shared requirement:

1. *Can the requirement be split up to isolate themes?* If it can, you could rewrite the requirement to better divide responsibilities between themes. The shared requirement in Figure 1–8 could not be split up and still remain an actual sentence.

2. *Is one theme dominant in the requirement?* If so, then the dominant theme should likely be responsible for that requirement rather than the requirement being shared between themes. *Transaction handling* dominates the shared requirement in Figure 1–8, since the requirement mainly talks about when transaction handling is needed.

3. *Is behavior of the dominant theme triggered by the other themes mentioned in the requirement?* If so, then you have identified a trigger relationship between two themes. **Transaction handling** behavior is triggered by the initiation of a **transfer**: When a transfer occurs, transaction handling is needed and so triggered.

4. *Is the dominant theme triggered in multiple situations?* If, across the requirements, the dominant theme is described as triggered in multiple situations, then it is crosscutting. The dominant theme becomes the aspect, and the triggering themes become the base. **Transaction handling** is needed in different situations (for transfers, for adding interest, etc.). **Transaction handling** is an aspect.

As mentioned above, theme and aspect identification activities are interleaved, as newly split requirements give way to new themes and as new themes give rise to newly shared requirements. If, as they often are, the requirements are live and changing, then new themes and responsibilities for themes will arise after you've moved on to design and implementation. Design and implementation may also cause you to revisit the choices you made about theme responsibilities, so you would come back and shift things around.

Designing Themes with Theme/UML

Theme/UML allows separate design models for each of the themes identified in the requirements. It is grounded in some important steps of aspect-oriented software development: modularize, relate, and compose.

Design the Themes

From a modularization perspective, the themes that were identified using Theme/Doc can be designed separately regardless of whether one theme crosscuts another or whether there are other kinds of overlaps in the themes. Examples of overlaps other than crosscutting might be when some core domain concept (perhaps associated with particular classes), such as loan account or savings account, is relevant for multiple themes. When designing the different themes, you need not be concerned with overlaps.

You can see in Figure 1–9 that each of the banking concerns described earlier is captured in its own theme.

You will use almost entirely standard UML to design each theme from its own perspective. All the classes and methods pertinent to each of those concerns would be designed within the themes, essentially as depicted in

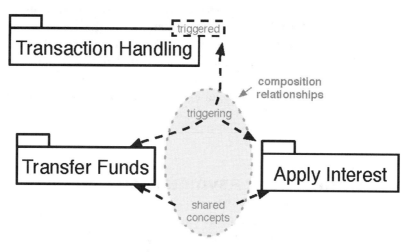

Figure 1–9   *Stylized Theme/UML composition.*

Figure 1–4. This is a considerable strength of the Theme approach. When you want to work with a single feature or concern, you have just one place to go—the theme. Within the theme, not only is every design element relevant for the concern, you can also be sure that you don't have to go anywhere else to find other relevant design elements. Aspect themes use a little nonstandard UML to capture parameterization of the behavior that is triggered by a base theme (shown as "triggered" in Figure 1–9).

Specify the Relationships

Where you will primarily notice some differences with the standard UML is in the area of specifying the relationships between the themes and in the composition capabilities that Theme/UML defines. In all aspect-oriented approaches, there must be a way to designate how the modularized concerns relate to the rest of the system. To provide this capability, Theme/UML has defined a new kind of relationship, called a *composition relationship,* that allows you to identify those parts of the theme designs that relate to each other and therefore should be *composed.* For themes that crosscut others, this means identifying when and where in those other themes the additional dynamic behavior should occur (shown as triggering in Figure 1–9). For other kinds of overlaps, this means identifying elements in the theme designs that correspond to each other and saying how they should be integrated (shown as shared concepts in Figure 1–9).

Theme/UML also provides semantics for model composition based on the composition-relationship specification. We think of this as a verification step to allow you to have a look at the overall system design, including the composition specification, to ensure that it makes sense. Of course, the composed design will have all the poor modularization that we've been trying to avoid! The developer can then take a step back and revisit the separate Theme/UML models with a view to implementation.

Theme: Symmetric or Asymmetric?

The Theme approach more closely aligns with the symmetric approach to system decomposition, since themes are individual concerns regardless of whether they are aspects or separated concerns that would be located in the core. However, the terms crosscutting and aspect are defined as in the asymmetric paradigm: as functionality that is triggered in multiple situations.

As we mentioned above, however, the symmetric decomposition described in this book does not dictate unnecessarily tiny concerns. In this book, we look at several examples: Some that have many concerns and some (particularly the final case study of the book) that have a more solid base. The important thing about the Theme approach is that you should choose the degree of separation that is right for you and your situation. The heuristics for aspect identification described above are the same regardless of whether you intend to implement your system using a symmetrical or an asymmetrical decomposition approach. Similarly, Theme/UML models can encompass functionality related to either a fine-grained concern or to the entire core functionality of your system.

Fitting Theme into Your Existing Development Process

The analysis and design activities described in the Theme approach can be split up and molded to fit into whichever development process you are happiest using. Later, in Chapter 3, "The Theme Approach," we briefly outline how that might work. Fitting the Theme approach into processes such as the iterative and waterfall approaches is quite straightforward. Figuring out how to work them into the family of agile processes[7] deserves further discussion. In Chapter 3, we go into some of the processes in more detail. Here, however, we discuss analysis and design in the context of agile processes from a high-level point of view.

The use of Theme/UML in agile processes mirrors the relationship between standard UML and agile processes, which is a much larger question. After sifting through rhetoric from experts on both sides (UML is crucial versus UML is useless), we found words of wisdom that struck many chords with us—Martin Fowler's paper entitled "Is Design Dead?"[8] which we highly recommend.

---

[7] Agile processes attempt to dispense with "heavyweight" development processes and focus on a lightweight approach that values immediate results over lengthy planning.

[8] Available from http//:www.martinfowler.com.

What we have taken from the "Is Design Dead?" article is that if you are the type of developer to find diagrams helpful, then you will continue to do so with agile processes, and if you are not, then you won't. In addition, it is especially important to recognize that diagrams can "actually cause harm" and therefore should be used judiciously. The use of diagrams has potential value from a number of perspectives: communication; as a means to explore a design before you start coding it; and documentation both ongoing and for handover situations. From a Theme approach perspective, we paraphrase or steal directly from "Is Design Dead?" in the following list of recommendations for managing both Theme/Doc and Theme/UML diagrams in an agile process environment:

- Capture the interesting analysis and design decisions in the diagrams. Not every class in every theme may be interesting and not every attribute or method in an interesting class may be interesting. Do, however, consider capturing all the composition relationships and crosscutting behaviors during your exploration phase.

- Keep the analysis diagrams and designs only as long as they are useful. Don't be afraid to throw away diagrams that have become outdated through refactoring or other reasons—they were useful for a time, but you can let them go. Since Theme/Doc views are automatically regenerated, generate new ones when changes occur.

- When you are coding, if you think diagrams would be useful for communication outside the immediate team or for capturing a point in time, then re-create them for that purpose.

- Even if you fall into the category of people who don't really find diagrams useful, bear in mind that there are others who do, and so when you are handing over the system to other people, then diagrams that represent the current state of the code may be appreciated.

What About Implementation?

The focus of this book is on aspect-oriented analysis of requirements and aspect-oriented design. Other books may be of better service if you're looking for detailed information about implementation in aspect-oriented languages. However, we spend a chapter delving into how you might follow to code from the analysis and design process described above.

There are two ways in which developers may implement a system designed using the approach presented here. As a developer, you may choose to carry through to implementation the separation of the design-level themes. Of course, you need to use a programming model that supports theme-based modularization and composition as designed using Theme/UML. Aspect-oriented languages provide such a model. Taking this approach yields the traceability benefits that we previously discussed as an advantage to using the Theme approach.

Alternatively, you may implement the composed design using an object-oriented language. It is likely that this approach would only be taken where there is a reluctance to use an aspect-oriented programming language. The resulting code will display the modularization characteristics, in which the themes are integrated into the straight object model, that aspect-oriented programming has been designed to avoid.

In either case, there is language support as well as development environments that would be helpful in implementation. Later in this book, we briefly review how to make the translation from the theme models to implementation languages, covering how to translate theme models into a selection of aspect-oriented languages.

Summary

In this chapter, we described the basic motivation for considering aspects early in the software lifecycle. We follow the symmetric approach to modularization, where features or concerns are each separated. We use the term "aspect" to refer to features or concerns that crosscut other features or concerns. We refer to all of these as themes.

In this chapter we also introduced the Theme approach, which consists of two parts: Theme/Doc, which relates to consideration of themes in requirements, and Theme/UML, which allows description of themes at design. Next, we look more closely at the motivation for the use of themes by applying the best object-oriented practices to solve a design problem and seeing where those practices fall short.

2

The Object-Oriented Way

Before we get into describing Theme in any detail, let's explore why it is that the object-oriented software paradigm does not provide us with encapsulation and reuse to the extent that we would like.

The basic point of this chapter is that requirements do not align with objects. To get from one to the other requires a leap or transformation of some kind. That leap hurts how easy it is to evolve a system. It is also an impediment to comprehensibility, reuse, and traceability. This is true regardless of how well you've designed your system. When a new requirement is introduced late into your development cycle, accommodating it is going to affect an unpredictable number of objects simply because your requirements and your objects don't align.

This chapter describes the basic motivation for aspect-oriented analysis, design, and implementation: We would like to be able to encapsulate units in the software that we recognize as units of interest from our understanding of the requirements. This provides us with a level of traceability between the software and the requirements that in turn helps us to ensure that we have covered all the requirements in the software and helps us to understand where changes to requirements will impact the software. We would also like to reuse such units when we come across the same requirement in different situations. Reuse is likely to significantly decrease the cost of development.

In this chapter, we explore the extent to which we can achieve software encapsulation of units of interest in the requirements with the object-oriented paradigm.

Differing Units of Interest

As with any large, complex problem, breaking the problem into smaller parts makes it easier to understand. Software engineering is no different in this respect, with the word *modularization* often used to capture this notion. We get modularized units when we wrap parts of the problem space together. To this end, we are interested in how a particular problem is divided into smaller parts. In this section, we show how requirements specifications and object-oriented specifications use different modularization units, making it difficult to match up one with the other.

Describing Requirements

A requirements specification is a description of an expected software system. It is generally the output of a requirements-gathering process that is likely to have considered a number of dimensions: The needs and requirements of the potential end users of the software system are elicited and documented; the business processes the software system must support are examined and the supporting requirements are documented; the technical environment and technical constraints within which the software system must run are assessed and documented; all existing software systems with which the new software system must interact are identified, and the requirements for their interaction are documented. Requirements specifications tend to be documented in a language that can be understood by eventual users of the system, which is generally a natural language.

Individuals and groups of individuals (for example, clubs or businesses) have different needs for software systems from both a business and personal perspective. The vocabularies and processes used to describe these needs are wide and varied, with numerous approaches to requirements gathering and documentation. Here, we look at two things: first, the differences in vocabularies used by various approaches to describe individual requirement units (e.g., features, functions, services), and second, some different approaches to dividing a requirements specification into smaller parts. Influences on this division relate to the different views or perspectives of the people who need the software.

Requirements Units

There are many words used to describe what a computer system is supposed to do: requirement, feature, functionality, facility and service are a subset that we look at here. In order to give a context for the vocabulary, dictionary[1] definitions for each of these terms are shown in Table 2–1, followed by a description of how the concepts are used in some requirements-engineering approaches.

Table 2–1 *Requirements Units*

Term	Dictionary Definition
Requirement	Need; depend on for success, fulfillment, etc.
Feature	Distinctive or characteristic part of a thing; part that arrests attention; important participant in.
Function	Mode of action or activity by which a thing fulfills its purpose.
Service	Provision of what is necessary for the maintenance of a thing or property.
Facility	Equipment or physical means for doing something.

Different requirements-engineering processes use different vocabularies to describe units of interest to the requirements gatherer. For example, the Unified Software Development Process[2] refers to requirements, features, and functionality, but in essence describes the process of capturing requirements as *use cases*. A use case delimits the system from its environment; outlines who and what will interact with the system and what

---

[1] *The Concise Oxford Dictionary.* Clarendon Press, Oxford.

[2] Ivar Jacobson, Grady Booch, & James Rumbaugh. *The Unified Software Development Process.* Addison-Wesley, 1999.

functionality is expected from the system; and captures and defines in a glossary common terms that are essential for creating detailed descriptions of the system's functionality.

Feature-oriented domain analysis (FODA) models domains in a *feature-oriented* way integrated with a use-case approach.[3] Its purpose is ". . . to capture in a model the end user's (and customer's) understanding of the general capabilities of applications in a domain," which, the point is made, "sounds like use-case modeling." The two approaches are integrated because they serve different purposes. The use-case model is *user oriented*, providing the "what" of a domain: a complete description of what systems in the domain do. The feature model is *re-user* oriented, providing the "which" of the domain: which functionality can be selected when engineering new systems in the domain.

Features, described as "an optional unit or increment of *functionality*," are also at the core of the Distributed Feature Composition (DFC) architecture.[4] The fundamental idea of the DFC architecture for the telecommunications domain is to treat features as independent components through which calls are routed from caller to callee. Examples of features in the telecommunications environment are call-waiting and third-party conference.

Services and *facilities* are part of the specification of the OMG work on CORBA.[5, 6] Systems that support distributed objects can conform to the CORBA standard by providing certain services. Two examples of such services are an object-naming service and an object-event service. Examples of common facilities provided for by CORBA are user interface facilities and data interchange facilities.

---

[3] Martin Griss, John Favaro, & Massimo d'Alessandro. "Integrating Feature Modeling with the RESB." In *Proceedings of International Conference on Software Reuse* (ICSR), 1998.

[4] Michael Jackson & Pamela Zave. "Distributed Feature Composition: A Virtual Architecture for Telecommunications Services." *IEEE TSE* Special Issue on Feature Interaction, 1998.

[5] Thomas Mowbray & Ron Zahavi. *The Essential CORBA: Systems Integration Using Distributed Objects.* Object Management Group, John Wiley & Sons, 1995.

[6] Jon Siegel. *CORBA Fundamentals and Programming.* Object Management Group, John Wiley & Sons, 1996.

Goal-oriented requirements engineering (exemplified by the KAOS[7] approach) involves the capturing of goals and agents. Goals are statements of intent about a program. Agents are "active components" or entities that play a role (humans, devices, and so on). Goals are refined into ever-finer grained subgoals until they can be realized and operationalized. Objects can be identified from goals by examining the passive entities involved in goal operation and by identifying the agents responsible for realizing the goals.

Motivation for Choosing Units

From the units' definitions and the approach of different requirements-specification techniques, requirements for computer systems can be seen to be *statements of what the computer system should do.* Opinions of what computer systems should do, even opinions of the same computer system, are dependent on the people who will use the system and for what the system will be used. Different kinds of people have different needs—and again, many different terms are used to describe the different motivations (for example, view, perspective, role). As before, in order to give a context for the vocabulary, dictionary definitions for these terms are described in Table 2–2.

Processes for requirements gathering take approaches based on the motivations of the end users of the computer system. Those motivations depend on the views, the perspectives, the roles, and the responsibilities of the end users. In requirements engineering, views have been described as allowing "development participants to address only those concerns or criteria that

Table 2–2 *Motivations*

Term	Dictionary definition
View	Manner of considering a subject, opinion, mental attitude; intention, design.
Perspective	Aspect of a subject and its parts as viewed by the mind; view.
Role	One's function, what a person or thing is appointed or expected to do.

---

[7] A. Dardenne, A. van Lamsweerde, & S. Fickas. "Goal-Directed Requirements Acquisition." *Science of Computer Programming,* 20:3–50, 1993.

are of interest, ignoring others that are unrelated."[8] One framework for requirements elicitation is based on the capture of multiple perspectives,[9] while the roles end users play under different domain-dependent circumstances are the motivation behind role-modeling.[10]

In summary, a requirements specification is modularized in terms of descriptions of required features, services, functions, and facilities. Potentially, each individual unit may be described to support multiple roles from different views and perspectives.

Describing Objects

The object-oriented paradigm supports modularization of software primarily based on the notion of an object as a representation of an entity, whether it's a "thing" in the real world, a software "thing," a system in and of itself, or an actor within a system. An object encapsulates the structural and behavioral properties that are core to that entity.

Object-Oriented Units

There have been many definitions of the units that are fundamental to the object-oriented paradigm. Table 2–3 illustrates some definitions for the main object-oriented concepts from a number of different sources.

The definitions for the individual units are much the same. Multiple definitions are listed here partially from a historical perspective to illustrate that even from the early days, there was some level of consistency as to what were considered to be the units of interest in the object-oriented paradigm. Essentially, there are "things" of interest to the design that encapsulate structure and behavior. Classes, objects, and attributes describe the structure of things. Operations, interfaces, and methods describe the behavior of things.

---

[8] Bashar Nuseibeh, Jeff Kramer, & Anthony Finkelstein. "A Framework for Expressing the Relationships Between Multiple Views in Requirements Specification." *IEEE TSE*, 20(10):760–773, October 1994.

[9] Steve Easterbrook. "Elicitation of Requirements from Multiple Perspectives." PhD thesis, Department of Computing, Imperial College, London. 1991.

[10] Trygve Reenskaug, Per Wold, & Odd Arild Lehne. *Working with Objects: The OOram Software Engineering Method.* Manning, 1995.

Table 2–3 *Object-Oriented Units*

Term	Definition
Object	A concrete manifestation of an abstraction; an entity with a well-defined boundary and identity that encapsulates state and behavior; an instance of a class. [a]
	A concept, abstraction or thing with crisp boundaries and meaning for the problem at hand. [b]
	The "is-a" abstraction, representing a part of a system. An object has identity and attributes and is encapsulated so that the messages it sends and receives constitute all its externally observable properties. [c]
Class	A description of a set of objects that share the same attributes, operations, relationships, and semantics. [d]
	Objects that share the same behavior are said to belong to the same class. A class is a generic specification for an arbitrary number of similar objects. [e]
	A description of a group of objects with similar properties, common behavior, common relationships, and common semantics. [f]
Attribute	A named value or relationship that exists for some or all instances of some entity and is directly associated with that instance. [g]
	A named property of a class that describes a range of values that instances of the property may hold. [h]
	A data value held by the objects in a class. [i]
	The information an object may store. [j]

[a] Grady Booch, James Rumbaugh, & Ivar Jacobson. *The Unified Modeling Language.* The Object Technology Series, Addison-Wesley, 1998.

[b] Derek Coleman, Patrick Arnold, Stephanie Bodoff, Chris Dollin, Helena Gilchrist, Fiona Hayes, & Paul Jeremes. *Object-Oriented Development: The Fusion Method.* Prentice Hall, 1994.

[c] Reenskaug, Wold, & Lehne, *Working with Objects.*

[d] Booch, Rumbaugh, & Jacobson, *The Unified Modeling Language.*

[e] Rebecca Wirfs-Brock, Brian Wilkerson, & Lauren Wiener. *Designing Object-Oriented Software.* Prentice Hall, 1990.

[f] Coleman et al., *Object-Oriented Development.*

[g] FOLDOC: *Free On-Line Dictionary of Computing.*

[h] Booch, Rumbaugh, & Jacobson, *The Unified Modeling Language.*

[i] Coleman et al., *Object-Oriented Development.*

[j] Reenskaug, Wold, & Lehne, *Working with Objects.*

Table 2–3 *Object-Oriented Units (cont.)*

Term	Definition
Operation	The implementation of a service that can be requested from any object of the class in order to affect behavior.[k]
	A function or transformation that may be applied to or by objects in a class.[l]
	A piece of code triggered by a message.[m]
Interface	A collection of operations that are used to specify a service of a class or a component.[n]
Method	The implementation of an operation.[o,p]

[k] Booch, Rumbaugh, & Jacobson, *The Unified Modeling Language.*
[l] Coleman et al., *Object-Oriented Development.*
[m] Steve Cook & John Daniels. *Designing Object Systems. Object-Oriented Modeling with Syntropy.* Prentice Hall, 1994.
[n] Booch, Rumbaugh, & Jacobson, *The Unified Modeling Language.*
[o] Ibid.
[p] Coleman et al., *Object-Oriented Development.*

Motivation for Choosing Units

The original motivations associated with the choice of "object" as the basic decomposition unit in the object-oriented software paradigm was to model real-world objects, thereby making software systems easier to develop and understand. Since then, objects have made sense as a unit of encapsulation because they allow decomposition and description in terms of a system's entities. Those entities can then be extended and reused. Additionally, the concept of working with objects at the software-specification level is familiar and intuitive, since we can relate it to the way in which we work with and describe real-world objects in daily life.

Comparing Requirements to Objects

The requirements-specification paradigm contains the notions of features, capabilities, services, functions, and so on, with generally no mention of objects and interfaces or any of the units of interest in the object-oriented design domain. The object-oriented paradigm contains the notions of objects, interfaces, and so on, with no mention of features, requirements, or any of the units of interest in the requirements domain. Object-oriented designs structurally match object-oriented code, because object-oriented programming languages such as C++ and Java explicitly provide programming constructs that map to object-oriented notions. This provides a measure of traceability between the design and coding phases.

Structurally, the units of interest in the requirements domain are fundamentally different from the units of interest in object-oriented software. Requirements units of interest generally are not, and cannot readily be, encapsulated in the software.

Achieving a mapping from requirements specifications to the object-oriented paradigm necessitates a transition from feature (or function, service, etc.) concerns in the requirements phase to the object/class concerns of the object-oriented paradigm. For instance, Figure 2–1 abstractly illustrates how requirements might not align with an object structure. Requirements are handled by multiple objects, and objects contain functionality pertaining to various requirements. Even the goal-oriented approaches listed above involve additional stages to make the transition from their basic unit (the goal) to objects.

This point is particularly important. *In general, most design paradigms are not sufficiently powerful to permit designs to match both requirements and code*—they allow designs to align with either the requirements or the code, but not with both. Let's look at the impact of this with an example.

Expressions Example

This example exposes some of the difficulties in making the transformation from requirements to objects. It involves the construction and evolution of a simple expression evaluation system (EES). A simplified software development process is assumed, consisting of informal requirements specification in natural language, design in UML, and implementation in Java.

The required EES supports the specification of simple expression programs. The set of tools needed to work with expressions is listed in Table 2–4.

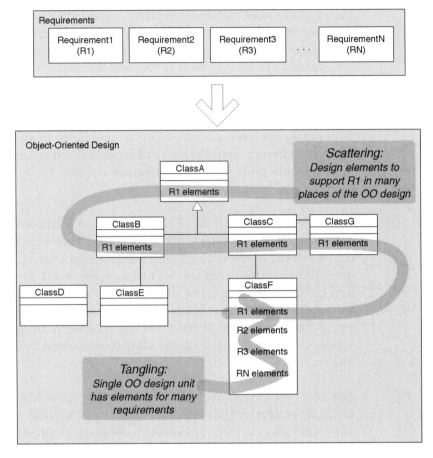

Figure 2–1   *Requirements to objects.*

Table 2–4 *Expression Evaluation System*

R No.	Requirement Text
R1	An *evaluation* capability that determines the result of evaluating an expression.
R2	A *display* capability that depicts expressions textually.
R3	A *check-syntax* capability that optionally determines whether expressions are syntactically and semantically correct.
R4	The check-syntax, display, and evaluation operations should all be logged.

The initial software system supports a small grammar for expressions as follows:

```
Expression := VariableExpression | NumberExpression |
   PlusOperator | MinusOperator | UnaryPlusOp | UnaryMinusOp
PlusOperator := Expression '+' Expression
MinusOperator := Expression '-' Expression
UnaryPlusOp := '+' Expression
UnaryMinusOp := '-' Expression
VariableExpression := ('A'| 'B' | 'C' | ... | 'Z') +
NumberExpression := ('0' | '1' | '2' | ... | '9') +
```

This grammar basically means that an `Expression` is either a `VariableExpression`, a `NumberExpression`, a `PlusOperator`, a `MinusOperator`, a `UnaryPlusOp`, or a `UnaryMinusOp`. A `PlusOperator` is made up of two `Expressions`, with a + symbol between them; a `MinusOperator` is made up of two `Expressions` with a - symbol between them; and so on. The grammar for expressions can be rewritten as requirements R5 through R11, as is shown in Table 2–5.

Table 2–5 *Expressions Grammar Requirements*

R No.	Requirement Text
R5	Expression is defined as a variableexpression or a numberexpression or a plusoperator or a minusoperator or a unaryplusop or a unaryminusop.
R6	plusoperator is defined as an expression and a plusoperator and an expression.
R7	minusoperator is defined as an expression and a minusoperator and an expression.
R8	unaryplusop is defined as a plusoperator and an expression.
R9	unaryminusop is defined as a minusoperator and an expression.
R10	variableexpression is defined as a letter and an expression.
R11	numberexpression is defined as a number and an expression.

This grammar is very simple to effectively illustrate two problems: first, even with a small grammar, the design of a supporting EES gets unwieldy, and second, adding new constructs to the grammar, such as a product or assignment operator, requires crosscutting changes to the design.

Object-Oriented Design

The EES design represents expressions as abstract syntax trees (AST). Each type of AST node is represented as a class, as shown in Figure 2–2.

Figure 2–2   *AST nodes as classes.*

When we examine the nodes of the tree for this grammar, we see that there may be common properties between different nodes that could be abstracted to superclasses. For example, the `PlusOperator` and the `MinusOperator` have similar properties in that they both have left and right operands, which could be abstracted to a class called `BinaryOperator`. Also, the `UnaryPlusOp` and the `UnaryMinusOp` are similar in that they both only have one operand, which could be abstracted to a class called `UnaryOperator`. Finally, `NumberExpression` and `VariableExpression` are literals, and so could be abstracted to a class called `Literal`. These classes are illustrated in Figure 2–3.

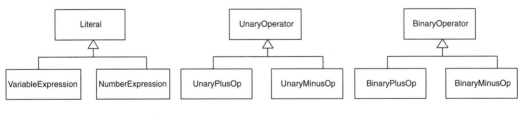

Figure 2–3   *AST classes with superclasses.*

The tree-structure nature of the AST is supported using the Composite pattern.[11] The intent of the Composite pattern is to "compose objects into tree structures to represent part-whole interactions." The idea is to provide a uniform interface to the objects within such a tree structure, be it a leaf or a composite object. Composite is centered around an abstract class that represents both primitives (in the EES case, literals) and their containers (in the EES case, operators, which "contain" one or two expressions). From the pattern, a container object maintains an aggregation relationship[12] with its parts. As shown in Figure 2–4, the abstract class that is used to represent literals and operators is called `Expression`. Since both `UnaryOperator` and `BinaryOperator` are containers of expressions, they maintain aggregation relationships with `Expression`.

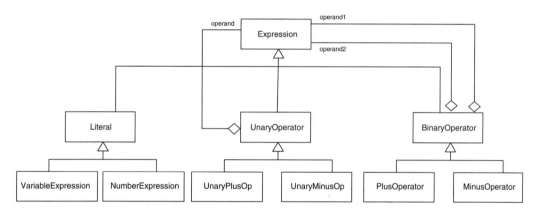

Figure 2–4   *Composite pattern for AST*

Now that we have the basic structure in place, let's look at how to fulfill the EES requirements. Several requirements identified in the specification must be realized in the design: expression support; the evaluation, display, and check-syntax tools, and a logging utility that can be included or excluded from the environment.

---

[11] Erich Gamma, Richard Helm, Ralph Johnson, & John Vlissides. *Design Patterns: Elements of Object-Oriented Software*. Addison-Wesley 1994.

[12] Booch, Rumbaugh, & Jacobson, *The Unified Modeling Language*.

There may, of course, be many approaches to the design and implementation of such a system. Since we are assuming the AST structure, a designer might first specify basic structural and accessor properties, as illustrated in Figure 2–5.

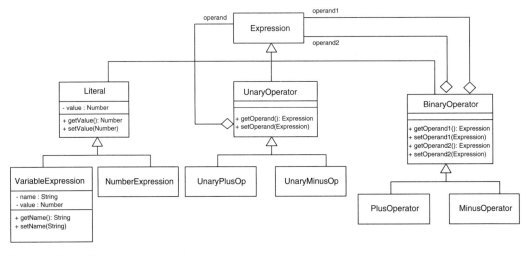

Figure 2–5   *Core expression design.*

It is likely that no behavioral models would be produced to capture any of these basic elements. On the other hand, checking expressions may have sufficiently interesting behavior to be designed using an interaction diagram. An interesting property of designing an interaction with a collaboration model such as a sequence diagram is that only elements relating to the collaboration need to be included. From that perspective, the object-oriented model provides a good level of modularization. Here, we assume a good design for the collaboration required to check the syntax of expressions. From a structural perspective, however, the operations and attributes that are relevant for checking expressions must be included in the core expression class model, as illustrated in Figure 2–6.

The design of the evaluate and display requirements is similar, and again, we assume a good design for the collaborations required. The impact on the EES class model is illustrated in Figure 2–7.

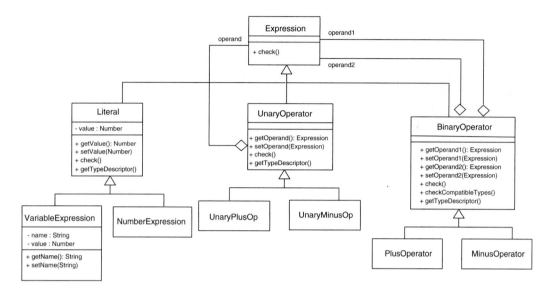

Figure 2–6   *Support for checking added to core expression diagram.*

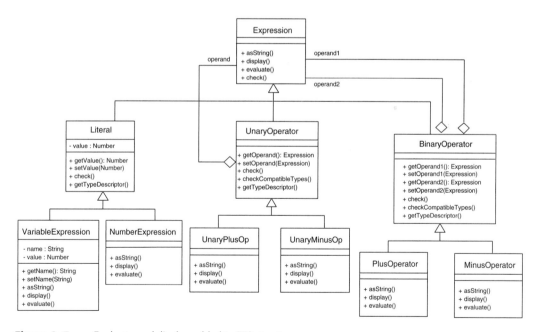

Figure 2–7   *Evaluate and display added to EES structure.*

The remaining requirement to be designed is the optional logging of operation execution. Figure 2–8 shows an example collaboration diagram for logging a check() operation. If the logging utility is turned on (modeled as a Boolean attribute loggingOn), each operation invokes Logger.beforeInvoke() prior to performing its action, then invokes Logger.afterInvoke() just before it terminates. The Logger permits applications to turn logging on and off with its turnLoggingOn() and turnLoggingOff() methods. This permits logging to be optional, as required.

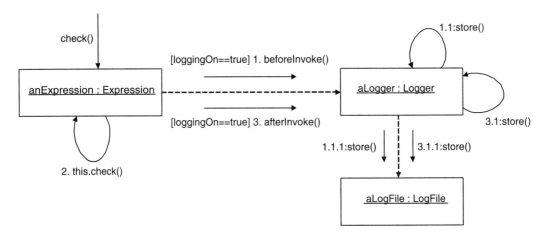

Figure 2–8   *Collaboration diagram for logging: example: check().*

The impact of the logging requirement on the structure diagram of the EES is illustrated on Figure 2–9. Logging is modeled as a separate, singleton class, Logger. The Singleton design pattern[13] ensures a class has only one instance, as is appropriate for a class performing a logging function that will always behave the same way regardless of what operation is being logged.

---

[13] Gamma, Helm, Johnson, & Vlissides, *Design Patterns.*

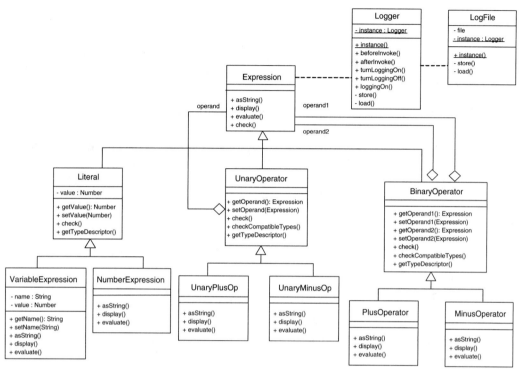

Figure 2–9   *UML class diagram for EES.*

Requirements Scattered and Tangled in the EES Design

Earlier in this chapter, we discussed the differing units of interest in the way requirements and objects are described. Requirement units are feature, function, and so on; object, operation, and so on, are the units of interest in object-oriented development. We asserted that while object-oriented designs align well with object-oriented code because of matching constructs, they do not align well with requirements units. This boils down to an issue of modularization. The structural differences in the units of interest between the EES requirements specification and the object-oriented design are central to the difficulties associated with mapping the modularization between the two. The transition between the two essentially results in discarding the encapsulation of requirements' units of interest in favor of units of interest mandated by the design and coding paradigms. The natural outcome is a *scattering* and *tangling* effect across the object-oriented design.

Scattering occurs when the design of a single requirement is necessarily scattered across multiple classes and operations in the object-oriented design. The EES requirements of expression evaluation, checking, and display, which are described as modularized concerns in the requirements specification, are not modularized in the design. In fact, these requirements are manifest across the AST classes—each class contains a method that implements these capabilities for its own instances.

Tangling occurs when a single class or operation in the object-oriented design contains design details of multiple requirements. If we look at almost any single class in the EES design, we see design elements from different requirements. Perhaps even more devastating is the tangling effect on one operation in particular: logging. The logging capability is realized as a first-class unit of interest in both the requirements and the design. Nonetheless, the protocol for logging requires cooperation from each method in each AST class to appropriately invoke `Logger.beforeInvoke()` and `Logger.afterInvoke()`. This is tangling—satisfying a given requirement necessitates interleaving design details that address the requirement with details that address other requirements.

Scattering and tangling imply insufficient modularization and are therefore negative from a number of perspectives. First, the *impact of change* to a single requirement, which may be well localized at the requirements level, can nonetheless be extremely high. This is because that change necessitates multiple changes across a class hierarchy. Second, there is a serious impediment to *software comprehension and reuse* because it is impossible to deal with the design details relating to one requirement without constantly encountering and having to worry about intertwined details relating to other requirements. Finally, there are significant difficulties with *traceability*, which is the ability to determine readily how a piece of one software artefact (e.g., requirement, design, code) affects others. Traceability makes it possible to look at a change to a requirement and find those parts of the design and code that are affected by the change. Without matching modularization between the software artefacts, traceability is obscured.

Interestingly, even with a system as small as the EES example, we see a significant level of scattering and tangling in the design. We might look at this particular design and think that it is not so bad, as it would not take long to figure out what is going on. However, extrapolate these problems to a system of any realistic size, and the difficulties are compounded.

We do not claim that recognition of the value of good modularity is new—developers seek new means to achieve better modularity all the time. For example, design patterns are one of the most important advances toward good modularity in the last decade. A major goal of design patterns is to allow changes to be made to a system in an *additive* rather than an *invasive* manner. This is a very important goal, the key to which is (as with many things!) modularity. In the next section, we look at how we might go about the task of evolving the EES. In order to assess the object-oriented way from a "best practice" perspective, we examine how the use of design patterns improves the basic EES of this section and assess how noninvasive the design patterns really are.

Accommodating Evolution

All useful software systems evolve over time. Evolution may occur because of, for example, changes to the organization processes manifest in the system or because of new requirements. Ideally, it would be nice to be able to change a system noninvasively—in other words, without having to "touch" the existing design. Design patterns[14] recommend approaches to supporting extensibility, some of which we look at here. In this section, we see that even when using good design practices, such as incorporating design patterns, evolution can still be difficult to accommodate.

First, though, let's look at the new requirements for the EES as shown in Table 2–6.

From a requirements-specification perspective, this change is additive—it need not affect any other requirement. At the design level, however, the change is not as straightforward, since the check feature is not encapsulated as a concern in the design. In fact, this change necessarily affects all AST

---

[14] Ibid.

Table 2–6 *Additional EES Requirements*

R No.	Requirement Text
R12	Check-def-use capability to ensure that all variables used are defined, and all variables defined are used.
R13	Check-style capability to ensure that expressions conform to local naming conventions.
R14	Mix-and-match checking capability to ensure that clients can choose a combination of check-syntax, check-def-use, and check-style to be run on their expression programs when they invoke the check tool.
R15	Check-style and check-def use should be logged.

classes in the design. One approach is to add new `defUseCheck()` and `styleCheck()` operations to each of the AST classes, with conditional execution based on `boolean` attribute options. This approach requires each class in the design to be changed, with corresponding significant potential for error introduction even to the first version of the EES system design. Another possible approach to designing the new forms of checking is to create new subclasses of the AST classes, where a given subclass overrides the original (syntax) `check()` method with one intended to provide def/use or style checking for a particular kind of AST class. While this approach is noninvasive, it is completely impractical, as it results in combinatorial explosion of classes with each new feature.

A better approach is to use the Visitor design pattern.[15] The Visitor pattern "represents an operation to be performed on elements of an object structure. Visitor lets you define a new operation without changing the classes of the elements on which it operates." This pattern definition with its corresponding description makes it a good candidate for solving the problem of adding new check operations noninvasively by having a Visitor to represent checking and to provide different visitors that correspond to the different kinds of checking. The Visitor approach, depicted in Figure 2–10, facilitates mix-and-match without combinatorial explosion of classes.

The use of Visitor requires, however, an invasive change to all of the AST classes to replace the `check()` methods with `accept(Visitor)` methods. Visitor also introduces a second complication. The logging feature requires the visi-

---
[15] Ibid.

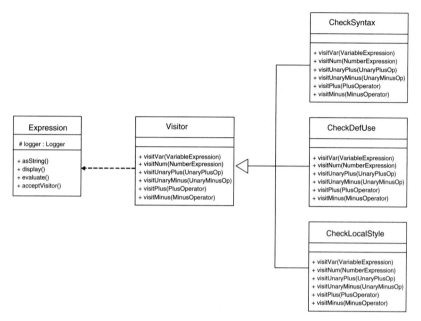

Figure 2–10   *Using Visitor to separate check functions.*

tors to invoke `Logger.beforeInvoke()` and `Logger.afterInvoke()` appropriately, further increasing the scattering and tangling problems associated with this feature.

Another possibility for the use of design patterns is in the design of the logger functionality. Our new requirements state that the new checking functionality should be logged. We would like this to be achieved as simply as possible. A mutation of the Observer pattern[16] appears as if it might be useful in capturing operations for logging. The Observer pattern supports an object that has changed state notifying other objects that have expressed an interest in its state. In Figure 2–11, this approach is evolved to capture all operations on an object by the interested object, which is the `Logger`.

In this design, before and after the execution of any operation call, a call is made to `notifyBefore()` and `notifyAfter()`. This approach has the advantage that any object other than an instance of a logger may express

---

[16] Ibid.

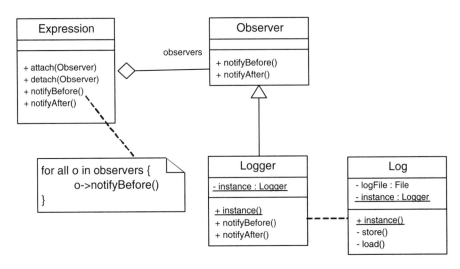

Figure 2–11   *Using Observer for logging.*

an interest in operations within the expression and attach itself as an observer to be notified before and after operation execution. For example, different kinds of audit trails may be attached with no change to the design of the expression AST.

Another approach to designing logging is to use the Decorator pattern.[17] Decorator supports the attachment of additional responsibilities to an object dynamically. Decorators provide an alternative to subclassing for extending functionality and reduce coupling, for example, in the logging case, by separating the logging functionality into separate, decorator objects, as illustrated in Figure 2–12.

Many other design approaches are possible for the EES, and some of them are likely to address some of the modularity issues. From the examples here, the judicious application of design patterns helps solve some problems. While it is impossible to exhaustively elaborate the possible design approaches (with or without design patterns), we've had a look at the most likely design pattern alternatives.

---

[17] Ibid.

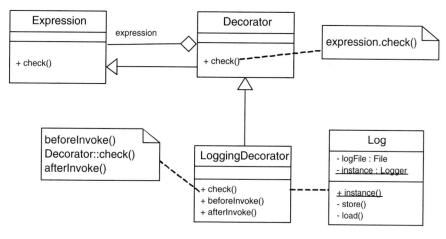

Figure 2–12   *Using Decorator for logging.*

Scattering and Tangling with Design Patterns

We've tried to use Visitor, Observer, and Decorator to improve the EES design. First, a look at Visitor: In hindsight, the initial use of the Visitor pattern to model checking, as illustrated in Figure 2–5, would have made it a lot easier to add new checkers—this is the case precisely because visitors provide encapsulation of features, which results in better alignment of design with requirements. That sounds great—but let's consider evolution to a unit of interest that is *not* a feature. For example, adding a new type of expression, like assignment, is simple in the original design in Figure 2–8, but it would necessitate invasive changes to *all* visitors in a Visitor pattern solution. While visitors promote some forms of evolution, they hinder other forms.

As for Observer, we used it to reduce coupling between the logger and the AST classes by having logging performed by observers. This approach does achieve looser coupling, which is good. However, it does not improve the scattering problem, as AST methods must notify any observers, thereby scattering the implementation of logging across all the AST classes. Used in conjunction with visitors for the AST tools (check, evaluate, display), the design for the EES becomes significantly larger and more complex, with many more relationships among the classes to be represented and enforced.

As an alternative to Observer, logging could be designed using the Decorator pattern, where decorators optionally perform logging. Decorator, like Observer, helps to reduce coupling, and unlike Observer, reduces tangling by segregating logger notification code into separate, decorator objects. Unfortunately, the Decorator solution is significantly more problematic than the Observer solution, because of the *object schizophrenia* problem. Object schizophrenia occurs when a class serves several roles, resulting in an object that has multiple personalities. In this case, to ensure that logging occurs consistently, it is necessary to ensure that *all* messages to all objects go through the decorator, *not* directly to the object itself. Even methods that are invoked from within the decorated object must go through the decorator. This means that the object must know about its decorator(s), which introduces a new form of coupling and tangling (i.e., each class must include code to implement interaction with the decorator).

Evolution the Object-Oriented Way

We added some requirements to the EES that appeared to be straightforward and additive from the client's perspective and from their impact on the requirements. The resulting design demonstrates, in a microcosm, the spectrum of problems resulting from differing units of interest between the requirements and the design. Scattering and tangling lead to weak traceability and poor encapsulation of requirements-level concerns within the design and, subsequently, the code. They also make propagation of requirements changes to design and code very difficult and invasive. It is even difficult to determine which design elements are affected by a given requirements change. The level of effort needed to propagate changes from requirements to design is increased because of the different units of interest.

Design patterns can help alleviate some, but not all, of the identified problems. Unfortunately, in diminishing some problems, they introduce other problems or restrictions. For instance, incorporating a design pattern into existing code will likely require invasive changes and refactorings. The only way to avoid those invasive changes is to pre-enable code with design patterns. It is, of course, impossible to anticipate every kind of change that might be required and every pattern you will benefit from using. Even if that kind of prescience were possible, flexibility always comes at a cost in terms of conceptual complexity and/or performance overhead, as the Visitor, Observer and Decorator patterns demonstrate. Enabling for some forms of change inhibits other kinds of change—for example, introducing visitors promotes the future addition of new types of checkers, but it greatly complicates the addition of new types of expressions.

Design patterns and other design approaches are very useful, but they cannot fully address the issues raised here. As long as object-oriented designs have to discard the separation manifest in the requirements, the consequences—weak traceability, low comprehensibility, scattering, tangling, coupling, poor evolvability (including high impact of change and invasive change), and so forth—will be present.

Summary

In this chapter, we showed how requirements do not align with objects, leading to difficulties in the object-oriented way of developing software. Requirements do not align with objects because the units of interest in the requirements for a software system are not the same as the units of interest in an object-oriented model of the same system. To get from one to the other requires a transformation of some kind that hurts evolution, comprehensibility, reuse and traceability. We walked through applying good object-oriented design practices in designing a simple expression-evaluation system. We found that problems arose, both in the initial design and upon evolution, because, ultimately, we had to adhere to objects as the main unit of modularity. In the next chapter, we apply the aspect-oriented Theme approach for designing the same system. We will see that by using themes, we can overcome the difficulties that are present with straight object orientation.

3

The Theme Approach

In Chapter 2, "The Object-Oriented Way," we worked through an example of applying good object-oriented principles to designing an expression evaluation system (EES). We found that there were some difficulties: Features couldn't be properly encapsulated; adding new features was difficult; choosing between active features involved a lot of work.

This chapter introduces the Theme approach to aspect-oriented analysis and design. We work through the same EES as a way to illustrate how themes can be used to encapsulate features, and how the approach is used to identify crosscutting concerns (aspects).

Structure and Relationships of Themes

The Theme approach involves identifying and designing separate *themes*, which are then combined to make a whole system. Themes can be thought of as analogous to features or concerns. So, in a sense, the Theme approach lets you design each feature of your system separately, and then offers a way to combine them. In the introduction, we discussed the nature of themes and how they relate to one another. We now review the nature of themes at a high level, but this time using the EES example from the previous chapter as a basis.

Themes at Analysis, Design, and Composition

Figure 3–1 depicts themes at analysis, at design, and then retangled after composition. Themes "look" different as you move from requirements to design. At the requirements level, the parts that make up a theme are fairly abstract: They are participants and actions, as described in a set of requirements. As you can see, at requirements analysis, a single theme is represented by a diamond and is linked to the description of a particular functionality from the requirements. As shown in Figure 3–1, a requirement for the EES from Chapter 2 was a feature for checking the syntax of expressions.

At the design level, these parts are more concrete, consisting of classes, methods, and relationships between them. These parts are both structural and behavioral: the "things" and "actions" that work together to provide a feature of your system. At the design level, many classes were needed to implement the check-syntax feature, including the `Expression` class and all its subclasses. If the check-syntax feature was described as a theme (as depicted in the middle column of Figure 3–1), all these classes would be included in the theme. However, each theme contains only the relevant portions of the design. You'll notice that the **check-syntax** theme does not contain the `asString()` method. The classes and methods related to the check-syntax feature provide only functionality related to checking syntax.

Relationships Between Themes

Themes can relate to one another in two ways: by sharing concepts and by crosscutting. It is also possible for themes to be completely independent. This is rare; independent themes relate in no way to the rest of the system.

Concept Sharing

Different themes may have design elements that represent the same core concepts in the domain. A design element might be a particular class, method, or attribute. A concept relates to something from the domain. In

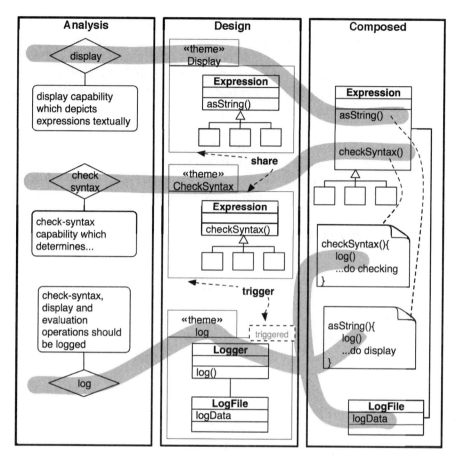

Figure 3–1   *Themes at analysis, at design, and then retangled after composition.*

the banking system, described in Chapter 1, a core concept might be a bank account. The concept of a bank account could be described by classes of varying names, such as `Account`, or `BankAccount`.

In the Theme approach, each theme describes the classes it requires from its own perspective, regardless of whether other themes also have classes that describe the same concepts. Conflicts and overlaps are resolved later, when deciding how to recombine the themes. For instance, you need an `Expression` class for most of the features in the system. You can see that both **check-syntax** and **display** have a version of the `Expression` class.

When considering each theme, you include the entities and behavior needed to capture the analysis and design of that theme, regardless of whether the underlying domain concepts have also been described elsewhere. The arrow labeled "share" in the middle column of Figure 3–1 depicts that the **check-syntax** and **display** themes share concepts (the `Expression` class, in this case).

You can see that the composed system has merged the different `Expression` classes into one single class: Both the `asString()` method from the **display** theme and the `checkSyntax()` method from the **check-syntax** theme are now included in the `Expression` class.

Crosscutting

Themes can also *crosscut* one another. One theme crosscuts another if its behavior is triggered by the behavior of the other theme. While independent themes and themes that share concepts can operate without knowledge of one another, crosscutting themes require an abstract knowledge of the themes they crosscut, and they cannot operate independently. The log feature in the EES system is a good example of a crosscutting theme. The logging behavior appeared throughout the system but could not operate unless other behaviors in the system were also in operation (otherwise, what would be logged?). The arrow marked "trigger" in the middle column of Figure 3–1 shows that the **log** and **check-syntax** themes have a crosscutting relationship. The **log** theme is parameterized to show that it contains the triggered behavior.

Crosscutting themes are also called *aspects*; noncrosscutting themes are the *base* upon which the aspects operate.

The trigger arrow between **log** and the other two themes depicts that the `log()` method is triggered by the behavior associated with those themes. In asymmetric separation parlance, it has been *woven* into those methods. You can see the result of the weaving in the composed methods: `log()` is called before the main functionality of the `asString()` and `checkSyntax()` methods.

Theme Process Overview

Now that you have a sense of what a theme is and how it looks at requirements analysis and design, we delve into how to get from a set of requirements to a set of modeled themes. This chapter provides a high-level glance at this process. The rest of the book goes into the process in far more detail.

The Theme approach helps you to identify and model themes. The approach also helps you identify which of those themes are crosscutting themes and which are not. The approach involves two representations: Theme/Doc, which is used for viewing and analyzing requirements, and Theme/UML, which is applied for design. Using Theme/Doc, you view the relationships between concepts described in a set of requirements and refine the concepts into features, or themes. You then apply Theme/UML to design the themes and to designate how shared structure and behavior should be recombined. You perform three main activities when applying the approach: analysis, design, and composition. The activities are depicted in Figure 3–2 and are described at a high level in the list below.

1. *Analysis.* The first step in the approach is to perform analysis of the requirements to identify themes. This involves mapping requirements to concerns in the system. Theme/Doc lets you view the relationships between behaviors. These relationships expose tangled concerns and lead you to identifying aspects.

2. *Design.* You then design the themes using Theme/UML. Use the themes you found using Theme/Doc to identify potential classes and methods, then fill in the design details and make changes that are needed to benefit the design. Other aspect themes are likely to emerge during detailed technical design.

3. *Composition.* You then specify how the Theme/UML models should be recombined. In many cases, some of the Theme/Doc views will help to determine how themes relate to one another: whether they overlap or whether they crosscut one another.

You'll notice that some of the arrows shown in Figure 3-2 are styled "automatic." These arrows depict actions that the Theme toolkit performs automatically. The Theme/Doc tool generates views of requirements and

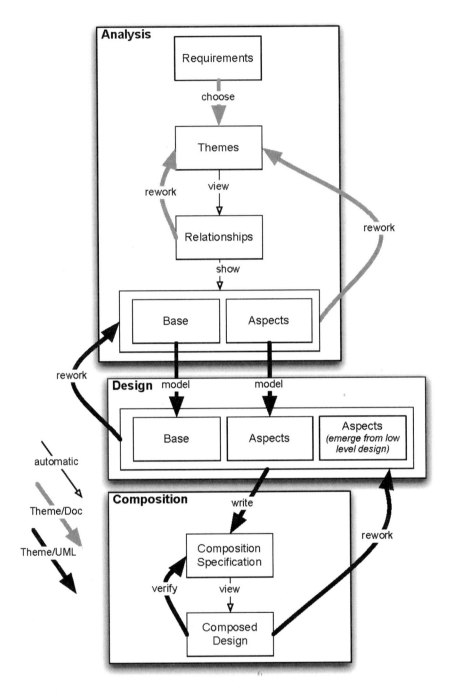

Figure 3–2   *Theme process.*

themes and their relationships. The Theme/UML tool allows design com-position based on Theme/UML composition relationships.

For the rest of this chapter, we work through each activity in more depth, using the EES from Chapter 2 as an example. Later, Chapters 4, 5, and 6 go into greater detail on a more involved example.

Finding the Themes

The first step in the Theme approach is to examine the documentation of the system requirements. At this stage, you are trying to identify features and crosscutting concerns (aspects) that are described in the requirements from the EES (rewritten in Table 3–1) and also to find out which portions of the requirements document pertain specifically to those features and aspects.

Table 3–1 *Expression Evaluation System Requirements*

R No.	Requirement Text
R1	An evaluation capability, which determines the result of evaluating an expression.
R2	A display capability, which depicts expressions textually.
R3	A check-syntax capability, which optionally determines whether expressions are syntactically and semantically correct.
R4	The check-syntax, display, and evaluation operations should all be logged.
R5	`Expression` is defined as a `variableexpression` or a `numberexpression` or a `plusoperator` or a `minusoperator` or a `unaryplusop` or a `unaryminusop`.
R6	`plusoperator` is defined as an `expression` and a `plusoperator` and an `expression`.
R7	`minusoperator` is defined as an `expression` and a `minusoperator` and an `expression`.
R8	`unaryplusop` is defined as a `plusoperator` and an `expression`.
R9	`unaryminusop` is defined as a `minusoperator` and an `expression`.
R10	`variableexpression` is defined as a `letter` and an `expression`.
R11	`numberexpression` is defined as a `number` and an `expression`.

Finding the themes for your system has four main activities:

1. Choose a starting set of potential themes.

2. Refine the set of themes.

3. Identify which of the themes are aspects.

4. Prepare for design.

These activities are depicted in Figure 3–3, numbered and shaded in gray. In this chapter we will describe the activities linearly. However, in practice, they will most likely be intertwined.

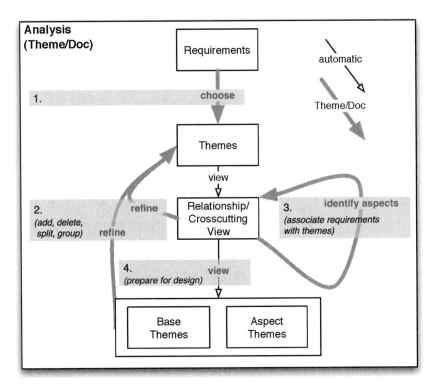

Figure 3–3   *Theme/Doc process, detailed view. Gray-shaded areas represent steps in the Theme/Doc process.*

Identify Potential Themes and Entities

In object orientation, classes, or entities, are the main unit of modularity. In the Theme approach, concerns are as much a unit of modularity as entities: They represent themes, either *base* or *crosscutting*. The first step is to identify a set of concerns from your requirements (see Figure 3–3, step 1). So, rather than just sifting through our requirements looking for key entities, we also look for key concerns. In the next step, you iterate over that set, deciding whether to add, delete, split up, or group themes. As in OO, where we use at least some of the entities to motivate classes, we use some of the concerns to motivate themes. There are several ways to arrive at a starting point of themes. You may choose names of features, services, or use cases of your system if you know what those might be. In the EES, we have no use cases described and have not analyzed the requirements in terms of features or services. Instead, we scan the requirements for identifiable pieces of functionality. We identify six potential themes:

- **evaluation**

- **display**

- **determine**

- **check-syntax**

- **log**

- **define**

We also identify nine entities:

- `expression`

- `variableexpression`

- `numberexpression`

- `plusoperator`

- `minusoperator`

- `unaryplusop`

- `unaryminusop`

- `plus`

- `minus`

The purpose in choosing potential themes and entities is to narrow down an eventual list of features and objects to design. Of course, this is a somewhat simplistic description of how to go about choosing those elements. Chapter 4, "Analysis," discusses in more depth how to go about choosing them.

Refine the Set of Themes

The Theme approach allows the individual design of different system features. In object orientation, not all the nouns in a requirements document are designed as objects or classes. Similarly, in the Theme approach, not all functionality is captured separately in its own theme. Some functionality is too minor to warrant separation. In this step, we set out to identify the themes of the system by identifying which of the potential themes are major enough to be modeled separately (once we get to the point of modeling). The operations that can be used for refining themes are shown in Table 3–2. The refinement step is depicted in Figure 3–3 as step 2.

Table 3–2 *Operations on Themes and Requirements in Theme/Doc*

Operations on Themes	Operations on Requirements
Add	Add/Split
Delete	Attach (to a theme)
Split	Associate (with a theme); selects the theme as an aspect
Group	Postpone (decision about requirement until design time)

For theme refinement, we use a Theme/Doc view called the *theme-relationship view*, or *relationship view*. The relationship view for the expression evaluator is shown in Figure 3–4. Relationship views are automatically created given a set of requirements and a set of themes. They represent requirements as rounded-corner boxes and themes as diamonds. If the name of a theme is mentioned in a requirement, there is a link from the requirement to that theme in the relationship view. R2, for instance, mentions **display** and so is linked to it in the view. Some requirements refer to more than one theme. R4, for instance, refers to four themes: **evaluation, display, log,** and **check-syntax**.

As you can imagine, relationship views can become quite large if there are many requirements and many themes. We discuss how you can mitigate the size of relationship views in Chapter 4 under the section entitled "Dealing with Large Relationship Views."

In this view, we can either see requirements as labels (their requirement number), or we can enlarge them to see their content, as we have for R4. The relationship view is nonhierarchical, so even though it looks as though some themes are "higher" than others, this is just a coincidence of layout.

At this stage, what you want to take from this view is what role the behaviors play in the requirements, to determine whether they should be themes or just behavior (perhaps methods) within themes. We scan the potential themes

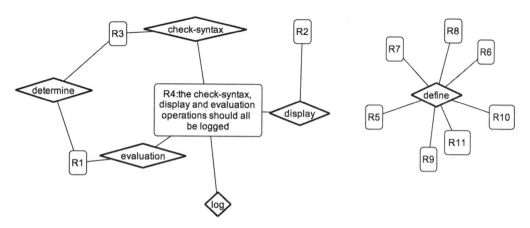

Figure 3–4 *Initial theme-relationship view for the expression system.*

and question whether it makes sense to have each of them as a feature in our system. If they are not feature-worthy, we remove them from our list.

The **log** concern makes sense as a theme: It is something that you would perhaps like to turn on or off, or at least model separately from the other actions you see in the view. A **check-syntax** feature makes sense for the same reason, as does a **display** feature. You can imagine that an **evaluation** feature would provide the functionality that R1 described, which is to determine results of an expression, and can imagine it as a group of classes and methods to perform that function. The **define** concern makes sense as a theme if you want to separate the grammar definition of the expressions from the rest of the implementation. The **determine** concern, however, does not seem to be as strong a potential theme as the rest. It is involved in two requirements, but in a relatively minor way, and it seems hard to imagine it as a collection of classes. It is more likely a method than a feature in and of itself. For this reason, we decide to remove **determine** from the list of potential themes.

Deciding which of the potential themes are too minor to be a theme is an intuitive and iterative process. This activity makes use of the operations on themes taken from Table 3–2: You may choose to remove, group, split up, or add new themes as you see fit. The changes you make are reflected in the relationship view, which may motivate you to make more changes. As usual in choosing the modules of your system, domain knowledge is helpful. Your set of themes may also continue to shift along with the development and aging of your system. It's probable that the next step in the analysis process (identifying crosscutting themes) will cause you to rethink and refine the themes you've chosen. Much more information on and examples of deciding on themes is provided in the Chapter 4 and in the case studies at the end of this book.

Identify Crosscutting Themes

As we discussed in the section "Structure of Themes," some of the themes we've chosen are crosscutting themes, or aspects, since their behavior is triggered by functionality found in other themes. The rest of the themes are base themes. This is depicted as step 3 in Figure 3–3.

You use the final theme-relationship view to help you determine which themes are base and which are aspects. This view is made up only of the remaining themes from the previous relationship view. You can see in Figure 3–4 that the **determine** node is no longer shown.

To identify aspects, you look for requirements that are shared between themes. R4 is an example of this, as is made clear by the fact that it is linked to more than one theme in the relationship view.

Generally speaking (though exceptions to this are discussed at length in Chapter 4, "Analysis," and Chapter 6, "Theme Composition"), requirements are "owned" by just one theme. As you can see, some requirements are already associated with only one theme. It's pretty easy to assume that whatever functionality is described in those requirements (even though you can't read it) should be provided by those themes. So, when we're designing the **check-syntax** theme, we know it should provide the functionality described in R3.

Shared requirements, however, represent a tangling of responsibilities and signal that we may have identified an aspect in our system. As described earlier, R4 (shown in Figure 3–5) is shared between several themes. You now have to decide whether this sharing represents an aspect-base relationship. But before jumping to any conclusions, you want to make sure that you

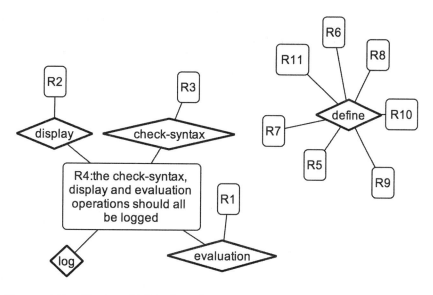

Figure 3–5   *Theme-relationship view with R4 enlarged.*

have not encountered a vaguely written requirement that is masquerading as a shared one.

In fact there are three rules you apply to identify an aspect:

1. *Splitting up doesn't work* (there is no rewriting that can isolate the themes and remove sharing).

2. *Dominance means association* (associating a requirement with a theme selects that theme as an aspect).

3. *Base triggers aspect* (aspects are triggered from within base behavior).

First, we check to see whether the requirement can be rewritten into several requirements that each refers to only one theme. You can see that in this case the only possible rewriting would be to break it into three sentences that each mention **log** and another of the themes (a log capability that logs the evaluation activity, a log capability that logs the display capability, etc.). There is no rewriting that gets a one-to-one relationship between themes and requirements: The **log** feature must be described with relation to the **evaluation**, **display**, and **check-syntax** features. We have passed the *splitting up doesn't work* rule.

Additionally, the **log** theme "dominates" this requirement—R4 mainly describes logging as opposed to the behavior of evaluation, display, or syntax-checking. Based on the *dominance means association* rule, the log theme is the aspect, since we would associate R4 with log.

It is clear from the requirement that these three themes trigger the log operation; logging happens at the time of syntax-checking, display, and evaluation. Once again, the log theme is the aspect due to the *base triggers aspect* rule.

We can now say conclusively that the log theme is appropriate as an aspect of **check-syntax**, **display**, and **evaluation**.

You denote that the **log** theme crosscuts the other three by associating the shared requirement, R4, with it. This association clips the links from R4 to the other three themes. In its place, a gray arrow indicating a crosscutting relationship is placed from the aspect theme to the base themes. These relationships are shown in a special Theme/Doc view called a *crosscutting-relationship view*, shown in Figure 3–6.

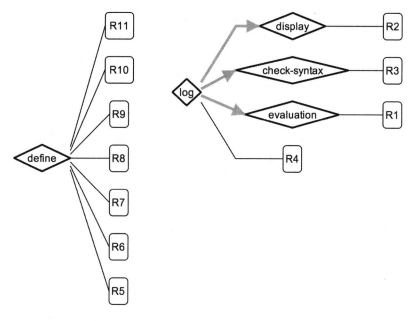

Figure 3–6 *Crosscutting-relationship view.*

There are no other shared requirements, so you can now move on to examining your themes individually and planning for design.

Preparing for Design

The *individual-theme view* (also called the individual view) helps determine which objects and behavior should be modeled in Theme/UML. Individual views show all the requirements connected to the theme of interest. Additionally, they include themes crosscut by the theme of interest, and depict the crosscutting relationships as shown in the crosscutting view. They also include structural components, or entities if they are specified and fed into the Theme/Doc view-generation tool. We now go over individual views for both base and crosscutting themes.

Viewing Base Themes

When we formed the crosscutting-relationship view shown in Figure 3–6, we associated particular requirements with particular themes. You may also recall that when we were picking the theme keywords, we also chose entity keywords: a set of *things* that might be considered participants or objects in the system. The individual-theme view is a combination of that list of keywords and the crosscutting-relationship view. Since base themes do not crosscut other themes, there will be no crosscutting relationships depicted. There may, however, be postponement relationships depicted between themes, as taken from the main crosscutting view.

Each theme can be viewed in an individual view, which shows the requirements associated with the theme, the actions (major and minor) derived from the requirements, and the entities we chose earlier. For instance, the theme view for **check-syntax** is shown in Figure 3–7.

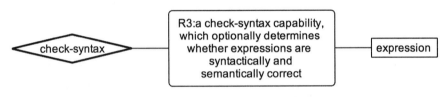

Figure 3–7   *Check-Syntax individual theme view.*

Notice that in the theme view for **check-syntax**, only R3 is shown, and not the requirement that **check-syntax** be shared with the **log** theme (R4). This is because you design the **check-syntax** theme without any regard for the logging functionality.

From this view, you can predict some of the classes and methods needed when you design your themes. Themes and other functionality described in the requirements loosely translate into methods, and entities loosely translate into classes. You can tell that you will likely have a class representing an expression. There will probably be a method specifically related to the **check-syntax** behavior.

Figure 3–8 shows the theme view for the **define** theme. This theme is made up entirely of the structural components of an expression. Once again, this

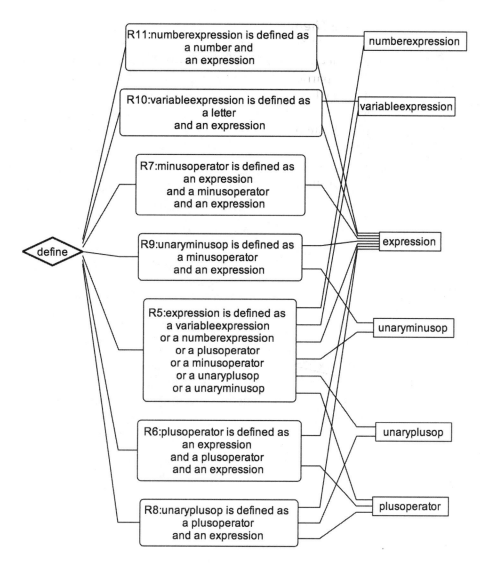

Figure 3–8   *Define individual-theme view.*

view helps you predict many of the structural entities in the design. It is likely that this theme will just define the structure of an expression, but will have no active components.

The **evaluation** theme is shown in Figure 3–9. It has two entities: result and expression. You can see that the **evaluate** theme shares a concept with the

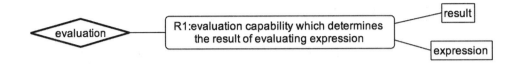

Figure 3–9   *Evaluate individual-theme view.*

---

check-syntax and **define** themes: the expression entity. As we discussed before, themes can share concepts freely. In Chapter 6, we discuss how to resolve sharing conflicts and how to recombine concepts.

Viewing Aspect Themes

Individual-theme views for crosscutting or aspect themes are a little different from those for base-theme views. As you can see in Figure 3–10, some nodes are shown in gray, indicating that these are external elements: elements that are crosscut by the **log** theme rather than elements that are unique or internal to it. You can see here that there actually are no elements described in the requirements that are internal to this theme. The **log** theme is described only in terms of how it affects other themes in the system. It will be up to the designer to determine all appropriate structure and behavior for logging.

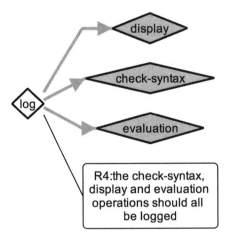

Figure 3–10   *Log theme view.*

Designing the Themes

By this point, you should be reasonably comfortable that you have a good set of themes identified from the requirements document. We now look at designing four of the themes that have been identified: **define**, **check-syntax**, **evaluate**, and **log**. First, though, a few words about the overall Theme/UML process.

The primary purpose of Theme/UML is to provide a means for you to consider the concerns of each theme separately. This allows you to work with separate design models for each concern. Bearing in mind, though, that all the concerns must work together in an executing system, you must at some point specify the relationships between the separate models and verify those decisions. Theme/UML, therefore, prescribes three high-level activities to add to the design process (depicted in Figure 3–11).

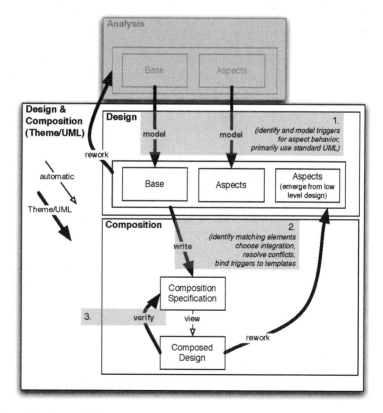

Figure 3–11   *Overview of the Theme/UML process.*

- Separately design the themes that were identified using Theme/Doc.

- Specify the relationships between the theme designs.

- Compose the themes for verification purposes.

This chapter takes you through these three steps. We begin in this section by designing the themes. As you can see in Figure 3–11, these steps are applied iteratively. Chapter 5, "Theme Design," and Chapter 6, "Theme Composition," discuss in more depth how to go about achieving these steps.

Theme Design

We look at the design of four of the themes identified: **define, check-syntax, evaluate**, and **log**. We do not have a lot to say in this book about how the internals of themes are designed; standard UML and standard object-oriented principles should be used. Except for small extensions to the UML required for designing crosscutting themes (aspects), there is no additional notation or semantics in Theme/UML for individual theme design. The main difference you will see is that when designing themes using Theme/UML, you do not have to worry about how an individual theme affects or is related to other themes.

The Define Theme

Figure 3–12 illustrates the structural design of the grammar required for expressions. This reflects the Theme/Doc representation of the specification from Figure 3–8. Of course, you are free to make detailed design decisions that result in design elements that might not be explicitly referenced in the requirements and shown in the Theme/Doc view. An example of this in the **define** theme is recognizing that this grammar represents a classic example for using the well-known Composite pattern, and that accessor operations (e.g., `getOperand()`, `setOperand()`, etc.) are likely to be useful. Another example is adding `name` and `value` attributes to the `Variable` class.

In addition, each theme design will probably have a behavioral specification. Indeed, any UML model determined to be useful for specifying the

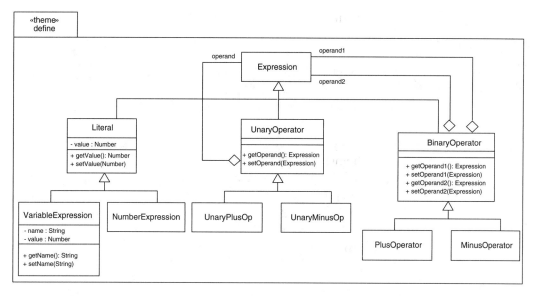

Figure 3–12   *Define theme design.*

design of the theme may be used here and considered part of the theme design. For the **define** theme, the UML class diagram is sufficient, as there is no particularly interesting behavior.

The Check-Syntax Theme

The requirements and the theme view do not thoroughly detail what "syntactically correct" means, so we take as a given that the **define** theme view indicates the correct syntax. As illustrated in Figure 3-13, the design has only the view of the grammar that it needs to successfully check the syntax of an expression. Notice that the hierarchy is different—when designing the **check-syntax** theme, we don't need to worry about the particulars of the grammar beyond what is needed to check the syntax. Anything else is handled by the **define** theme. This is the structure that emerges from designing the syntax-checking algorithm. When working through the details of the algorithm, you will determine which of the structural elements need to specify their own checking behavior. This hierarchical difference is a little contrived, perhaps, for this example, but the point is nonetheless important, as we will see throughout the book. You worry about the structure and

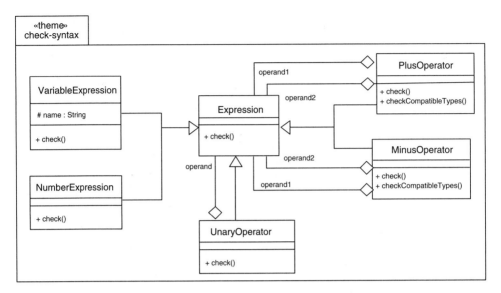

Figure 3–13   *Check-syntax theme design.*

behavior of the problem domain only as they apply to designing the theme of interest.

As before, any other design models may be added to the theme design. For example, we are likely to add an interaction diagram representing the syntax-checking algorithm.

The Evaluate Theme

As before, the design illustrated in Figure 3-14 reflects the needs of evaluating expressions and does not concern itself with other issues. Only those classes that evaluation directly deals with appear in the structure diagram. We assume that the **evaluate** theme will probably also have a behavioral design to describe the evaluation algorithm from which the required structure emerges.

You might notice that since each theme was designed from its own perspective, each theme has its own view or version of the Expression hierarchies. We learn how to unify those versions when we discuss composition.

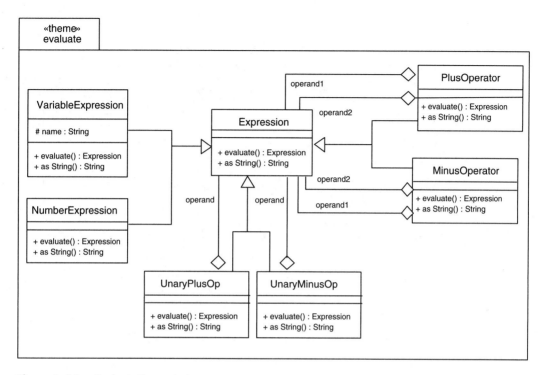

Figure 3–14   *Evaluate theme design.*

The Log Theme

The Theme/Doc individual view of the **log** theme (Figure 3–10) illustrates that this theme is triggered by behavior found in other themes in the expression system—in particular, the **evaluation**, **display**, and **check-syntax** themes. This makes it a classic example of a crosscutting theme, or aspect. However, we want to be able to design the **log** theme by reasoning about operations requiring logging without actually referring to them explicitly. This is where we find the first diversion from the standard UML.

The thing to keep in mind when designing an aspect theme is that some behavior in the theme is being *triggered* from the base themes. Notice in Figure 3–15 the dotted template box in the corner of the theme package box. In that template box, you specify a handle for the operation that triggers the aspect behavior. The triggering operation handle is a *template*

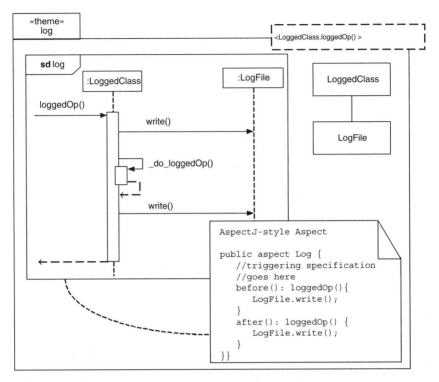

Figure 3–15   *Log theme design.*

parameter. In this case, the triggering operation is an operation being logged, and hence is called `LoggedClass.loggedOp(..)`. At this point, you needn't worry about how to hook up this handle of the triggering operation to the actual triggering operation. You just design the behavior relevant to the theme and worry about composition later.

A sequence diagram details the triggered behavior of the theme (the response to the triggering operation). For the **log** theme, the requirements tell us that the execution of operations in the affected themes should be logged. The requirements do not state exactly what this means, but in this case, we make a judgment call and say that before and after any operation is executed, a note will be written to a file. The actual logging behavior has no particular interest in the semantics of an operation being logged—just that it is executing.

You can see the handle for the triggering behavior (loggedOp()) starting off the sequence in Figure 3–15. Next, the LogFile.write() method is called, which performs the actual logging of the operation. Then, since we still haven't executed the actual logged operation, we make a special call to _do_logged_op(), which represents the invocation of the actual triggering operation. When the triggering operation completes, there is another LogFile.write(), and then the triggering operation returns to the base flow of execution.

The **log** theme also includes a note to show how an AspectJ[1] version of the sequence would look. Parts of the sequence diagrams that describe crosscutting behavior in a crosscutting theme map to *advice* in the asymmetrical separation paradigm, of which AspectJ is an implementation language. Advice is code that is executed before, after, or as a replacement for a trigger. Once again, we leave until later how to identify what the triggering operation is. For now, we concentrate on how the sequence diagram translates to AspectJ-style code.

The **log** theme has become an aspect. In the aspect, you can see two pieces of advice: before and after. In each advice there is simply a call to LogFile.write(), just as there is in the sequence diagram. Notice that there's no AspectJ equivalent for the _do_loggedOp() call. That's because before and after advice imply the execution order in relation to the trigger. In AspectJ, unless you are using an around advice (discussed in later chapters), you do not have to explicitly invoke the triggering operation. When a method represented by the loggedOp() is reached in the base of the system, the before advice is called, then the loggedOp() itself, then the after advice. Chapter 7 discusses mapping your Theme/UML designs to AspectJ in more depth.

Composing the Themes

By now, we have expended considerable effort modularizing the EES design, separating concerns wherever possible. The result is a set of theme designs, each containing all and only those design elements that relate to the requirement(s) the theme represents. In other words, there is no scattering

---

[1] http://www.eclipse.org/aspectj.

or tangling manifest in the theme designs. However, as we know, the EES software as a whole is the amalgam of all the requirements and all the themes that contain the designs for the requirements. You must consider where the modularized theme designs relate to each other and how they interact. In all aspect-oriented approaches, there must be a way to designate how the aspects relate to the rest of the system. In this section, we look at how you designate the relationships between theme designs in Theme/UML and examine the impact of these relationships.

Specify Relationship Between Themes

Theme/UML defines a new kind of relationship, called a *composition relationship*, that allows you to identify the overlaps in the different themes, specify how to resolve conflicts between overlapping elements, and specify how overlapping elements should be integrated in a composed model. You can see two kinds of overlap. The first is the classic aspect-oriented crosscutting, where dynamic behavior in one theme is triggered in tandem with behavior in other themes. The second category of overlap is concept sharing, where different themes have design elements to represent the same core concepts in the domain. For example, the **evaluate** and **check-syntax** themes both talk about plus operators and minus operators, and they both have an `Expression` class. A composition relationship can be used to handle both kinds of overlap.

Relating Themes That Share Domain Concepts

A domain concept is represented as structural and/or behavioral elements in the design. A particular class is an example of a representation of a concept. As discussed above, themes can each provide designs for the same core concepts, each from its own perspective. For instance, both the **check-syntax** and **evaluate** themes have an `Expression class`, but each class only has methods relevant to the theme in which it resides.

Composing elements that represent the same core concepts and that have been given the same name (the name `Expression` is used in both **check-syntax** and **evaluate**) is the simplest composition case. All you need to do is draw a composition relationship between the relevant themes with a `match[name]` tag. The elements are merged in a composed design, with matching elements appearing once. Where the matching element is a container like a class, the elements in all matching containers appear in the one composed container. The simplest case is appropriate for this expression example, and Figure 3–16 illustrates how to specify a composition of the **define**, **check-syntax**, and **evaluate** themes. The `ThemeName["base"]` tag shows that a theme called **base** will be the product of the merged themes.

Of course, the simplest case will probably not be applicable in every situation. Theme/UML has a means to match elements with different names, exclude elements that may coincidentally have the same name but are not a representation of the same concept, and specify how to reconcile any conflicts in matching elements. These capabilities are discussed in later chapters, and we also describe an integration policy based on overriding elements in one theme with elements from another theme. This is useful for late-introduced themes that contain design changes to possibly obsolete elements in the existing design.

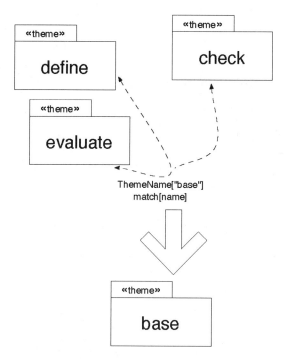

Figure 3–16   *Composition relationship: shared concepts.*

Relating Themes That Crosscut

As described for the **log** design, a theme that contains a design for crosscutting behavior specifies templates as placeholders for real design elements. The **log** theme, for instance, has a template parameter called `LoggedClass.loggedOp(..)`. `loggedOp(..)` represents the actual method that triggers the logging behavior, as described in the sequence diagram in the **log** theme. We now specify which operation is the real trigger for the logging behavior. When we compose the **log** theme with its base theme (**check-syntax**, in this case), we want the trigger from the base theme to actually replace the references to `loggedOp(..)`.

To specify that replacement, you use the `bind[]` tag for the Theme/UML composition relationship. You can see an example of binding in Figure 3–17. In this case, we want logging to occur when expressions are checked, when they are displayed, and when they are evaluated. These operations are handled by the `Expression.check()` method, `Expression.asString()` method, and `Expression.evaluate()` method, respectively. So, we list each method that we're interested in logging, each of

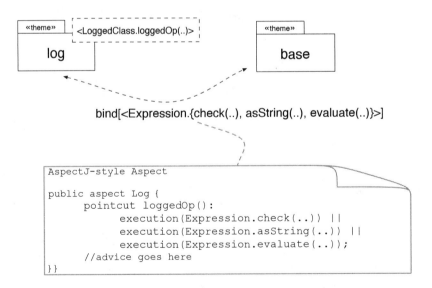

Figure 3–17   *Composition relationship: crosscutting.*

which will separately replace the `loggedOp(..)` template. If these methods were the only ones in the `Expression` class, we could have simply used used a wildcard to represent all operations using `Expression.*(..)`. The `*` is a wildcard that means any string, and the `(..)` is a wildcard that means any parameters. See Chapter 6 for details of how more interesting bindings can be achieved with the bind annotation.

Figure 3–17 also shows a note containing some AspectJ code that specifies which operations are the triggers for the logging behavior. Just as with the Theme/UML bind tag, we're looking for the execution of three particular methods: (`Expression.check()`, `Expression.asString()`, and `Expression.evaluate()`) regardless of their parameters (`(..)`). In AspectJ, you use a `pointcut` statement to capture all those methods. A pointcut is a way to specify the points of execution at which advice behavior should be triggered. Based on this pointcut specification, when the AspectJ code is compiled, the code in the advice is woven into the execution of the program before and after every specified method.

Composed Themes

At this point in the design process, you understand the internals of individual themes and have defined where you see overlaps between themes—both in terms of how they each may have elements that describe the same domain concept and also relating to crosscutting behavior. You can apply the composition relationships to compose the design. The composed design can be helpful for checking whether the composition relationships are written as intended or can be used as a guide for implementing your system in a non-aspect-oriented language. The composed design will, of course, display the nonmodular (tangling) characteristics that this whole approach is designed to avoid.

Shared Concepts Composed

The result of composing themes as specified in Figure 3–16 is illustrated in Figure 3–18. Design elements that have the same name are deemed to relate to the same concept, and so are merged in the output. In this case, all classes except the `Literal` class from the **define** theme design have a matching class in at least one of the other two themes being composed. For

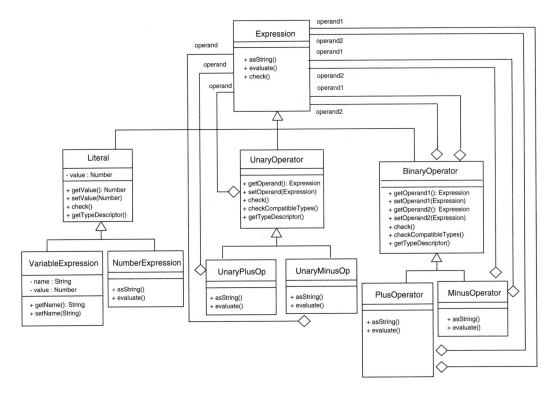

Figure 3–18   *The base theme: shared concepts composed.*

each class, attributes and methods from all matching input classes appear in the composed output.

Note also that all of the relationships defined in the input themes are added to the output, with redundant relationships excluded and duplications added just once. An example of a redundant relationship is a generalization between two classes in one theme that has an additional layer in another theme. Say `ClassA` inherits from `ClassC` in one theme, and in another theme, `ClassA` inherits from `ClassB`, which inherits from `ClassC`. In this case, the inheritance relationship from `ClassA` to `ClassC` is redundant in a composed hierarchy. You will also need to watch out for circular inheritance relationships that may appear. For example, `ClassA` inherits from `ClassB` in one theme, and `ClassB` inherits from `ClassA` in another theme. Such circular relationships will have to be removed. An example of a duplicate relationship is an aggregation relationship between two classes with the same role names that has been defined in more than one input theme. Aggregation relationships that appear for a subclass and also for its superclass are not duplicates, and are each added. Composing the themes gives you an opportunity to examine the relationships between classes in the input themes, and decide which relationships should be made explicit in an implementation.

Crosscutting Behavior Composed

The result of composing themes as specified in Figure 3–17 is illustrated in Figure 3–19. You may recall that aspect themes have template parameters, specified in angle brackets (< >), that specify the triggering operation. For each triggering operation, there is a sequence diagram specified in the composed theme. When we bound the template parameter operation to

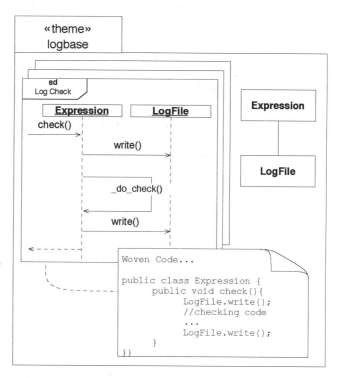

Figure 3–19   *Crosscutting behavior composed.*

the actual triggering operation (found in the **base** theme), we were actually telling Theme/UML to generate a new sequence diagram for each bound operation in which the template parameter behavior and structure would be replaced with the bound operations.

For instance, one of the bindings we specified was of `<LoggedClass.loggedOp()>` to `Expression.check()`, denoting that a sequence diagram should be generated in which all occurrences of `LoggedClass` are replaced with references to `Expression`. In Figure 3–19, you can see that there is no `LoggedClass` shown. Instead, there is an `Expression` class receiving the triggering call in the sequence diagram. All design elements in `LoggedClass` are added to the `Expression` class.

Additionally, all occurrences of `_do_loggedOp()` will be replaced with references to `_do_check()`, with the triggering call changed from `loggedOp()` to `check()`.

Hidden behind the `Expression.check()` sequence diagram are corresponding diagrams for `Expression.asString()` and `Expression.evaluate()`.

Once again, you can see a code snippet to illustrate what happened in the composition. In this case, we see the `check()` method of the `Expression` class. The `LogFile.write()` call is made before and after the code related to checking the syntax of expressions.

Revisiting Evolution

In Chapter 2, we noted that evolution was particularly difficult when you are faced with adding certain functionality to the object-oriented design for the expression system. We now revisit that evolution, this time applying the Theme approach.

The additional requirements are as follows:

- R12: Check-def-use capability to ensure that all variables used are defined, and all variables defined are used.

- R13: Check-style capability to ensure that expressions conform to local naming conventions.

- R14: Mix-and-match checking capability to ensure that clients can choose a combination of check-syntax, check-def-use, and check-style to be run on their expression programs when they invoke the check tool.

- R15: Check-style and check-def-use should be logged.

Now that we have these new requirements, let's see how to absorb these changes using the Theme approach. We start by finding any new themes that arise out of these requirements, and then design and compose those themes.

Finding the Themes

We follow the first steps of the Theme/Doc process again and arrive at some additional likely themes:

- **check-def-use**

- **check-style**

- **mix-and-match**

Once again, we look at the relationship view to see how the addition of the new potential themes affects the system. The new relationship view is shown in Figure 3–20. Each of the shared requirements has been expanded so that we can investigate them further.

Choose Initial Themes

First, we look at the themes and consider whether to keep them. In this case, we chose potential themes that seemed to be of the same style as the successful ones from the previous development cycle. It is not necessarily the case that your themes will always be the same size or style. In this case, though, we are happy with the new themes that we have chosen.

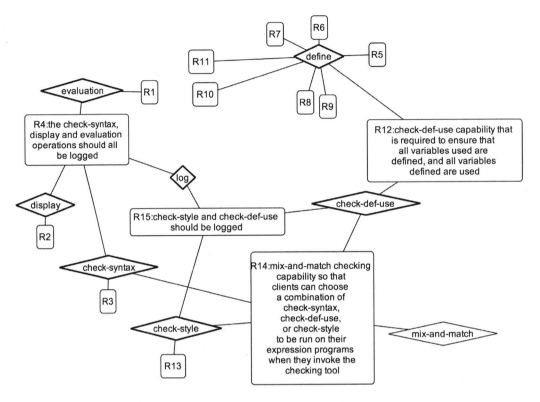

Figure 3-20   *SEE relationship view, with added themes and requirements.*

Examine Shared Requirements

Once you have settled on a set of themes that you're happy with, you move on to examining shared requirements to see if they reveal aspect behavior. As before, you apply the three rules (*split if possible; dominance means association;* and *base triggers aspect*) to help identify which themes are crosscutting. If those rules fail, you may need to rework either themes or requirements to handle requirements sharing. When you can't even do that, you can postpone the decision until later, when it becomes possible to deal with it.

Identify Aspects

We've already made the decision that **log** dominates and is triggered in R4. But this does not mean that **log** will necessarily be the aspect theme when looking at its other shared requirement, R15. Rather than just restating the rules, this time we ask the questions you would ask when looking at a shared requirement.

> *Can it be split?* First, R15 is checked to see whether it can be split. Like R4, splitting it into two requirements (**check-style** should be logged, and **check-def-use** should be logged) does not completely remove requirement sharing.

> *Does one theme dominate?* Once again, this requirement seems to be mostly about logging and the situations in which it's used.

> *Is the dominant theme triggered by the other themes?* Logging, the behavior dominant to R15, is triggered by **check-style** and **check-def-use**.

Based on this reasoning, we associate R15 with the dominant theme, **log**, and so denote that **log** is an aspect of **check-style** and **check-def-use**.

Figure 3–21 shows the new crosscutting relationships from **log** to all the checking themes.

Rework Themes and Requirements

R12 is shared between **define** and **check-def-use**. We now examine R12 to assess whether it reveals crosscutting.

Can it be split? Not really. The requirement describes **check-def-use** with relation to **define**, and there is no rewriting that will change that.

Does one theme dominate? Once again, not really. While the theme is mainly about **check-def-use**, the **define** behavior is also quite central to the requirement. Since this test has failed, it's not necessary to move on to

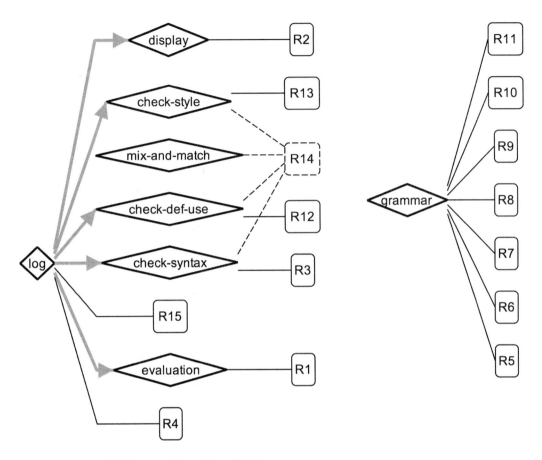

Figure 3–21   *Evolved crosscutting-relationship view.*

whether one theme triggers another. Instead, we need to look closer at this requirement to see how we can handle the sharing.

Most importantly, the sense in which **define** is used in R12 (variables must be defined and then used) is not the same sense in which it is used in R6 through R11 (an operator is defined as a . . .). We have encountered a synonym that needs to be resolved to remove the erroneous sharing. We can split the **define** theme to remove the sharing. Or, we could rename the **define** theme to something more specifically about grammar definition. The string "is defined as" is how each operation in the SEE is described. If we rename the **define** theme to **is defined as**, the sharing will be removed.

Since **is defined as** isn't a very good name for a theme, we can rename it to reflect its design-level name, **grammar**.

Figure 3–21 displays the new **grammar** theme and shows that R12 is no longer shared.

Postpone as Needed

R14, as is visible in Figure 3–20, is shared between **mix-and-match**, **check-style**, **check-def-use**, and **check-syntax**. On first reading, it's clear that this is actually a requirement about which themes to compose; we would not design its implementation. This requirement is a good candidate for postponement. We can then be reminded to use it later when we are choosing which of the check themes to compose together. Postponing R14 changes its outline to dashed. The links between R14 and its constituent themes are also changed to dashed. The dashed postponement is shown in Figure 3–21.

Planning for Design

You can now look at the theme views for the new themes to advise you on how to design them, and you can use this crosscutting-relationship view to plan the theme bindings.

Designing and Composing the Themes

As we showed in Chapter 2, your options for adding new functionality to existing designs using standard object-oriented techniques are limited. The solutions considered either resulted in combinatorial explosions of classes when a noninvasive, subclassing approach was taken or required invasive changes to the existing design when we tried to retrofit the Visitor pattern. Here, we show how new functionality can be added to a system without making any changes to the existing design. You can do this because each new concern (as derived from the new requirements) is considered to be a theme in its own right. The new themes can be designed separately and composed with the full design using a composition relationship.

The previous step in the Theme process of finding the themes using Theme/Doc identified three new themes: **check-def-use**, **check-style**, and **mix-and-match**. The first two require a design, while the third will influence the composition. There is nothing different about designing **check-def-use** and **check-style** that is specific to the Theme approach, and so we do not show their detail. Suffice to say that for each, there will be an appropriate set of design models (structural and behavioral) that captures their design without consideration of any other expression concerns. As with the initial design, design decisions such as the nature of the class hierarchies will be specific to the theme under design.

Handling composition of the two theme designs with the existing expression design is more interesting. The output from the Theme/Doc process, as illustrated in Figure 3–20, tells you that inclusion of any of the three checking themes is optional, leading to any combination of checking possible. This means we would simply include only the desired checking themes in the composition process. As these are domain concept-sharing themes, the composition relationship to be used is similar to that shown in Figure 3–16. In Figure 3–22, we show all three checking themes included in a composition relationship with another theme. As an example, this other theme is the **grammar** theme, but could be any other (set of) theme(s)—even the output theme of a previous composition.

For illustrative purposes, we show just the `Expression` class from the four themes in the composition and the impact of the composition on those classes. Each individual checking theme names the operation that does the checking `check()`. Therefore, the `match[name]` tag in the composition relationship deems these operations as matching. When operations are merged, the behaviors of each of the matching operations are joined together. This means that the execution of any one of the matching operations results in the execution of all matching operations. **Mix-and-match** behavior is achieved because any of the checking themes included in the composition will be included in any checking process. In Theme/UML's composition process, the specification of this behavior is achieved by generating interaction diagrams realizing the composed operation as delegating to each of the matching input operations when it is invoked. The order of operation execution specified in the interaction diagram is random. As

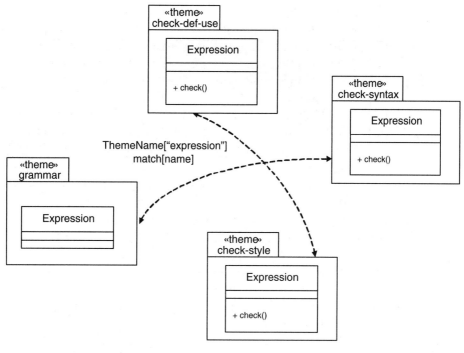

Figure 3–22 *Composing new themes.*

you can see in Figure 3–23, input operations are renamed to avoid a name clash. Excluding any particular kind of checking entails simply removing it from the composition specification using the composition relationship.

In Chapter 6, "Theme Composition," we show how to match elements in input themes that may not have the same name, but should be considered to match. We also show how to define a specific order of execution for matching operations.

A Final Word on Evolution

A major selling point for aspect-oriented software development is the improvements gained in the software evolution process. As manifested in the Theme approach, evolution suggests that there just happen to be some

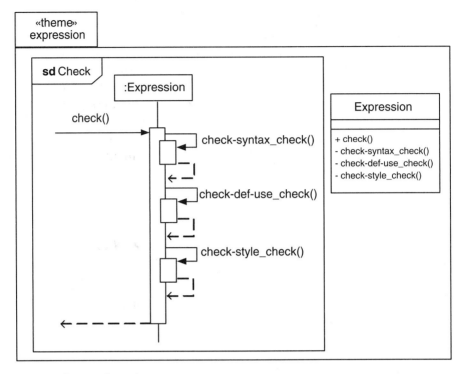

Figure 3–23 *Composed mix-and-match.*

more themes to be composed with other themes. The whole approach is designed to ensure that separate themes are designed from their own perspective, without reference to other themes. Therefore, whether a theme design was created during the development of an initial version of the system or for later versions of the system makes no difference to the composition process. This is true whether the themes are concept-sharing themes or crosscutting themes.

What Is the Right Size for a Theme?

The Theme approach does not explicitly recommend any particular "size" for a theme. If a theme is measured by the number of design elements contained within, then the size will be dictated by what is necessary to support the particular requirement under design by that theme. Other design approaches provide some guidelines as to the size of their different models.

For example, the OORam model provides some loose guidelines for the size of role models based on the notion that human short-term memory can manage seven plus or minus two notions at the same time. The suggested guideline, therefore, is that a role model should consist of between five and nine roles, where fewer than five roles should be synthesized into a larger role model, and where consideration should be given to further breaking up a model with greater than nine roles. The Theme approach, however, focuses on modularizing designs based on logical separations as ascertained from examination of the requirements specification, and not what the ultimate size of the theme might be.

Fitting Theme into Your Existing Development Process

The analysis and design activities described in the Theme approach can be split up and molded to fit into whichever development process you are happiest using. We briefly outline how that might work.

Waterfall

With the waterfall approach, you have very distinct phases of requirements analysis, design, implementation, and testing. Each one feeds into the next, with little, if any, jumping between them. The Theme approach can be fit into this model by extending your analysis process to include analysis with Theme/Doc followed by doing your design with Theme/UML.

Iterative Approach

With the iterative lifecycle, you divide your system into a number of different parts (most commonly by end-user-recognizable function, but sometimes by technical component). You then design and implement these parts consecutively, each in its own iteration. This approach has the advantage of allowing you to get early feedback from the end user (or other programmers using the services of the component that makes up the iteration), which can be incorporated into the design of the next iteration. The

Theme approach supports this style of development, as each iteration can be designed separately in its own (set of) themes.

Agile Processes

Agile processes are lightweight approaches for software development. They are intended to get away from the heavyweight approaches (such as the waterfall approach) in which there are significant analysis and design before implementation begins. Agile processes stress the use of appropriate methodology, and *people over process.*

There are several offerings of agile processes. Although these processes are quite different, the Theme approach can be flexibly used within them. We discuss three of them here: extreme programming (XP), test-driven development (TDD), and feature-driven development (FDD). For each, we outline how the Theme approach can be applied.

Feature-Driven Development

FDD involves the development of individual features of a system. Developers take ownership of certain features and see them through from modeling to implementation. Themes fit in with FDD[2] quite naturally. Themes can be used to represent features in a system, so using the theme approach for AO-FDD would work well. There are five steps in applying FDD with the Theme approach:

> *Build an overall model.* In this step, developers and domain experts provide a high-level overview of the system and its scope. This step happens as usual when applying the Theme approach.

> *Build a features list.* This step works with the "identify themes" phase of the Theme analysis process. The descriptions of features is used to generate a Theme/Doc relationship view to identify relationships between themes. Feature

---

[2] Available from http://www.thecoadletter.com/article/0,1410,29684,00.html.

clusters, as identified in FDD, translate to groups of themes. The "aspect identification" phase also occurs here, where the heuristics about shared feature responsibilities are assessed to determine whether aspect features (aspect themes) are required.

Plan by feature. This happens the same way as in vanilla FDD.

Design by feature. Here, the only change to the vanilla FDD is that each feature is designed as a separate theme, and the composition semantics are also specified. Class ownership (in which a developer claims responsibility for a pertinent range of classes) could become theme ownership.

Build by feature. Each theme is translated into code, then tested.

Test-Driven Development

In TDD, tests are written before coding begins, then enough code is written to fail and then pass the test. Refactoring happens and is tested along the way. The first phase of TDD is the "think about what you want to do" phase. If, during this phase, you appeal to any written documentation for motivation (requirements for a feature, for instance), or if you write your thoughts down, you enhance the thinking process by looking at a Theme/Doc view of that document, seeing which themes you would like to implement, and identifying requirements that might reveal aspect behavior. In the thinking phase, you also identify themes that should be implemented as aspects.

If you normally use a design language like UML to enhance the thinking process, then here you would use Theme/UML.

Then, you write your tests, write your failure code, and start to write your "hoping to pass" code. If decisions you made during your thinking were wrong, the changes you need to make to fix the problems are reflected back to your list of themes, their responsibilities, and the relationships between themes. The new list of themes and responsibilities is used to regenerate the Theme/Doc relationship view, which might reveal relationships you hadn't foreseen and that would drive further implementation.

If you encoded your design in Theme/UML, then you alter your Theme/UML as well.

This process continues until your tests pass.

As you think about your next collection of functionality, you integrate any documents you were using and generate a Theme/Doc view to predict relationships between functionality in your system. This helps you anticipate how you might accommodate old functionality at implementation, and also reminds you about code reuse: If a behavior is already present in the Theme/Doc view, then you already have a theme that implements it.

Extreme Programming

XP is a highly collaborative, team-based approach to software development. It stresses collaboration between programmers and customers. XP, like the other agile processes described above, prioritizes pragmatic design over design for long-term change.

XP uses TDD for its "inner loop." As such, you would apply TDD for Theme as described above.

XP uses "user stories" to describe functionality to be implemented in the current cycle. These are high-level use-case-style-descriptions of new features to add to the system. While traditionally, user stories are written on note cards, they could be translated to electronic text and used to generate a Theme/Doc view of all the user stories combined, or for a selection, or of just one.

Themes are identified from pieces of functionality included in a user story during the planning-for-implementation phases, and aspects are identified from the relationships between themes.

Alternatively, a single user story can be chosen as corresponding to a theme. Relationships between the texts of user stories may give rise to aspects and would be revealed by a check of a Theme/Doc relationship view.

Class-responsibility-collaboration (CRC) cards informally record developers' planning for implementation in terms of programming language structure.

CRCs (again, electronicized) could also be used as input to the Theme/Doc tool to identify where behavioral overlaps occur. Groups or portions of CRC cards would comprise a theme; the scope of the group (entire or partial user story) would depend on your earlier choice about theme scope. If you chose to break up your user story into multiple themes, then one theme per piece of functionality would work well as a starting point. Concept-sharing and crosscutting relationships could be recorded in the collaboration part of the CRC card.

Theme/UML is used in place of UML to capture the themes regardless of whether they were entire user stories or smaller functionality found within. Theme/UML can be used to encode the CRCs for a cycle.

The Theme approach fits well into the "do the simplest thing" and "you aren't gonna need it" philosophies. At the design level, each theme needs to contain only the minimal set of structure and behavior to carry out the responsibilities identified through analysis.

If your project necessitates requirements tracking, in which you must show your customer that the functionality they have requested has been considered from user story to implementation, then a requirements theme to design theme (either in Theme/UML or on CRCs) to code mapping would likely help.

Summary

In this chapter, we continued with the EES example described in Chapter 2. We walked through using the Theme approach to find themes, design those themes, and evolve the system.

Finding the themes involved refining the set of themes to include in your system, and then looking at shared requirements to determine whether they revealed an aspect. To assess this, you

- ensure that the requirement cannot be split up,

- assess whether one theme dominates the requirement, and if so,

- assess whether the dominant theme is triggered by the other themes (that it is externally triggered).

If all these tests pass, then you have identified aspect functionality. Later, in Chapter 4, we describe another aspect-identification rule: The theme must be externally triggered in multiple situations to be an aspect.

Designing the themes then involves modeling the noncrosscutting (base) themes in individual package-like modules. Crosscutting themes are designed in parameterized packages. Their template parameters expose their triggering behavior.

Themes are then composed using a composition relationship that allows you to

- identify overlapping design elements within the themes,

- specify how the themes should be integrated,

- specify how conflicts should be resolved between overlapping design elements,

- identify triggering behavior in a base to bind to templates in an aspect.

This chapter provided a very high-level example of how to map designs to implementation. Detailed instruction about that are provided in Chapter 7, "Map to Implementation," and an example of implementing themes is described in the second case study at the end of this book.

Next, we give the details of a more in-depth example system that will serve as a basis for a detailed description of the Theme approach in Chapters 4 to 7.

4

Analysis

This chapter describes the Theme approach to requirements analysis. In earlier chapters, we described what a theme is: an encapsulation of a concern. In this chapter, we look at themes at the requirements-level. Requirements describe behavior associated with concerns. Portions of a requirements document may all describe a particular concern. Grouping those portions encapsulates them in a requirements-level theme. Requirements may describe more than one concern, and so may seem to fit in more than one theme's group of requirements. Some care must be taken to try to achieve theme-orthogonality: themes should not overlap in their requirements groups. At times, rewriting the shared requirement is needed, and at other times, handling the overlap in design is necessary.

An aspect is a special kind of theme: a concern that is triggered by one or more other concerns. So, at this point, we take a requirements-level view of aspects: We consider aspects to be concerns that possess four main traits:

- a concern whose description within a requirement is tangled (irreparably) with the description of other concerns,

- the dominant concern in the tangled requirement,

- concern functionality that is triggered by the other concerns in the requirement,

- concern functionality that is triggered in more than one situation as described in the requirements.

Figure 4–1 depicts scattering and tangling in requirements taken from the set of requirements for the Crystal Game (see the sidebar "Crystal Game" and the appendix). In this figure, some of the pieces of functionality are circled. If they're in more than one requirement, then their circles are linked with a solid line. The solid line indicates scattering of functionality between requirements. If two pieces of functionality appear together in a requirement, they are linked with a dashed line to indicate tangling. This is just a small example, but it conveys the difficulty of trying to mentally disentangle requirement-level relationships. For instance, it takes a minute to see that the "shown" functionality is indirectly related to the "duel" functionality. The

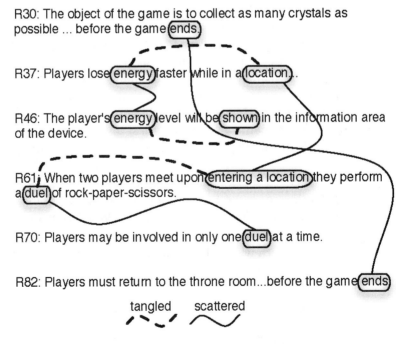

Figure 4–1   *Concerns mixed between requirements.*

Crystal Game

The Crystal Game is a location-aware game. Each player is equipped with a handheld device (PDA) through which they interact with the game world. Players explore the physical world using their PDA to tell them which game elements are present in sensor-equipped locations.

The Object of the Game

The object of the game is to collect as many virtual crystals as possible before time runs out. Virtual crystals are distributed around the game-play area at the start of the game. There are also magical items scattered around the game-world. Those figure differently into game-play.

Players

Players can take on three roles: wizard, warrior, and sage. There are also nonplayer characters (NPCs) in the world. NPCs are also wizards, warriors, and sages.

Starting a New Game

One player (the "host") creates a new game. Other players can then join the game. When the players join, they are sent to locations around the game-area. The host's location becomes the "throne room" that figures into the end of the game.

Game Play

Crystals can be discovered by players when they enter a new location. Players can (nonviolently, of course) duel one another for crystals. The winner of the duel receives the wagered crystals from the losing player.

Players interact with NPCs in different ways depending on their role-type, and the role-type of the NPC.

NPCs sometimes demand that players locate magical items in order to receive a crystal that the NPC is hoarding.

As the game progresses, players lose or gain energy. Different acts cause energy levels to go up or down.

Winning and Losing

When the game time is up, all the players must go back to the location deemed to be the throne room to find out who won. The player with the most crystals wins. If two players have the same number of crystals, the one with the most energy wins. If there is still a tie, a duel decides the winner.

Refer to the appendix, "The Crystal Game," for a complete set of requirements.

purpose of Theme/Doc is to help you better visualize the relationships between tangled functionality and make decisions about how it should be encapsulated in your system.

In the "Finding the Themes" section of Chapter 3, "The Theme Approach," we walked through a simple example of how to identify themes in a set of requirements. Finding themes is a broader task than finding aspects. Finding themes involves identifying groupings of functionality that make sense. As we discussed in Chapter 3, some of these units may be aspects, and some may be base. We looked at how to find a starting list of possible themes, how to narrow those down to a list of actual themes, and then how to decide which themes are crosscutting (aspect) themes and which are base themes.

In this chapter, we delve into these concepts in much greater detail. As a basis for this, we use the Crystal Game example system, described in the appendix, "The Crystal Game." As you will see, the requirements for the crystal game example are not as simple as those we use in the EES from previous chapters. This chapter walks you through applying the Theme/Doc part of the Theme approach when faced with requirements that are not ideal.

We also go over how to know when you are done with the analysis process, or at least when you are "done for now."

First, however, we go over some basics of the Theme/Doc. We start by describing the Theme/Doc views that are used as well as the tool support available to create those views. Then, we take a high-level look at the Theme/Doc process.

Theme/Doc Views and Tool Support

Before we start going over the process of applying Theme/Doc views for aspect-oriented analysis, we're going to go over the Theme/Doc views themselves. There are three Theme/Doc views: the relationship view, the crosscutting view, and the individual view. Later (in the section "Overview of the Theme/Doc Process"), we discuss what the views are used for. Here, we mainly outline what they look like and what information they present.

Kinds of Requirements

Requirements can be written in various ways, from various points of view, and can describe differing units, such as features or services.

In terms of applicability to the Theme approach, this variability makes no difference. As long as requirements are written in text, the Theme approach can be applied to them.

If they are expressed diagrammatically, as use cases sometimes are, their associated text can be used in the Theme approach or might be described textually, and those descriptions can then be used when applying the Theme approach.

Some requirements are written more formally, using systems of logic. The Theme approach can be applied to requirements in this form, since each requirement will have lexically identifiable elements and behaviors.

The granularity of a requirement can be arbitrarily chosen. Typically, in natural language texts, a single sentence is treated as a requirement. But paragraphs might also be a natural choice. Really, any block of text (regardless of its grammar) can be set as a requirement. The Theme approach allows for certain flexibility in this because it supports requirement refinement: If a requirement can be split into smaller units to achieve better separation of concerns, then this becomes obvious in the early phases of analysis.

Theme/Doc views are created automatically by the Theme/Doc view-generation tool. For each view we describe in this section, we also discuss what inputs are needed for the tool to construct it.

Theme-Relationship View

The theme-relationship view shows, as you would expect, relationships between themes. Figure 4–2 shows an abstract example of a theme-relationship view (sometimes called simply a relationship view). Themes are

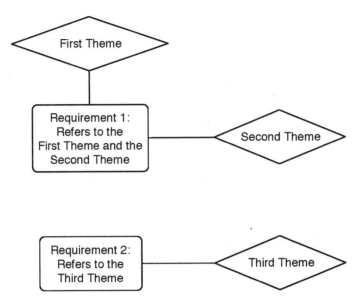

Figure 4–2   *Abstract example of a Theme/Doc-relationship view.*

each shown in diamond-shaped nodes. The theme's name is the label for the node. Requirements are also displayed in this view, shown in rounded-corner boxes. Requirements can be labeled with their entire text or simply with the requirement number. Most of the views in this chapter show just the requirement number.

The relationship view is formed by providing a list of theme names and a list of requirements to the Theme/Doc view-generation tool. The relationship view doesn't show *direct* relationships between themes. Instead, it shows how themes relate to requirements. If a requirement's text contains a reference to a theme name, a link is depicted connecting the requirement to that theme. If a requirement mentions more than one theme (like Requirement 1 in Figure 4–2), then it is linked to more than one theme node. Requirements that refer to more than one theme are called *shared requirements*. If two themes are linked to the same requirement, we say that these themes *share* that requirement and that the themes are related.

It will most likely be the case that some requirements do not contain any references to the themes listed. If that's the case, then those requirements are not linked to any themes in the views. We call these *orphaned* requirements. Later in this chapter, we talk about how to use the features of the Theme/Doc tool to resolve synonyms to help deal with orphaned requirements.

Crosscutting Theme View

Shared requirements often describe crosscutting behavior. We don't get into what crosscutting behavior really is at this point, or how you might identify it. Instead, we go over how this view can represent choices you make based on shared requirements.

As in the relationship view, themes are shown as diamonds, and requirements are shown as rounded boxes. These elements are present in Figure 4–3.

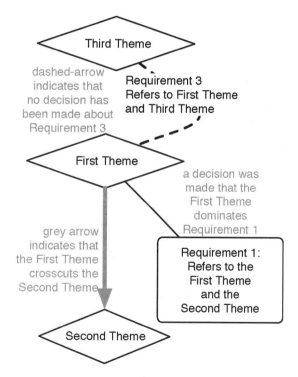

Figure 4–3   *Abstract example of a Theme/Doc crosscutting view.*

Generally, behavior described in requirements has to be "associated" with just one theme, which is to say that a theme is held responsible for a requirement's behavior. This is not a hard and fast rule, as you will see both later in this chapter and in the discussion of overriding behavior in one theme with behavior in another (Chapter 6, "Theme Composition"). But in the initial phases of the analysis process, we try to sort out which themes are basically responsible for which functionality in the system, so it's useful to think of it as an N:1 requirement to theme relationship.

There are two choices about how to associate a shared requirement. The first is to associate it with the theme that you believe to be the "aspect" in the situation. Associations are depicted in the crosscutting view as thick gray arrows extending from the aspect theme (the one held responsible for the shared behavior) to the base theme (the one with which the requirement is no longer associated). Figure 4–3 depicts a crosscutting relationship from **First Theme** to **Second Theme**. Association relationships alter the links between a requirement and the themes to which it refers. If a requirement is associated with a theme (the aspect theme), it is shown as linked only to that theme. All the other themes to which the requirement refers (the base themes) are shown as crosscut by the aspect theme. There are no links from the theme to the base themes, though textual references to those themes are still present in the requirement. Notice that there are no links from Requirement 1 to **Second Theme**.

The second choice is to postpone the decision about how the shared theme should be associated. Postponements are depicted in the crosscutting view with dashed lines, labeled with the requirement whose association has been postponed. You can see an example of a postponed requirement association in Figure 4–3. The dashed line linking **First Theme** and **Third Theme** denotes that association of Requirement 3 (which refers to both **First Theme** and **Third Theme**) has been postponed. Just the requirement number is used to label the postponement relationship, rather than the requirement's text.

The crosscutting view and the relationship view are actually just two extremes of a continuum. The relationship view extreme includes all the relationships between themes and requirements, but it includes no crosscutting relationships. The crosscutting view extreme includes association relationships between themes and requirements, and depicts those as associations between themes. It includes no shared requirements. In practice, though, these views are integrated so that you'll likely be looking at a relationship view that has some crosscutting relationships but also some shared requirements. You can think of the relationship view as the starting point and the crosscutting view as the eventual goal.

The crosscutting view is created by the Theme/Doc view-generation tool by providing four inputs: a list of themes, a list of requirements, a list of associations, and a list of postponements.

Individual View

The individual view is the crosscutting view extreme (no shared requirements) for just one theme. Additionally, it includes key entities. The Theme/Doc view-generation tool forms the individual view by taking all the inputs given to the crosscutting view (themes, requirements, associations, postponements, and entities). An abstract example of the individual view is shown in Figure 4–4.

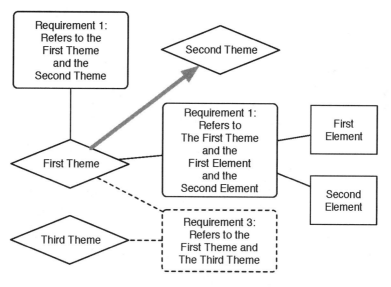

Figure 4–4   *Abstract example of a Theme/Doc individual theme view.*

Associations affect requirement–theme links in the individual view in the same way they do in the crosscutting view. Postponement relationships are depicted a little differently to accommodate viewing of the text of requirements rather than just the requirement label, as is usually used in the crosscutting view. Notice that Requirement 3 is depicted as a requirement shared by First Theme and Third Theme, and that dashed lines are used to indicate that its association has been postponed. Formation of the individual view has a few subtleties when grouped themes are involved. Those subtleties are discussed in the sections entitled "Viewing Base Themes" and "Viewing Aspect Themes."

Overview of the Theme/Doc Process

The Theme/Doc portion of the Theme approach contains three main components: deciding on a set of themes to include in your system, determining the responsibilities of those themes, and planning for design. These three activities are depicted in Figure 4–5.

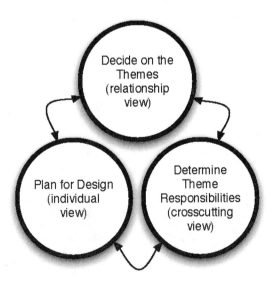

Figure 4–5   *General view of the analysis process.*

The activity at the top of the figure is Decide on the Themes. In that part of the process, you attempt to arrive at different pieces of functionality, each described separately.

Moving clockwise, the bottom right activity is Determine Theme Responsibilities. This is a more general way to say, "Decide which themes are aspects and which are base." The reason we describe it as deciding on responsibilities is that if a theme is responsible for behavior that is triggered in another theme, than the first theme is an aspect of the second.

Finally, there is the Plan for Design activity in which you consider the structure and behavior that you will model using Theme/UML.

It is likely that, at least at first, these activities will take place in the order shown, so that you first think about which themes you want to implement, then decide what those themes will do (which requirements they will cover, how they relate to other themes, whether they are aspects or base), and then do initial designs for the themes. But once that initial iteration is over, it's likely that you'll choose to mix up the process a little. For instance, after thinking about the design of a theme, you may realize that you're not happy with the responsibilities of that theme, and you may backtrack and assign the theme different responsibilities (by associating it with different requirements). Or, you may decide that you don't think the theme works at all and that you'd rather get rid of it. In that case, you review the themes you plan to keep and reconsider how to split up the responsibilities from your unwanted theme.

You may have noticed that in Figure 4–5, the activities have particular Theme/Doc views associated with them. The relationship view is suggested as a way to help you decide on which themes should be included in your system; the crosscutting view can help you determine the responsibilities of a theme (and hence which themes crosscut other themes); the individual view is suggested to help you plan for design. However, it is not the case that you have to stick religiously to those suggestions; any of these views might be helpful when performing the other activities. Just as you will likely have to iterate between the three main activities, you will probably find that switching between views is helpful.

A more realistic look at how views might be used for tasks is shown in Figure 4–6. The relationship view is depicted as being useful for both deciding on which themes to have and determining theme responsibilities. The

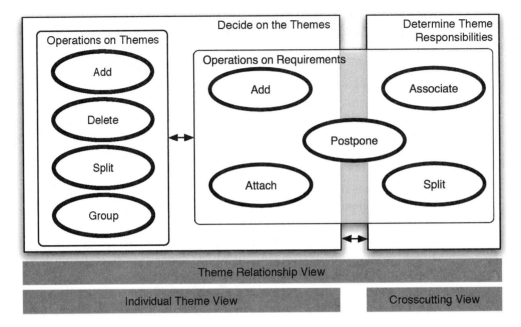

Figure 4–6   *Focused look at the activities involved in choosing themes and deciding on their responsibilities.*

individual view seems most relevant when looking at whether the themes you have chosen are appropriate (part of the process of deciding on themes). The crosscutting view is what reflects choices about requirements associations (and postponed associations), so that view is mainly useful when deciding on aspect-base relationships. All three views, however, are useful when planning for design.

Figure 4–6 shows operations you can perform on requirements and themes as ovals. These operations are available when using the Theme/Doc view-generation tool regardless of the view you are using. Four operations can be performed while adjusting themes: adding themes, deleting themes, splitting up themes, and grouping themes. Five operations can be performed on requirements: adding a new one, splitting them up (essentially adds new ones to the end of the list of requirements and marks the requirement as "split"), attaching them to a particular theme, associating them with a particular theme (to specify crosscutting), and postponing their association until more information becomes available.

The rest of this chapter looks at how these operations are used when analyzing the requirements from the Crystal Game (provided in the appendix). The description of the approach in this chapter is very linear: first we describe deciding on the themes, then determining which themes are aspects and which are base, and finally, preparing for design. The application of the views in this chapter is also simplified such that all the views in the chapter are used in the task context depicted in Figure 4–5. As we discussed above, you should not feel limited to the ordering of events as described below. The case studies at the end of this book provide examples of mingling these activities, using views in different contexts, and interleaving these activities with design.

Deciding on the Themes

The first step in the Theme/Doc requirements analysis process is to figure out what functionality relates to which theme. Once you've done that, you can look at the overlap between the themes and see whether making some themes aspects would be beneficial to the design. There are lots of ways you might parcel your requirements into a set of themes, and many approaches for refining and parceling requirements into features, concerns, or goals. Some of those approaches were described in Chapter 2, "The Object-Oriented Way." Theme/Doc views can also help with this task because they can give you, at a glance, a sense of which requirements have been assigned to a theme and which themes might not actually be effective. This section goes over how Theme/Doc views (specifically, the theme-relationship view) can help with assigning themes to requirements.

Choosing Initial Themes

The starting point for the Theme/Doc approach is finding a set of potential themes, or features, of your system. This is not the same as finding the *eventual* themes or concerns of your system. That comes later, and likely after much iteration. This initial step is to identify all the behavior described in your requirements that could potentially be a theme. To get a list of potential themes, you pick out key concerns described in your requirements.

How you choose your initial themes likely depends on the kind of requirements you have. If your requirements have been translated into one or more use cases, you might start with each use case becoming a theme; or, if the use case covers a great deal of functionality, you might try starting with each action in the use case as a theme.

If you have a set of formally specified and refined goals, as you would if you had applied a goal-oriented requirements engineering approach, then you might choose key terms from the goal or subgoal behaviors to represent themes.

If you have a set of requirements like the one we have (See appendix "The Crystal Game" for the full list), which are quite informal and written in natural language, there is a spectrum of approaches you might apply. The two extremes of the spectrum are the "choose-carefully-up-front" approach, and the "start-with-everything" approach. In the first, you begin with some well-chosen themes, but may break them up later to form smaller ones as needed. In the second, you begin with a potentially huge set of themes, then reduce that set by grouping and removing themes from your list. Somewhere in the middle of the spectrum is the more moderate and likely useful way. It combines the two extreme approaches.

We now go over each one in detail and look at the kinds of initial themes you can expect to identify with each one. Along the way, we use the example described in the appendix, "The Crystal Game."

The Choose-Carefully-Up-Front Approach

With this approach, you read through the set of requirements and identify key bits of functionality that are likely to become features in your implementation. This approach takes some time up front, since to choose well you must carefully assess what concerns your requirements describe. With this scheme, your main task is to split up themes that are too general or that have requirements that, when grouped, do not form a cohesive set of functionality.

If we look at the Crystal Game example in the appendix, we may choose the following potential themes:

    begin, end (the game)

join, leave (the game)

win, lose (the game)

prompt, display (user interface information)

enter (locations)

gain (energy)

meet (players and characters)

duel, challenge (behavior of character interaction)

The Start-with-Everything Approach

In this approach, you might choose all verbs, or action words, written in the requirements. This is a straightforward approach and can even be automated to some extent. There is a multitude of tools that identify nontrivial verbs in a textual document. A good place to look for those tools and the products that are built to work with them is Edinburgh Language Technology Group (LTG) at http://www.ltg.ed.ac.uk/. Automatic indexers can also identify all "important" terms in a document.

This approach saves time during the first step of going through the documentation. However, with this approach, you will have lots of potential themes. You are working to eventually get to a set of well-chosen themes, which may or may not correspond well to a set of automatically chosen terms. This means that your main analysis job is to narrow down which of the terms are real themes and to group verbs to form bigger actual themes.

If we looked for nontrivial verbs in the Crystal Game requirement, here is what we might come up with:

accumulate	carry	collect
ask	challenge	comes
assign	choose	create

decide	interfere	reach
depend	join	respect
display	leave	restore
dissipate	locate	return
distribute	look	reward
drop	lose	run
duel	mean	see
encounter	meet	select
end	obtain	send
enter	own	set
equip	permit	show
expire	pick	split
explore	placed	start
find	played	take
force	pose	tap
give	proceed	track
grant	prompt	wager
honor	provide	win
identify		

A Combination of the Two Approaches

In reality, your approach will probably be a mixture of the two described above. You'll likely read through your requirements document and pick out anything that looks like a behavior, concern, or feature of some kind. This is a little more conservative an approach than just choosing any nontrivial term, and a little freer than picking only concepts that look highly promising. You may miss some smaller bits of behavior, or you may have broken features up a little too much, but that's fine; this is only a starting point. The next few steps of grouping and segmenting themes (described in the next several sections) will help you converge on a good set of themes regardless of whether you have chosen too many or too few initial ones. As a compromise, we use a set of themes that are not as high level as those in the choose-carefully category, but not as fine-grained as the list from the start-with-everything approach:

begin	explore	populate
challenge	gain	prompt
create	initiate	scatter
display	join	sent
distribute	leave	show
drop	lose	start
duel	meet	wager
end	pay	win
enter		

Looking at the Theme-Relationships View

Now that you have an initial set of themes, you can take a look at the theme-relationships view, also called the relationship view.

Figure 4–7 shows the relationship view if we had started out with the choose-carefully set of themes. As you can see, each theme we listed is shown as a diamond. However, many requirements do not explicitly mention any of the themes we've chosen. You can tell this because there are lots of orphaned requirements in the view—that is to say, they're floating on their own rather than having a link to one of the diamond-shaped theme nodes. The orphaned themes form a grid on the right hand side of Figure 4–7. As mentioned above, the main job with this starting set of themes is to visit each orphaned node to determine with which of the themes it rightly belongs.

You can also see that some requirements are linked to more than one theme. These are called *shared requirements*. They represent functionality overlap between the themes, since in their text they mention the name of

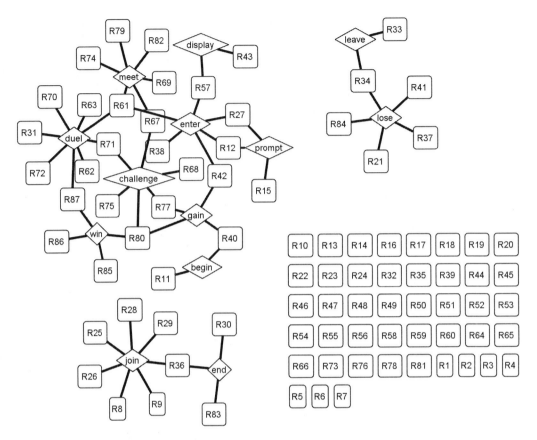

Figure 4–7 *"Choose-carefully" initial theme-relationship view.*

more than one theme. At a later stage (described in the section "Identify Aspect Themes"), a decision must be made about which theme actually owns that overlapped functionality.

The start-with-everything initial relationship view (shown in Figure 4–8) is the other extreme from the choose-carefully view. Here, there are very few orphaned requirements and many shared requirements. Considering that there were only a handful of themes listed using the choose-carefully approach, it's unlikely that all of these would end up being themes. It's more likely that they would be merged into groups and that some would be discarded all together.

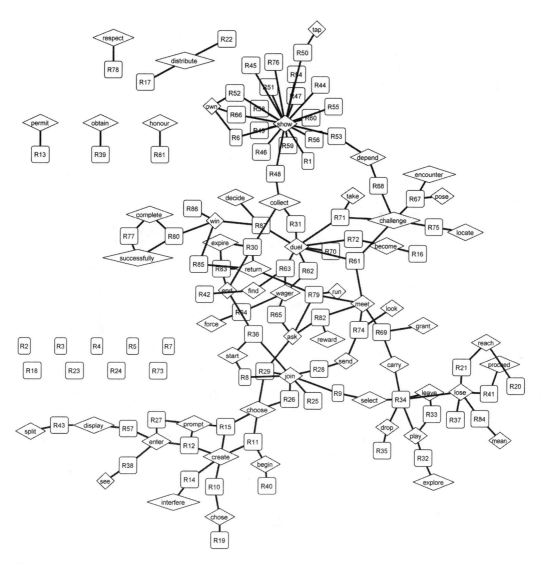

Figure 4–8   *"Start-with-everything" initial theme-relationship view.*

The relationship view for the compromise approach is shown in Figure 4–9. As given, it doesn't have the multitude of themes in the start-with-everything view and also has fewer orphaned requirements than the choose-carefully approach. For the rest of this chapter, we will use this set of themes as a basis for discussion. If we refer to one of the other views, we point that out explicitly.

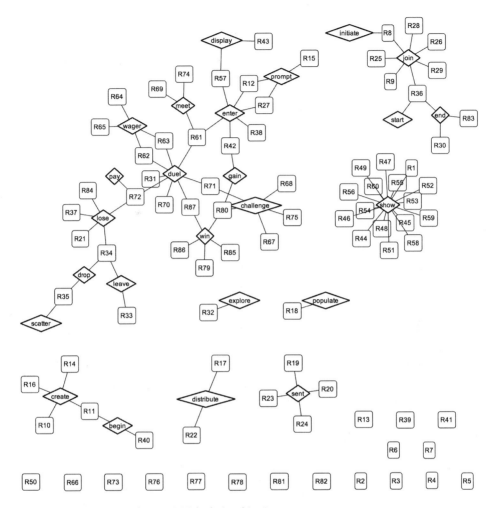

Figure 4–9   *Compromise themes: initial relationship view.*

You should also note that if you specify a theme that does not appear in the text (if there is no lexical match for the keyword), then it would not appear in any of the Theme/Doc views. These views are just representations of the text; they neither interpret it in any way nor do automatic synonym detection. Later (in the section "Unifying Synonym Themes"), we go over how to compensate for the lexical nature of the Theme/Doc view-generation.

Dealing with Large Relationship Views

If the number of themes and requirements is very large, the relationship view is also very large: There is one node for each theme and one node for each requirement. One way to handle the size of the view is by grouping sets of themes. Grouping is quite straightforward. It involves selecting a theme to be the main theme of a group, and then specifying the other themes as subthemes of that main theme. Grouping collapses all the subthemes into the main theme. Later in the chapter, we talk about grouping themes to actually arrive at a *better* set of themes. But grouping can also be helpful for reducing complexity and clutter in large relationship views. If, for instance, you wanted to focus on just the requirements and themes related to join (shown in the top-right of Figure 4–9), you might collapse the big, connected group of themes (which includes **meet**, **duel**, **challenge**, **pay**, **enter**, etc.) into one big theme called **play**. Regenerating the view then produces a far less cluttered view. You can then remove the grouping later to see the themes as they originally were.

You can also play with the options of the Theme/Doc view-generation tool to change the sizes of the theme and requirement nodes. For instance, you can enlarge some requirements (connected to certain themes) while making others smaller. This would help you if you were trying to focus on one portion of the view. Examples of partial view enlargements are presented later in this chapter.

Operating on Themes

Figure 4–6 showed that there are four operations you can perform on themes. You can split them up if you feel they are too general, you can add new ones if you feel one is missing, you can delete a theme that seems unhelpful or irrelevant, or you can group themes that seem similar (combining them into one larger theme). We now go over when you might apply each of these operations.

Split Themes If They Are Too General

Regardless of how you went about choosing your initial set of themes, you'll find that you have behaviors associated with a particular theme that do not belong together. It's important to remember that you want themes that are coherent and cohesive, which means that one theme should not try to fulfil many unrelated requirements.

The **enter** theme consists of the following requirements:

- R12: The player is then prompted to enter a port number for the new game.

- R27: They will then be prompted to enter the machine name or IP address of the other player's device.

- R38: If a player enters a location that has no players or characters in it, they may pick up any crystals or magical items they see.

- R42: Energy is gained by two units when they find a crystal upon entering a location.

- R57: Once a player enters a location, a local map is displayed on his or her handheld device.

- R61: When two players meet upon entering a location they perform a duel of rock–paper–scissors.

As you can see, some of these requirements are about a player entering a location, whereas others are about a player entering information. The **enter** theme could be split into two more cohesive themes: one about entering a location and the other about entering information.

To perform this split, you make two new themes: **enter-location** (consisting of R38, R42, R57, and R61) and **enter-input** (consisting of R12 and R27). You then choose to explicitly *attach* the requirements to the appropriate themes. Attaching explicitly links a requirement to a particular theme even though the theme is not mentioned in the requirement. Figure 4–10 shows that we have attached the four requirements for **enter-location**, but did not do so for **enter-input**. As you can see, **enter-input** is not attached to R12 naturally (since neither requirement contains the text "enter-input"), and so it appears isolated in Figure 4–10. In the next step we will use **enter-input** as

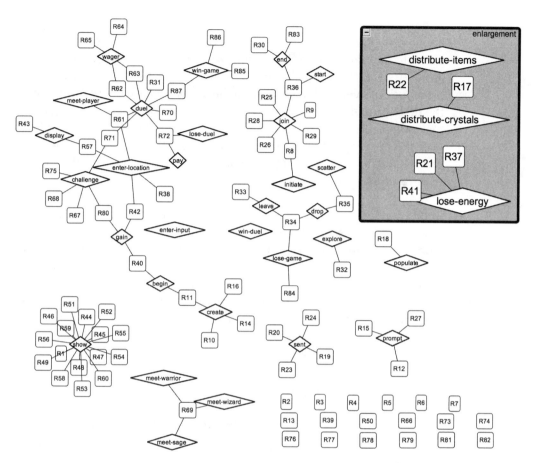

Figure 4–10 *Results of theme operation: split.*

an example of how we can link requirements to themes without explicitly attaching them.

Another example of a theme to split is the **distribute** theme, which is initially made up of two requirements:

- R17: The new game randomly distributes crystals throughout the game area.

- R22: Magical items are cloaks, swords, keys, and rings, and are randomly distributed around the location.

The first requirement is about distribution of crystals, and the second is about distribution of magical items. While this might seem fine now, it's possible that later in the design phases, you might decide these activities are better modeled separately; the functionality to accommodate crystal distribution is very different from the behavior for item distribution. Maybe the **distribute** theme is two themes masquerading as one. Once again, we make the new themes (**distribute-crystals** and **distribute-items**) and reattach the appropriate requirements with those themes. In Figure 4–9, you can see the result of splitting some of the themes. You can see that the **distribute-crystals** theme is on its own.

Additionally, you might choose to split the **lose** theme into **lose-duel, lose-energy** (which essentially keeps track of energy levels of a player), and **lose-game** (which involves the final showdown of the game), since these are three very different concepts. Similarly, the **win** term is used in two senses, encompassing both winning of duels and winning of the game itself. Finally, the **meet** theme encompasses meeting characters and meeting players. You may choose to split these also.

Figure 4–10 shows the following changes:

- **enter** is now **enter-location** and **enter-input.**

- **enter-location** has been attached to R38, R42, R57, and R61.

- **enter-input** has no requirements.

- **distribute** is now **distribute-crystals** and **distribute-items** (shown in enlargement).

- **lose** is now **lose-duel, lose-game,** and **lose-energy** (shown in enlargement).

- **win** is now **win-game** and **win-duel.**

- **meet** is now **meet-player, meet-wizard, meet-warrior,** and **meet-sage.**

Group Similar Themes

If you applied the start-with-everything approach, it is likely that you have many finely grained themes. Some of the names of these themes may have the same literal meaning, but since different words were used, they showed up separately in the relationship view. Others may not have the same literal meaning, but are synonymous in the sense that two events or behaviors always happen together. In either case, you don't want them to remain separate themes. Instead, you want to group them into one larger theme.

We actually use two terms to refer to grouping of themes. One is straightforward *grouping*, in which subthemes are essentially encompassed by another theme. The relationship and crosscutting views display only the main theme of a group and redirect all requirements connections from subthemes to the main theme. Subthemes are not displayed. The subthemes are displayed in the individual view, however. The other kind of grouping is a special case called *unifying*, which is mainly used for handling synonyms. Unified themes are displayed only by their main term in all views. We look first at situations in which you might want to unify themes and then at situations where grouping might be appropriate.

Unifying Themes

While the unify operation is mainly used for resolving synonyms, it is handy to use in any case where you would like to essentially "replace" references to one theme with references to another.

First, let's consider some themes that have the same literal meaning. These are relatively easy to spot. Of course, you can't be sure just by looking at the terms themselves that they refer to the same concept. To be positive, you have to inspect the requirements that describe them to compare their meanings. One that stands out is the set of themes related to distributing crystals around the game location: **populate**, **scatter**, and **distribute-crystals**. The requirement attached to **populate** is R18: *When the game environment is initially populated with crystals, a random number of random locations are populated with a random number of crystals up to 10.* The **scatter** requirement is R35: *Dropped crystals are rescattered throughout the game area.* We saw R17 above: *The new game randomly distributes crystals throughout the game area.* All of these terms refer to the distribution of crystals, so we unify all these themes under the **distribute-crystals** head-

Table 4–1 *Distribute-Crystals Theme*

R No.	Requirement Text
R17	The new game randomly distributes crystals throughout the game area.
R18	When the game environment is initially populated with crystals, a random number of random locations are populated with a random number of crystals up to 10.
R35	Dropped crystals are rescattered throughout the game area.

ing. This unification results in the **distribute-crystals** theme found in Table 4–1. Notice that R18 and R35 do not mention **distribute-crystals** explicitly. Still, the unification means that R18 and R35 will be attached to the **distribute-crystals** theme.

Other themes we might think about unifying are the themes associated with game creation, such as **start**, **create**, and **begin**, and those associated with the user interface, such as **display** and **show**.

Dealing with synonyms doesn't have to happen just on the theme level. For instance, a theme might not catch all the requirements it should because they use synonyms of your theme and not the theme name itself. For instance, when you look at the set of **meet-character** themes (**meet-wizard**, **warrior**, and **sage**), you can see that they are not connected to the **challenge** theme in any way. This seems odd, since characters pose challenges to players. It makes sense that these should have been linked in the requirements. Sure enough, when we inspect R67, it says, *When a player encounters a character, the character poses a challenge to that player.* Meet and encounter are synonyms, and R67 should relate to each of the **meet-character** themes. Since the **meet** theme has been split into the three **meet-character** themes and **meet-player**, we must attach R67 to the three **meet-character** themes in addition to unifying it with **meet**.

Unified themes appear in all views only under their unified heading. When you look at Figure 4–11, you can see in the enlargement marked "unify" that R18 and R35 both point to the **distribute-crystals** theme . Essentially, what you have done by choosing to unify a set of themes is set up a dictionary of synonyms in which there is one dominant term for each collection of synonymous ones. When the Theme/Doc view is created, only the dominant term is used.

Unifying (or grouping) themes can be used to attach a requirement to a theme implicitly. Recall that at the end of the split-theme operation **enter-input** was linked to no requirements. Here, we unify the word "tap" with **enter-input** and as a side effect, attach **enter-input** to R50 (*the player can tap on the dots to see the options available*).

Figure 4–11 shows the following changes:

- **populate** and **scatter** are now unified under **distribute-crystals** (shown in unify enlargement, top-right).

- **initiate**, **create**, and **begin** are unified under **start** (shown in the lower-right corner of the figure).

- R67 is attached to **meet-wizard**, **meet-warrior**, and **meet-sage** (shown in the middle of the right-side of the figure).

- "tap" is unified under **enter-input** which links R50 to **enter-input**.

- "errand" is unified under **challenge**, which links R77 to **challenge** (shown in the center-right of the figure).

Grouping Themes

Grouping a set of themes collapses those themes together into one theme. The main theme of a group is the only theme displayed in the relationship and crosscutting views. The individual view ignores the grouping and displays all the subthemes. This operation is useful for grouping closely related behavior that you would like to design as one theme. You can also use groupings to capture a decision to essentially demote behavior from being its own theme to being a method. Grouping can also be used as a convenient way to collapse portions of the relationship and crosscutting views temporarily while focusing on other areas (see the section "Dealing with Large Relationship Views" for more information).

Now, let's take a look at some themes that seem to describe closely related behavior. One such set is behavior related to **energy**. The **gain** and **lose-energy** themes capture two opposite but closely related concepts. You can imagine that these two themes would share a lot of underlying structure (all

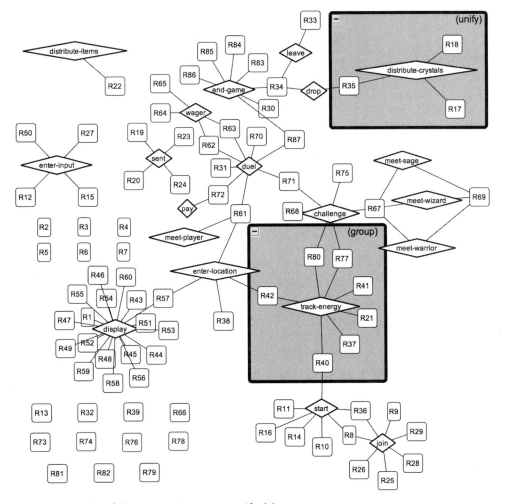

Figure 4–11 *Results of theme operations: group, unify, delete.*

the **energy**-related state). The difference between them would be relatively small. These could be grouped quite naturally in a **track-energy** theme. In that case, you would create a new theme, **track-energy**, and designate **gain** and **lose** as its subthemes. If you reach design and decide that these two themes are better off separate, it is fine to backtrack and split them up again.

Another set of behaviors you might want to group is the **end-game** functionality. There are currently two themes, **win-game** and **lose-game**, that deal with the **end-game** scenario.

Finally, you might consider grouping all the user-interface-style themes into one. These are currently the **display**, **enter-input**, and **prompt** themes. They all deal with input to the game-play device. Once again, this grouping involves creation of an **end-game** theme and specification that the other themes are subthemes of **end-game**.

Figure 4–11 shows the following changes:

- **gain** and **lose** energy are grouped under **track-energy** (shown in the group enlargement in the lower right of the figure). This change obscured other unifications made in the previous step:

  - "provide" was unified under **gain**, linking R77 to **track-energy**

  - "dissipate" was unified under **lose-energy**, linking R41 to **track-energy**

- **end**, **win-game**, and **lose-game** are grouped under **end-game** (top-center of the figure)(for instance, R86 is now linked to **end-game** and not **win-game**).

- **win-duel** and **lose-duel** are grouped under duel, shown in the upper-center of the figure (**win-duel** and **lose-duel** no longer appear).

- **prompt** is grouped under **enter-input**, shown in the left-center of the figure (has the side effect of attaching **enter-input** to R12, R15, and R27).

- **show** is grouped under **display,** shown in the lower left-corner of the figure (all of **show**'s requirements are now attached to **display**).

Delete Unwanted Themes

As you refine your themes, chances are that you will find some themes too trivial or too unrepresentative of the system's functionality to keep.

The only really trivial theme that can be identified in Figure 4–9 is the **explore** theme. It has only one requirement, R32: *Players explore the world by walking around the game-play area.* While this theme is important from a user perspective, it is not useful in terms of its impact on the design. So, we omit the **explore** theme and deal with the now-orphaned R32 in the next section.

Figure 4–11 shows the following change:

- the **explore** theme is no longer shown, and R32 is now orphaned (R32 appears in the lower-left corner of the picture).

Operating on Requirements

Figure 4–6 depicts five operations that can be applied to requirements. Two of them are part of the process of deciding on the themes to include in your system: adding new requirements and resolving or refining requirements that can be made more concrete. A third, postponing requirements, spans both deciding on themes and determining theme responsibilities. We discuss situations in which you would apply these three operations and limit our discussion of postponement to how it's applied when deciding on your themes. The other two requirements operations (association and postponement of association) are discussed in the section "Deciding on Theme Responsibilities." More on the use of postpone in terms of determining theme responsibilities is also discussed in that section.

Postponing Requirements

At this point, we can *postpone* requirements that are not interesting from a design perspective (or until more information becomes available). Recall R32, which describes that players will roam around the game area. This feature is nice to have in a high-level requirements document just to give a sense of the overall system to the reader. It isn't, at this point, a useful requirement for moving forward to design. The best way to deal with this requirement is to postpone it and see if later in the development process more insight arises (or other requirements are introduced) to advise how to handle it. Postponing it changes its outline to dashed, which signals to us that it is a requirement that we are choosing not to deal with right away.

Figure 4–12 shows the following change:

- Postponed R32 (its outline turned to dashed). R32 appears on the lower-right corner of the figure.

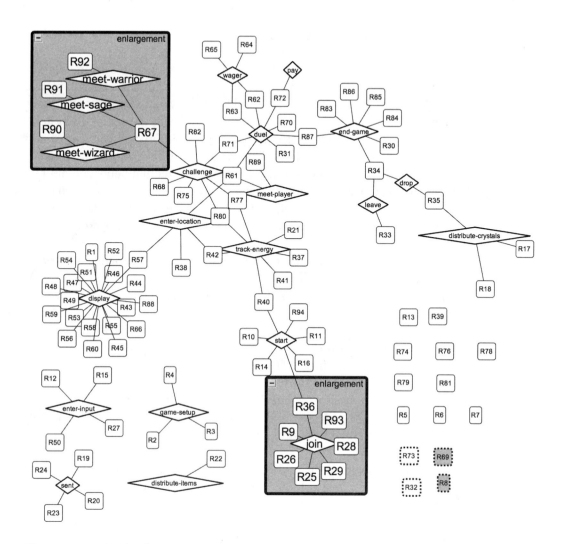

Figure 4–12   *Results of operating on requirements.*

Adding Requirements

Requirements can be added either by introducing new requirements into your set or as a product of splitting up an existing requirement.

Incorporating New Requirements

Depending on the kind of approach you use to develop your system, requirements may or may not crop up after you've already begun the analysis process. If they do, then you need to be able to add them to your existing set of requirements in order to see how they can be integrated with the rest of the system. Adding new requirements in Theme/Doc is straightforward; you simply add them to the set of requirements and then regenerate the relationship, crosscutting, and individual views as required. If the new requirements contain text that refers to pre-existing themes, the text will be automatically linked to those themes in the views. The new requirements may give rise to new themes, causing you to rethink the themes you already have or to change their groupings.

How deeply you reassess your existing theme breakdown depends on how far into the development process you are. If you are at the beginning of your requirements elicitation process, then adding new requirements is no big deal.

However, perhaps you have designed and implemented many of your themes already. If so, then new requirements can be included in a way similar to that described in the "Revisiting Evolution" section of Chapter 3, which involved the creation of new themes to handle the new requirements. Those themes instead of the themes they replaced were then composed together with the rest of the system. More on how to perform compositions is described in Chapter 6, "Theme Composition."

If you're somewhere in the middle, you probably can add the requirements and see how they relate to the existing themes and make adjustments accordingly. It's of course impossible to predict how a hypothetical requirement will impact the functionality of a system, but the Theme/Doc views provide a starting point for assessing that impact.

Splitting Requirements

Some requirements are added as a result of splitting up requirements already in the set. Splitting is sometimes appropriate for requirements that are not written concretely enough to link to any particular behavior. Take, for instance, requirement R73: *Wizards are magical beings*. It is, of course, up to you to decide how to deal with requirements that are this abstract. One possibility is to refine the requirement to try to make it more concrete and to perhaps split it into several requirements that get at its real intent.

Perhaps this requirement refers to wizards interacting using terms specific to a magical being. Players can choose to be personified in the game as wizards. R73 tells us that the user interface display differs depending on a player's chosen persona. One interpretation of requirement R73 is that the user interface for a wizard-player should have magical-seeming terms and icons. Taking that interpretation, this requirement could be refined into *Players that are wizards should have magical icons and terms displayed in their user interface.* This requirement would automatically be linked to the **display** theme already in the list of themes.

Or, requirement R73 might mean the language that wizard-NPCs use should be magical-seeming: *When wizard characters meet players, they should speak to them using magical language.* This requirement would automatically be linked to the **meet-wizard** theme.

Since R73 would be diminished by altering it, you may choose to preserve it in its original state and add a new requirement that represents the refinement. You could then postpone it, as we discuss next. So, we add two new requirements: R88 (*Players that are wizards should have magical icons and terms displayed in their user interface*) and R89 (*When wizard characters meet players, they should speak to them using magical language*) to reflect the additional requirements that we want to incorporate.

Figure 4–12 shows the following changes:

- Postponed R73 (its outline turned to dashed).

- Added R88 (*Players that are wizards should have magical icons and terms displayed in their user interface*), which is attached to **display**.

- Added R89 (*When wizard characters meet players, they should speak to them using magical language*), which is attached to **meet-player**.

Attaching Requirements to Themes

We saw examples of attaching requirements to themes earlier in the theme-operations section. We now discuss how attachment can be used from a requirement-operation perspective. In particular, we look at how it can be used to remedy orphaned requirements.

As described earlier, orphaned requirements appear as requirement nodes that are not connected to a theme node in the relationships view because they do not specifically name any term that was included in the list of themes. Ultimately, we would like to completely rid ourselves of orphaned requirements, since they represent elements of behavior that are not covered by any system feature. Orphaned requirements might rightly belong to an existing theme or might motivate the addition of new themes. If neither case applies, you can also postpone decisions about orphaned requirements, as described earlier.

R2 is orphaned in Figure 4–11. It reads *Location is defined by four points, forming a rectangle, and is outdoors.* We currently have no theme that defines the game-play area. We could attach this requirement to an existing theme, such as the **start-game** theme, if we felt it was appropriate. As described in the section "Split Themes If They Are Too General," attaching a requirement to a theme explicitly places a link between the two by automatically annotating the requirement with that theme name.

However, since the spirit of the **start-game** theme is more about setting up the game itself than defining the game as a concept, this option might not suit our needs. Instead, we could introduce a new theme called **game-setup**, which would allow us to capture some of the static game-infrastructure requirements. Other requirements that fit well into that theme are those from the same section of the requirements document (R2–R7), namely, R3: *The game boundaries are defined by four points,* and R4: *Not all points within the game boundaries are inside game locations.* We add the new theme and attach to it R2–R4.

Figure 4–12 shows the following change:

Added **game-setup**, with R2–R4 attached.

Deciding on Theme Responsibilities

A goal for the theme approach is to arrive at multiple themes, each responsible for implementing a cohesive set of system requirements. This more or less means that while themes can implement many requirements, requirements should be implemented by only one theme. There are, of course, exceptions, and we discuss ways to deal with those exceptions both in this chapter and Chapter 6. However, in general, it is helpful to think of the theme-to-requirement relationship as one-to-many.

At the beginning of this chapter, we said that an aspect is functionality whose description within a requirement is tangled with the description of other functionality. We push this into Theme parlance and say that an aspect is a theme whose description within a requirement is tangled with the description of another theme. Requirements that are linked to more than one theme (shared requirements) are where this intertwining occurs.

It is not, however, safe to say that all shared requirements mean that one of the sharing themes is an aspect and the rest are base. There are essentially four rules to guide how to handle shared requirements. The first is, *Split the requirement if possible*. Some requirements are written in such a way that they can be split up so that the descriptions of the themes are disentangled.

The second is, *Dominance means association*. If a requirement cannot be split, and you can ascertain that it is mainly about one of the themes, then it should be *associated* with its dominant theme. Associating a theme with a requirement denotes that the dominant theme is an aspect, and the others referred to by the requirement are base. This rule holds only if the third rule also passes, however.

The third rule is, *Base triggers aspect*. If two themes are mentioned in a requirement, then the triggered theme is the aspect theme, and the triggering theme is the base. Once again, if you locate the triggered theme, then you associate the requirement with that theme. All three of the aspect-identification rules should apply for you to have located an aspect theme. There is also one final aspect-identification rule to apply once you're done sifting through your shared requirements. This is described in the section "Is the Aspect Crosscutting Enough?"

If any of these rules cannot be applied (you can't split the requirement up, and it seems to mention all themes equally, where none are explicitly triggered), you should *postpone* its association (*postpone when all else fails*). More information may arise about the system that can help decide which theme should actually be responsible for that requirement. Or, you may be

Identifying Aspects in Requirements

Aspects are revealed by requirements that describe two themes in a tangled way. These requirements are called *shared requirements*. Test to see if a shared requirement reveals an aspect by seeing if these rules hold true:

- The requirement cannot be split to untangle the themes.

- One theme dominates the requirement.

- The dominant theme is triggered by the other themes mentioned in the requirement (*externally triggered*).

- The triggered and dominant theme is externally triggered in multiple situations (perhaps as described in other requirements).

If all these rules pass, then the shared requirement has revealed the triggered theme to be an aspect. The triggering themes are crosscut by the aspect theme.

able to handle postponed associations straightforwardly at design. This section talks in detail about how to assess shared requirements and how to capture the decisions that you make.

Split Shared Requirements If Possible

Looking at Figure 4–11, you can see that many requirements refer to more than one theme. These requirements essentially serve to link themes together. We call these shared requirements because they refer to two or more themes.

However, our goal for this process is to associate requirements with just one theme. We do not want functionality repeated in different themes. So, we go through each shared requirement to see if it is possible to rewrite it in order to disconnect the themes. Splitting a requirement adds new requirements to the end of the requirements list, attached where appropriate, and displays the split requirements as dashed and shaded gray.

Take, for instance, R69 from Figure 4–11: *However, if a player meets a character of his or her same type, the character grants the player any crystals that it carries*. Because we split the concept of meeting a character, we see that R69 is now associated with **meet-sage**, **meet-wizard**, and **meet-warrior**. These requirements can be split into three distinct requirements:

- R90: If a wizard type player meets a wizard character, the wizard gives them any crystals the wizard carries.

- R91: If a sage type player meets a sage character, the sage gives them any crystals the sage carries.

- R92: If a warrior type player meets a warrior character, the warrior gives them any crystals the warrior carries.

Splitting up R69 would result in R90 being linked to **meet-wizard**, R91 being linked to **meet-sage**, and R92 being linked to **meet-warrior**.

R8, which links the **join** and **start** themes, can also be split up. It reads, *Players can either initiate a new game or join an existing game*. This could be made into two explicit requirements: R93: *Players can join an existing game*. and R94: *Players can start a new game*

As you can see in Figure 4–12, the split of R8 has resulted in the **join** theme the split of R8 has reduced overlap for the **join** theme to just R36, and the R69 split has greatly decoupled the various meet-character themes.

Figure 4-12 shows the following change:

- split R8 into R93 and R94, and R69 into R90, R91, and R92 (shown in expansions). R8 and R69 are still shown in the view, but their outlines are now dashed, and their nodes shaded gray.

Identify Aspect Themes

After ensuring that a shared requirement cannot be split to untangle multiple themes, there are three rules to apply to see if the requirement reveals an aspect. The first rule, *dominance means association*, means that the theme that a requirement is most "about" (or is dominated by) is the one that may be the aspect. The second is the *base-triggers-aspect* rule, which means that if two themes are mentioned in a requirement, the one that is being triggered is the aspect, and the one responsible for the triggering is the base. The third is the *crosscutting-enough* test, which states that only behavior triggered in multiple situations is an aspect. After all those rules pass, you can associate the requirement with the aspect theme.

Dominance Means Association

As discussed above, the first line of defense for shared requirements is applying the rule, *Split up if possible*. However, you may be faced with a requirement that looks like R42: *Energy is gained by two units when they find a crystal upon entering a location*. This requirement refers to two themes: **enter-location** and **track-energy**. In trying to split this requirement, we could identify the **enter-location**–related information and add a new requirement to the end of our list that reads *Players may find crystals upon entering a location*. But this doesn't really help us split up R42. We would still be left with describing when energy-gain occurs, which leads us back to our original text: *Energy is gained by two units when a player finds a crystal upon entering a location*. No matter what rewriting is done, these **enter-location** and **track-energy** themes must be described with relation to one another.

This leads us to the next rule: *Dominance means association*. If one of the themes dominates a shared requirement, then the dominant theme may be an aspect.

You can try various techniques to assess whether a theme dominates a requirement. One is looking at the requirement in terms of which theme should "know about" its behavior. If you think about logging a set of method calls, you'll notice that you don't really want the logged methods to know that they're being logged. You want them to behave as normal, regardless of extra behavior attached to them. However, you do want a logging module to know what it's logging and to be able to tailor its behavior accordingly. In a requirement that stated "Log all method calls" in which there was a **log** theme and a **method calls** theme, the **log** theme would need to know about the behavior described, and hence would dominate the requirement. In the case of R42, think about which theme should know that energy is gained when a player enters a game location. Should the concept of entering the location know about energy gain? Or should the **track-energy** theme know that energy change happens in certain situations?

Another way to decide which theme is dominant is to look at the other requirements associated with each theme in order to get more of a sense of the identity of the theme. The **track-energy** theme contains ten requirements, six of which are shared with other themes. The requirements are shown in Table 4–2; the shared requirements are boxed in gray. Underneath each of the shared requirements is the list of themes that share the requirement. The theme considered to dominate the shared requirement is shown in bold.

All of the shared requirements in this set (R40, R42, R77, and R80) refer to gain or loss of energy in certain situations. Additionally, R21, which is not shared, refers to loss of energy. Just like our hypothetical logging theme would want to know which behaviors are being logged, it makes sense that the **track-energy** theme would want to know when energy is changed.

Thinking again about R42, the **enter-location** theme (Table 4–3) should only be concerned with location-entering behavior (as described in R38): seeing if there are other players in the location and dueling with them, or looking for crystals in the location and picking them up.

Table 4–2 *Track Energy Theme Requirements*

R No.	Requirement Text
R21	If players do not reach their initial location within the specified time, they lose 1 energy point.
R37	Players lose energy faster while in a location: they lose energy two units per five–minute period.
R40	Players gain 10 units of energy when the game begins. (**track-energy** *triggered by start*)
R41	As they proceed throughout the game, their energy dissipates by one unit for each five-minute period.
R42	Energy is gained by two units when they find a crystal upon entering a location (**track-energy** *triggered by enter-location*)
R77	Completing an errand successfully provides four units of energy to the player. (**track-energy** *triggered by challenge*)
R80	When a player completes a physical test challenge successfully, they gain three units of energy and win a crystal. (**track-energy** *triggered by challenge*)

Table 4–3 *Enter-Location Theme Requirements*

R No.	Requirement Text
R38	If a player enters a location that has no players or characters in it, the player may pick up any crystals or magical items they see.
R42	Energy is gained by two units when they find a crystal upon entering a location. (**track-energy** *triggered by enter-location*)
R57	Once a player enters a location, a local map is displayed on his or her handheld device. (**display** *triggered by enter-location*)
R61	When two players meet upon entering a location, they perform a duel of rock, paper, scissors. (**duel** *triggered by enter-location*)

From this, we decide that R42 is dominated by **track-energy**.

Base Triggers Aspect

The next test to see whether you've picked the right theme as the aspect is to apply the base-triggers-aspect rule. Aspect behavior is triggered by some behavior in the base. Aspect orientation allows triggering of aspect behavior to happen implicitly at trigger locations. If there were no aspect/base relationship, then the behavior would have to be triggered explicitly from the location in the base. In this case, four of the **track-energy** requirements (Table 4–2) mention some situation in which the **track-energy** behavior is triggered: reaching a location, starting a game, time passing, picking up a crystal, and so on. Since base behavior triggers aspect behavior, all themes that are representative of triggering behaviors are base, and **track-energy** is the aspect. In this case, we're looking at R42, in which the **enter-location** theme triggers the **track-energy** (gain) behavior.

Both the dominance and trigger rules need to pass to confidently identify an aspect theme. In R40, R42, R77, and R80, the dominant theme is **track-energy**, and the triggering theme is the other theme that shares the requirement. **Track-energy** has been determined to be an aspect of **start**, **enter-location**, and **challenge**.

Is the Aspect Crosscutting Enough?

Of course, every rule has exceptions, and the split/dominance/trigger rules do too. Before moving forward to design, we have to make one final check of all the themes we found to be aspects and consider whether they are crosscutting *enough* to warrant being designed as aspects.

Lots of behavior is triggered by other behavior—unless that triggering is crosscutting, it would be absurd to split it out. If you were to separate out every triggered behavior, you would simply have replaced all your method calls with aspect-invocation. Even the term crosscutting implies that you only want to separate out behavior that spans across the system.

It is a matter of experience to know how widely crosscutting a theme should be before you make it an aspect. To say that a theme must crosscut at least x number of themes is meaningless because the granularity of a theme is not fixed: one theme may crosscut another theme but be triggered from that theme in many places. It's also meaningless to say that if a theme is an aspect in x number of requirements, then it is crosscutting enough: one unsplit requirement might describe several situations in which a theme is triggered.

Instead, perhaps it's better to think of whether the theme is triggered in several *situations*. If a theme's behavior is triggered in only one place, then it doesn't make sense to make it into an aspect. The theme can still be a separate theme, but the call to the triggered behavior can be placed in the correct location in what would have been the base theme. Beyond that, it's a judgment call.

In a way, it's similar to thinking about when to refactor duplicated functionality into its own method—how many repetitions are too many? Perhaps if the exact set of statements is used more than once, then capturing that behavior in its own method is a good idea. Maybe it's a matter of system maintenance: At what point would it be difficult to go back and refactor?

For this system, we've decided that one trigger is too few to make a theme an aspect, but two is enough. If we later find that a theme crosscuts more broadly, then dealing with one hardcoded trigger is manageable.

Let's consider an example. R61, which is shared between **enter-location** and **duel**, reads, *When two players meet upon entering a location, they perform a duel of rock, paper, scissors.* R61 cannot be split to isolate the themes fully. This requirement is dominated by **duel** and triggers **duel** behavior. The triggering behavior is described in the situation description of the requirement: Two players meeting (**meet-player**) upon entering a location (**enter-location**). Looking at this, **duel** should be an aspect of **meet-player** and **enter-location**. By the split/dominance/trigger rules, **duel** is definitely an aspect.

But is **duel** crosscutting enough? Table 4–4 shows the requirements for the **duel** theme. Notice that **duel** is only triggered in one situation (when two players meet), as described in R61. In its other shared requirements, it is

Table 4–4 *Duel Theme Requirements*

R No.	Requirement Text
R31	Crystals can be collected by discovering them in a location in the world, interacting with characters, or dueling other players for them.
R61	When two players meet upon entering a location, they perform a duel of rock, paper, scissors. (**duel** *triggered by meet-player and enter-location*)
R62	Each player wagers a crystal on the outcome of the duel. (**wager** *triggered by duel*)
R63	If one player has no crystals they will wager the promise of the first crystal they find on the duel outcome, or they may wager two magical items in their possession. (**wager** *triggered by duel*)
R70	Players may be involved in only one duel at a time.
R71	If there are both another player and an NPC in a location when a player arrives, the other player takes precedence over the NPC, and a duel occurs, followed by the challenge from the NPC. (*no dominant theme*)
R72	Duel losers pay their debts immediately, or, if they cannot, their debts are automatically repaid when they become able. (**pay** *is triggered by duel*)
R87	If more than one player has the same number of crystals and energy, then they must duel to decide which wins. (**end-game** *not triggered by duel*)

either the base (of **wager** and **pay**) or there is no dominant theme present (as in R71).

Duel fails the final crosscutting-enough test and so is not carried through as an aspect to design. To capture this, we remove the association from R61 to **duel** (if we had made one) and instead postpone R61. As you will see, R61 then becomes visible, but appears dashed, in all relevant views, reminding us at design time that we need to place calls to dueling into their behavior.

Track-energy (shown in Table 4–2), however, passes the test (it is triggered in several situations, including when crystals are obtained and when challenges occur). It makes it past the final test to become an aspect.

Make the Association

We have decided that **track-energy** dominates R42 and that the other theme involved in R42 (**enter-location**) triggers **track-energy**, and so we associate R42 with the **track-energy** theme. We do the same for R40, R77, and R80.

When you associate a requirement with a particular theme, this is reflected in the relationship view by a gray arrow extending from the aspect (crosscutting) theme to the other themes referred to in the requirement (the triggering base themes). None of the links from the requirement to the crosscut themes are depicted. You can see by looking at Figure 4–13 that R42 is no longer linked to **enter-location**. Instead, it is linked only to **track-energy**. Gray arrows have also been inserted between **track-energy** and **start**, and **track-energy** and **challenge**, since those themes were mentioned in the R42.

Using the split/dominance/trigger rules, we can go through the rest of the shared **track-energy** requirements and see that all of these requirements are dominated by and trigger **track-energy**. Finally, we arrive at a **track-energy** theme that crosscuts the **challenge**, **start**, and **enter-location** themes, and that shares no requirements with other themes.

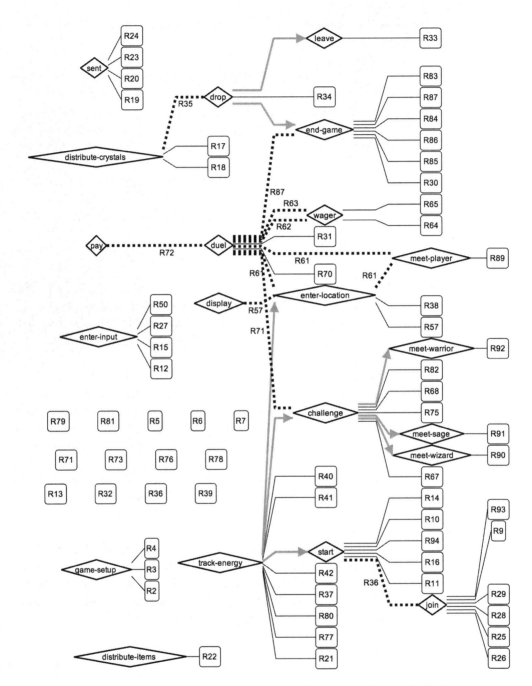

Figure 4–13 *Crosscutting and postponement relationships for the Crystal Game (display's requirements not shown).*

Figure 4–13 shows the following changes:

- R40, R42, R77, and R80 are now associated with, and linked only to **track-energy** (shown in Table 4–2). **Track-energy** appears in the lower-center of the figure.

- **track-energy** now crosscuts **enter-location**, **challenge**, and **start** (shown with gray arrows from **track-energy** to the other three themes).

- R34 (*when players leave game-play ot select leave-game from the options menu, they automatically lose the game and drop all the crystals they carry*) associated with, and linked only to, **drop**, (**leave-game** and **end-game** trigger **drop**), visible in the top-center of the figure.

- **drop** now crosscuts **leave** and **end-game**, visible in the top-center of the figure.

Chains of Crosscutting

Just because you have identified a theme as crosscutting another theme (as **track-energy** crosscuts **enter-location**), it does not mean that the crosscutting theme you chose will always crosscut others or that the base theme you chose will always be the base theme. It's fine for a theme to be crosscut and crosscutting at the same time.

For instance, examine R67 (in Figure 4–12), the requirement sitting between the **challenge** theme and the three **meet-character** themes. Although you have decided that **challenge** is the base theme in R77 and R80 (crosscut by **track-energy**), it does not mean that it will be the base theme when considering R67 (*When a player meets a character, the character poses a challenge to that player*). In fact, by applying the aspect identification criteria, we will associate R67 with **challenge**: Challenging needs to know when it happens (when two players meet), but the **meet-character** themes don't need to know about all the functionality to do with carrying out a challenge. So R67 is dominated by **challenge**; the three **meet-character** themes trigger **challenge**; challenging happens in three situations: meeting with wizards, warriors, and sages.

Associating R67 with **challenge** means that **challenge** crosscuts the **meet-character** themes. Now, **challenge** is both a base for **track-energy** (energy is gained or lost due to a challenge) and an aspect for the three **meet-character** themes. **Track-energy** is now an aspect of an aspect, since it crosscuts **challenge** (which is also an aspect). You can see this chain depicted in Figure 4–13, in which a gray arrow extends from **track-energy** to **challenge**, and three gray arrows extend from **challenge** to the three **meet-character** themes.

Looking ahead to implementation, you may wonder whether it's okay to have aspects of aspects, and whether they can be implemented that way. Later in the book, you will see that there's no problem implementing aspects of aspects. For an example of this, refer to Chapter 9, "Case Study 2: Usage Licensing." In Chapter 6, you will see the order in which chains of themes should be composed.

Figure 4-13 shows the following changes:

- R67 is associated with **challenge**.

- **challenge** now crosscuts **meet-character**, **meet-sage**, and **meet-wizard**.

Postpone Some Decisions

Some requirements are difficult to either split or associate. Take R71, for example. It reads, *If there is both another player and an NPC in a location when a player arrives, the other player takes precedence over the NCP, and a duel occurs, followed by the challenge from the NPC.* This describes ordering and precedence between themes rather than which theme operates on another theme or needs to know about another theme. This requirement has no dominant behavior, though there is triggered behavior. Because R71 fails one of the split/dominancy/trigger rules, we postpone it and decide how to handle its sharing at design.

When you read Chapter 6, "Theme Composition," you'll see that there are various ways of relating themes. One relationship is crosscutting, which corresponds to the aspect–base relationships we talked about in the previous section. Another is *merging*, in which behaviors residing in different themes are merged, sometimes including ordering specifications. The ordering considerations described in R71 might be best handled with such a construct. If so, rather than making an association decision at this point, we can postpone the decision until we create the composition specifications later in the design process. As you can see in Figure 4–13, dashed lines show requirements to be decided upon later.

Figure 4–13 shows the following changes:

- R71 (Table 4–4) (linking **duel** and **challenge**) is postponed due to no dominant theme. This is shown with a dashed-line in the center of the figure.

- R62 and R63 (Table 4–4) (linking **duel** and **wager**) are postponed because **wager** crosscuts in only one situation. This is shown with dashed lines in the center of the figure.

- R36 (*if a player's game device fails they may rejoin the game...*) (linking **start** and **join**) is postponed because **join** crosscuts in only one situation. This is shown with a dashed line in the lower-right corner of the figure.

- R57 (Table 4–3) (linking **display** and **enter-location**) is postponed because **display** crosscuts in only one situation. This is shown with a dashed line in the center of the figure.

- R61 (Table 4–4) (linking **duel, enter-location,** and **meet-player**) is postponed because **duel** crosscuts in only one situation. This is shown with dashed lines in the center-right of the figure.

- R72 (Table 4–4) (linking **pay** and **duel**) is postponed because **pay** crosscuts in only one situation. This is shown with a dashed line in the left-center of the figure.

- R87 (Table 4–4) (linking **duel** and **end-game**) is postponed because the dominant theme (**end-game**) is not triggered by the base (**duel**). This is shown by a dashed line in the upper-middle of the picture.

- R35 (*dropped crystals will be rescattered throughout the game area*)(linking **distribute-crystals** and **drop**) is postponed because **distribute-crystals** crosscuts in only one situation. This is shown by a dashed-line in the top-left of the figure.

Knowing When You're Done

Of course, it's likely that you'll never *really* know when you're done with all these decisions. There are some general rules to follow though. Ultimately, you're trying to get to a point where each theme is isolated, except for either crosscutting or postponement relationships. So, if you've associated or postponed all the shared requirements and read every requirement to make sure it's associated with the appropriate theme, then you are probably done.

A good idea, though, is to look at the relationships between the final set of themes and assess whether they make sense. If they don't, then you might have some rework to do. Sometimes an absence of a relationship is as interesting as an erroneous one, such as between the **start** theme and the main user-interface theme, **display**. A look at the **start** theme reveals a mixing of user-interface and game-start behavior. Its requirements are as follows:

- R10: One player is chosen to create a new game.

- R11: To create a new game, a player chooses *Begin New* from the Options menu.

- R14: Multiple games may be created in the same location at the same time and not interfere with one another.

- R16: The host player's location at the time the game is created becomes the throne room.

- R36: If a player's game device fails, as may happen in a power failure, the player can rejoin the game with the same number of crystals and the same game state as long as he or she restarts before the end of the game (shared with **join**, and postponed).

- R94: Players can start a new game.

All of the requirements except for R11 involve game setup. R11 is a user-interface requirement. There are, in fact, several requirements that mention the user-interface element, menu:

- R11: To create a new game, a player chooses *Begin New* from the Options menu (**start** theme).

- R26: The new player should choose *Join Existing* from the Options menu (**join** theme).

- R34: When players leave the game-play area or selects "leave game" from the Options menu, they automatically lose the game and drop all the crystals they carry (**drop** theme).

It makes sense that we would want all the menu-related behavior to be in the user-interface theme, **display**. So, we make a new theme, **menu**, and group it under **display**. Because of this new grouping, these three requirements become shared between **display** and their original themes. So, you need to check whether they motivate the promotion of **display** to "aspect-hood." In this case, they don't. None of these requirements are clearly dominated by **display**, and neither do they describe a trigger for **display** behavior. Rather than leaving them shared, however, we postpone them to be handled at design. **Drop** was an aspect before, because it dominated and was triggered in R34. It remains an aspect now, and as a result of this new attachment, crosscuts **display**.

It's also likely that you'll reach design and realize some of the decisions that you made weren't completely appropriate. That's fine too. Moving forward is often a way to test out whether or not your choices were wise. You can continue to modify themes as long as your system is undergoing change.

For instance, you can always disassociate requirements from particular themes if you are unhappy with your decisions later on, you can unsplit requirements or themes as you see fit, and you can also group themes late in the process. The **sent** theme, for example, has been ignored in our process up to now. This might be because it shared no requirements with other themes, so we never really considered it. When we come to design it, however, we realize that it doesn't make much sense as a theme. Its requirements are as follows:

- R19: Each other player is sent to a randomly chosen location.

- R20: Players have a set amount of time to reach the location to which they are sent.

- R23: Not more than one NPC is sent to any one location.

- R24: NPCs are randomly sent to locations.

These actually refer to two different kinds of behavior: Setting up players with locations and initializing NPCs. These changes are easy to make: Just attach R19 and R20 to a new **setup player** theme and attach R23 and R24 to a new **setup NPCs** theme, then move forward to design with the adjusted theme responsibilities.

Though in this chapter we describe this process as a very step-by-step application, in fact, there is no particular order in which these activities should occur. Chapter 9 includes an example of how rethinking and backtracking is done during design.

Regardless of when you make your decisions about themes and their responsibilities, it's a good idea to reflect on your choice at the Theme/Doc level so that your Theme/Doc views will align with your Theme/UML designs.

A cautionary note, however: Trying to design themes that still have shared requirements is a headache. You may end up with unwanted duplication of functionality in your design. If you want to move forward with designing a particular theme, it is best if all its shared requirements have been associated one way or the other or explicitly postponed.

Figure 4–14 shows the following changes:

- R19 and R20 are now attached to the **setup players** theme (left-center of figure).

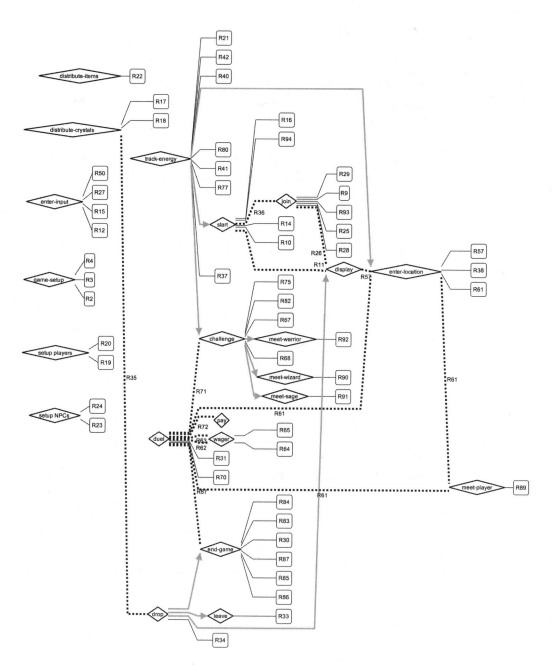

Figure 4–14   *Themes as used in Chapter 5, "Theme Design."*

- R23 and R24 are now attached to the **setup NPC**s theme (left-center of figure).

- R11, R26, and R34 are all included in the **display** theme (**display** is shown in the center of the figure; its requirements are not shown).

- **Drop** now crosscuts **display**, since R34, is associated with the **drop** theme (visible as a gray line extending from the lower-center of the figure to the center of the figure).

- The orphaned requirements and the requirements attached to **display** are excluded for the sake of the graph size.

Viewless Theme/Doc

The Theme/Doc approach can be also be applied without making extensive use of Theme/Doc views. We find the graphical approach easier, but it's not the only way.

For instance, if you have a general sense of which features you will include in your system, you can read each of your requirements to see whether any describe features in a tangled way. If one does (as is probably the case) the aspect identification rules can be applied in the same way as they would if you were using the Theme/Doc views. The difference is that you'll have to manually keep track of which requirements are going to be implemented under which themes.

Theme-identification and design-planning stages can be carried out without views when necessary. A simple textual search will reveal which requirements describe which themes. The tables of requirements provided throughout the book were formed in just this way. Unfortunately, this approach doesn't handle synonyms, and doesn't help you visualize overlap between themes. But if your requirements set is small, or if you have bookkeeping mechanisms of your own, then this viewless approach might work well for you.

Planning for Design

To this point, we've been looking at the relationships between themes and trying to minimize the overlap between them in order to be able to move to design. Now that they have been isolated (except for crosscutting and postponement relationships), you may want to see each theme individually so that you can see what you've got and how to move forward to design.

To do this, you use the individual-theme view. This view provides a depiction of the requirements associated only with one theme. It shows not only the overarching themes that were displayed in the relationship view, but also all the subthemes that you grouped under more major themes. Unified themes, however, remain unified in this view. In the case of crosscutting themes, the individual view also shows which elements of the theme are abstract and where crosscutting might occur as well as the "things" that are described in the requirements.

Identify the Objects

In Chapter 3, we identified a list of "things" as nearly the first step in our Theme/Doc analysis process. That would have worked fine, but actually, you don't need to single out the things (which are likely to become design-level objects) until you are planning for design.

You can look for objects in whatever order you would like: on a theme-by-theme basis or by reading the original requirements document again and looking for all the object-worthy keywords. These keywords are then used to identify objects when forming the individual theme views.

Here, we look at two themes: **enter-location** and **track-energy**, and pick out objects. By the end of our association phase, **enter-location** winds up with only two requirements associated with it: R61 (*When two players meet upon entering a location, they perform a duel of rock, paper, scissors*), which was eventually postponed, and R38 (*If a player enters a location that has no player or character in it, they may pick up any crystals or magical items they see*). From these requirements, we can identify objects such as *location, player, crystal,* and *magical item.*

In the **track-energy** theme, we identify *unit, point* (those are synonyms that can be unified in the same way as themes can be unified), *location,* *crystal*, and *player*. The requirements for **track-energy** are shown in Table 4–2.

Some of these objects, such as player and crystal, appear in both themes. That's fine. In Chapter 5, we go over how themes can include design elements to represent concepts that may also be represented in other themes without causing any problems, and in Chapter 6 we talk about how to resolve and compose design elements that represent the same concepts (or requirements-level things).

Viewing Base Themes

Base themes are made up of the requirements associated with a theme, the list of things identified for that theme, and all the behaviors associated with the theme.

Figure 4–15 shows the individual-theme view for the **enter-location** theme. Object nodes, which are particular to the individual view, are shown as boxes. R61, which is shared between **enter-location** and **duel**, has been postponed, so its outline is shown as dashed. The **duel** and **meet-player** themes, which R61 also mentions, are shown in this view.

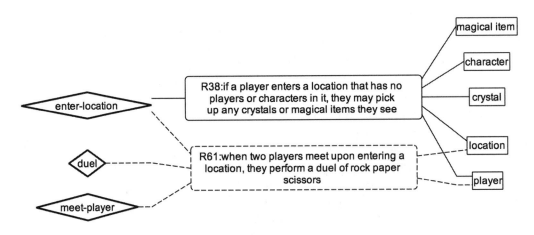

Figure 4–15   *Enter-location individual view.*

Viewing Aspect Themes

Individual views for aspects are the same as those for base themes, except they have a little more information. Before the theme view is constructed, a check is performed to see whether elements to be used in the view are also found in other themes. If they are, those elements are grayed out. Figure 4–16 shows the **track-energy** individual-theme view. You can see that none of the *lose, gain, unit, point,* and *energy* nodes are in gray. This is because they are all unique to this theme. There is no other theme that mentions these concepts. The rest of the nodes, such as *crystal, enter, challenge,* and *location* are all found in other themes (such as **enter-location** in Figure 4–15)and so are grayed out here. The point of the graying is to help you keep in mind that these are concepts that might be modeled abstractly in the design. The nongray elements can be modeled directly.

You might also have noticed that there are crosscutting arrows present in this view. These are the crosscuts that you specified when looking at the relationship view in the "Make the Association" section. In the relationship view in Figure 4–16, you can see that **track-energy** crosscuts **challenge, start,** and **enter-location.** You can also see a link between **start** and **begin,**

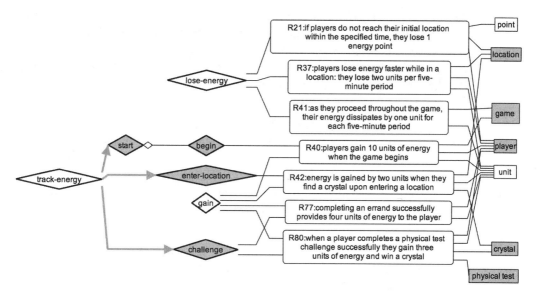

Figure 4–16   *Track-energy individual view.*

showing that they have been grouped. The diamond at the **start** end of the link denotes that **begin** has been grouped under **start**.

Summary

In this chapter, we discussed how to find themes and how to identify them as aspects and base.

General case theme-identification involves deciding on the major concerns described in a set of requirements, and then ensuring that the appropriate requirements are grouped with those concerns. Themes are groups of requirements that all describe a particular concern. At the end of the theme identification process themes will not overlap; that is to say, two themes will not share a requirement. To arrive at orthogonal themes, requirements may be rewritten to ensure that they are grouped under only one theme. If such a rewriting is not possible, then special attention must be paid to the requirement. The requirement may reveal that design-level choices must be made in order to account for the functionality it describes. Or the requirement may reveal aspect-behavior.

Aspects are a special case of theme, and require additional analysis to identify. Identifying aspects involves looking at requirements that are shared between themes. Shared requirements may represent tangling and may reveal aspects. When considering shared requirements to identify aspects, three questions should be asked:

- *Can the requirement be split?*
  If not, then you may have encountered tangled behavior.

- *Is there a dominant theme in the requirement?*
  If so, then the dominant theme of the requirement may be an aspect of the other themes mentioned in the requirement.

- *Is the dominant theme triggered by the other themes described in the requirement?*

If it is, then the requirement has revealed that the dominant theme is an aspect.

We then noted that you perform another check of your aspects:

- *Are aspects you have identified crosscutting enough to be modeled as aspects?*
  If they are triggered in more than one situation, it may be a good idea to keep them as aspect behavior. Otherwise, making them shared-concept themes may be better.

Finally, we looked at individual themes with design in mind.

In Chapter 5, we discuss how to model the themes you have isolated in the requirements analysis phase. Chapter 6 then explains how to compose themes, both base and aspect, using composition relationships.

5

Theme Design

Our focus in this chapter is aspect-oriented design as an extension to object-oriented design, an approach we call Theme/UML. Theme/UML's aspect-oriented extensions are built on top of the standard object-oriented design language, UML. There are numerous excellent "how-to" sources for object-oriented design and the UML, so we assume that you are well-versed in good object-oriented design practices. Indeed, everything you know about the subject is probably useful for you when you embark on an aspect-oriented development project.

At a high level, the aspect-oriented design process is simple. First, you design the individual themes and check them against the Theme/Doc views described in Chapter 4, "Analysis." Then, you describe how the themes should be composed and check the composed result. We divided a description of this work into two chapters. This chapter describes how to work with the individual themes. Chapter 6, "Theme Composition," describes everything to do with composing themes.

Overview of Designing with Theme/UML

Having gone through the Theme/Doc process, you have a good idea of where to start with designing your system, as each individual theme-view maps to a Theme/UML theme. Most of these themes are likely to be base themes, and some will be crosscutting or aspect themes. The primary strength of the Theme approach is that it allows a designer to work with individual themes in the system separately, considering only those design elements that are relevant for the theme at hand. As illustrated in Figure 5-1, here's where you use your standard UML modeling process to come up with the Theme/UML designs. In addition, there are some extra things to think about when you design aspect themes, relating to capturing the crosscutting behavior that happens as a result of triggers that are external to the aspect theme.

Let's look at an overview of designing both kinds of themes.

Overview of Designing Base Themes

It is likely that you already inspect any existing analysis models for the system when you are embarking on your object-oriented designs. Similarly here, a good start for designing your base themes is to include a look at the Theme/Doc individual theme-view. This view illustrates the requirements

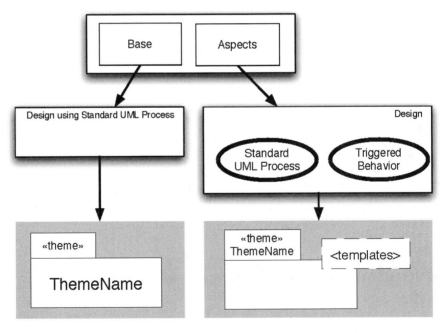

Figure 5–1 *General view of the design process.*

for which the theme is responsible and highlights the behaviors and objects that the requirements describe. We use gray shadows to show how elements from the Theme/Doc views correspond to design elements in Theme/UML. From an object-oriented design perspective, objects generally map to structural design elements such as classes or attributes, and behaviors are likely to map to some methods on objects. Figure 5–2 illustrates a generic Theme/Doc individual theme view with behavior nodes illustrated as diamonds and object nodes illustrated as boxes. As the designer, you decide whether each object is a class or an attribute of a class in your model. For illustration, all objects in Figure 5–2 except `object4`, which is an attribute, map to different classes. You make the decision about `object4` as an attribute the way you normally would in an object-oriented design: Probably based on a view that `object4` has, in itself, no other defining characteristics or behavior in which you are interested.

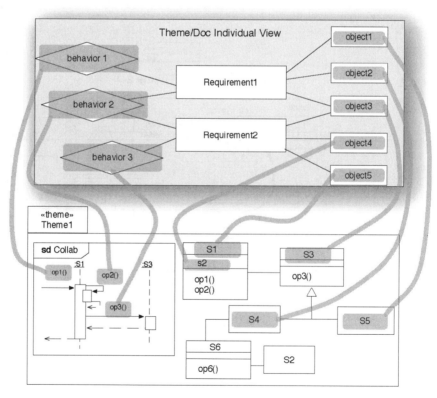

Figure 5–2   *Mapping individual theme view to theme design.*

You may notice that Figure 5–2 also contains some structure and behavior that are not directly mapped from nodes in the Theme/Doc individual view. We included these to illustrate that you may require supporting design elements to capture low-level design of the system. Such design elements may emerge, as you'd expect, because of the particular environment you are working on or because of more technical system concerns that are not directly manifest at requirements level.

Another way to think of the design of a base theme is as a standard UML package. In it, you have structural models such as a class or object diagrams, and behavioral models such as sequence diagrams or state machines, and so on. Though we stereotype UML's package with a stereotype called «theme», there really is no conceptual difference between the two. As illustrated in Figure 5–3, each separate theme package holds all the relevant design models to capture the design of the individual theme responsibilities.

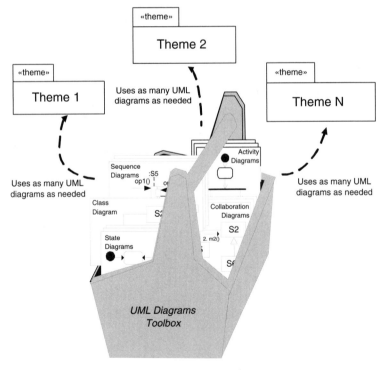

Figure 5–3   *Base theme designs.*

When you are designing any individual theme, you are using standard UML. You should use the same object-oriented development methodology that you are comfortable with for determining which structural and behavioral design elements best capture the set of requirements for which the theme is responsible. These requirements are clearly listed in the Theme/Doc views. Of course, for most, if not all, systems, the same domain concepts come into play for lots of different themes in the system. You would probably notice fairly quickly that in our Crystal Game, the notion of a "player" is relevant in lots of places—for example, when the game is being set up, when crystals are found, when a duel happens, and so on. Without giving too much away, you might therefore expect a class called Player to appear in a number of different themes, and you would be right—it does. You should not concern yourself with this apparent duplication when you design the individual view. If your requirements for the individual theme talk about players, then have a Player class if it makes sense. Bear in mind that you are designing the theme from the perspective of its own requirements, with the design in other themes containing specifications for such elements as players designed from their own perspectives. How you compose themes containing such elements is addressed in the next chapter.

Overview of Designing Aspect Themes

Where you'll start to see something new in this chapter is in the design of crosscutting themes. As with base themes, crosscutting themes may also share structural and behavioral concepts with other themes, and in addition (and here lies the difference), they may define behavior that is triggered by behavior in another theme. As illustrated in Figure 5–4, the extra

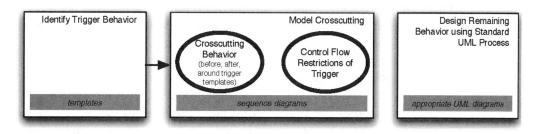

Figure 5–4   *General view of the aspect design process.*

things you need to think about for aspect themes relate to this triggered behavior. First, you should identify where triggered behavior needs to be modeled, and capture the triggers as templates (of which, more later). You will then be able to model the crosscutting behavior relative to those templates, and indicate whether there are control flow restrictions associated with the triggers. Of course, you will use your standard UML design process again for any other structure and behavior not impacted by the triggered behavior.

The individual aspect-theme views indicate where triggering occurs. Figure 5–5 illustrates a generic Theme/Doc individual aspect-theme view with some of the behavior nodes and object nodes filled in with dark-gray, indicating that they are all found in other themes. More explanation of the grayed-out nodes is provided in the "Planning for Design" section of Chapter 4.

Nongray structural nodes (e.g., the shadowed `object1` and `object5` from Figure 5–5) and nongray behavioral nodes with no link to a gray behavioral node (e.g., the shadowed `behavior3` from Figure 5–5) are conceptually the same as for base themes, and you should design them using a similar process. As for gray-filled object nodes (e.g., `object2`, `object3`, and `object4` from Figure 5–5), at this stage you should include a minimal specification of them in your design, because you will need to refer to them in the design of this aspect. Bear in mind that you expect that they are found in other themes, and so you needn't be too concerned about capturing information about them other than as much as you need to for the aspect. Indeed, this is true for all theme design—you specify only what you care about to capture the requirements for which the theme is responsible.

Gray arrows in Theme/Doc views indicate crosscutting; this is where aspect themes get interesting. These arrows extend from triggered aspect behavior to their trigger (a gray node). This brings us to the first change to the UML with Theme/UML. We need a way to talk about the triggering behavior in other themes without explicitly referring to it. While the gray-filled behavior nodes do indicate what that behavior is, we don't want to couple the design of the aspect with the base, triggering behaviors. To this end, we extend UML's notion of templates to allow you to reference those design elements that are outside the crosscutting theme. You can then refer to the template name as the trigger to initiate the crosscutting behavior to be defined within the aspect. You also need a way to express when the actual triggering base behavior should happen. As illustrated in Figure 5–5 for

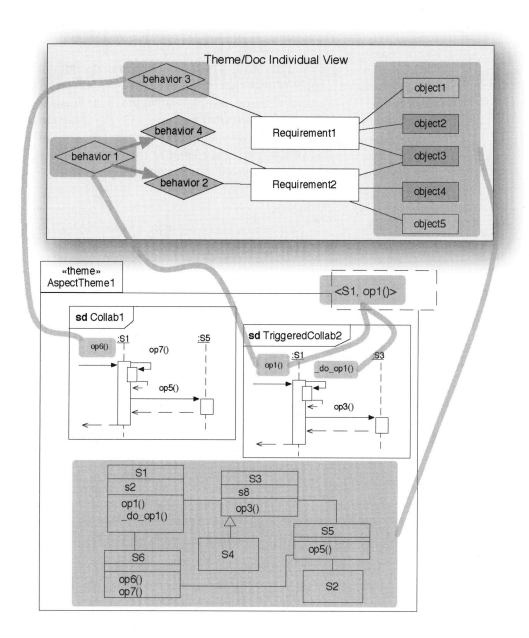

Figure 5–5   *Mapping individual aspect-theme view to aspect-theme designs.*

`op1()`, within a sequence diagram, you can prepend `_do_` to the template name to indicate its execution relative to the crosscutting behavior.

The overall aspect-theme design is similar to the overall design of a base theme, except that some of its behavior is triggered by behavior in other themes that is referenced using templates. Figure 5–6 illustrates an aspect-theme design as a standard UML package with the usual structural and behavioral models and just one notable difference. Templates are listed in a dotted box in the top right corner of the theme package box, with a sequence diagram for each template grouping in the box.

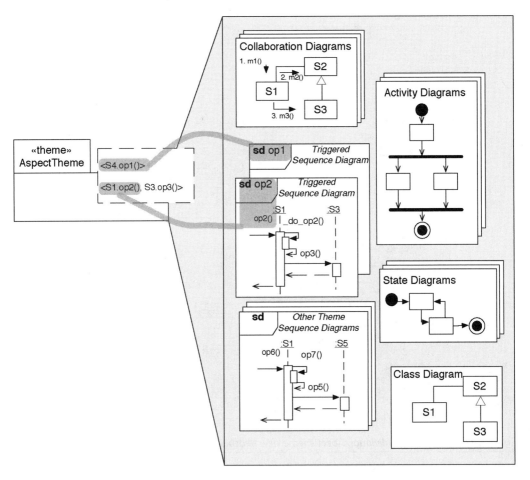

Figure 5–6   *Aspect-theme designs.*

It's important to note that it is perfectly normal to have other behavioral models within the aspect theme that are not triggered by other themes. The requirements for the theme are grouped in terms of encapsulating a concern or feature of the system, not by trying to encapsulate only triggered behavior.

We now move on to the design of the Crystal Game, first with examples of concept-sharing themes designed using standard UML, then with examples of designing crosscutting themes.

Designing Base Themes

If we consider just the themes illustrated in Figure 4–14, our base themes for the Crystal Game are

display	game-setup	pay
distribute-crystals	join	setup NPCs
distribute-items	leave	setup players
duel	meet-player	start
end-game	meet-sage	wager
enter-input	meet-warrior	
enter-location	meet-wizard	

We can list these from the theme diamonds, excluding those that have crosscutting relationships to other themes, since we deal with those separately later.

Kicking off our design, we know that we want to have a theme package for each base theme identified, as illustrated in Figure 5–7.

There are a lot of themes here, and the conceptual basis of the Theme process comes strongly into play in terms of how you manage their design. One of the strengths of Theme/UML is that you can design the requirements that are the responsibility of each individual base theme entirely

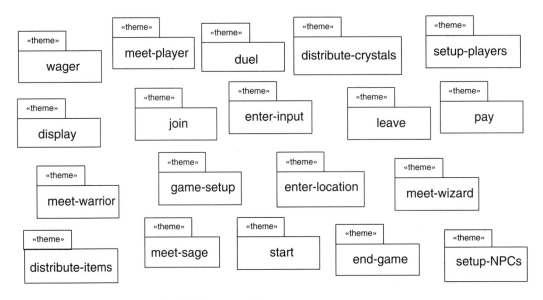

Figure 5–7   *Base themes identified during analysis.*

from the perspective of that theme. An implication of this is that different designers can design the themes at the same time. The lack of dependencies and critical paths for the overall design may be very useful for your design plan. In the "Some Comments on Process" section of Chapter 6, "Theme Composition," we talk a little more about whether and how the designers should communicate with each other along the way.

For an individual designer of any of these themes, the first step is to examine the Theme/Doc individual theme view to understand the responsibilities of the theme. After that, use your favorite object-oriented design methodology to come up with the appropriate structural and behavioral models required to capture the requirements. In this section, we choose a subset of the theme designs selected on the basis of their usefulness to illustrate composition in the next chapter. The internals of the base-theme designs are not interesting from a Theme/UML perspective, as it is standard object-oriented design. Indeed, we show you only a likely structural design for each, which is enough for the purposes of this book. The base themes we've chosen for this section are **start**, **distribute-crystals**, **setup-NPC**, **enter-location**, and **duel**.

Game Architecture

Before we go any further, though, let's look at the architecture of the Crystal Game, which was an important influence on many of the design decisions. In general, we view decisions on the architecture of your system to be reasonably orthogonal to the Theme process. However, some architectural concerns may influence how you group requirements into themes in the first place.

We've opted for a fairly standard architecture for mobile systems—see Figure 5–8 for an overview.

As you'd expect, there's the usual user-interface and logic layers. In addition, we reuse a GPS component from which we can obtain a reasonable approximation of a player's location by getting the GPS coordinates from this component. Of particular note in the architecture is the means by which players communicate with each other. Given the outdoor, mobile nature of the game, we chose a peer-to-peer (P2P) solution. In P2P systems, every party has equal capabilities (in essence, each party can be considered both a client and a server), and the communications model allows any party to initiate communications. Communication between players is event-based, which leads us to an important assumption. In designing our game logic, we assume that the underlying group communication system provides total-order, atomic multicast. From a game-logic perspective, totally ordered events mean that every player who receives events receives them in the same order. Atomic multicast means that for any event, every player receives it or no player receives it. For example, when a player takes

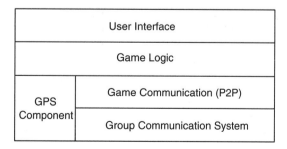

Figure 5–8   *Game architecture.*

crystals from a location, that information is multicast to the other players in the group. With total-order (and atomic) communication, no other player will be in conflict for the same crystals at the same location.

Those of you who are expert in group communications for distributed systems will agree that in a mobile, wireless, P2P environment, totally ordered, atomic multicast is a tall order, but in terms of illustrating Theme/UML, it's not important.

In general, the themes selected for illustration in this chapter belong in the game logic and the game communication layers of the architecture. In this base-theme section, we generally omit the behavioral designs, as you may assume standard UML behavior modeling that may, of course, be included in a theme design. In "Designing Crosscutting Themes," we include the behavioral designs, because they are interesting from an aspect-oriented design perspective.

Enter-Location Theme

The **enter-location** theme is responsible for handling what can happen when a player moves. The top part of Figure 5–9 illustrates the Theme/Doc individual theme view for **enter-location**, which tells us which requirements should be handled. R38 tells us that if the player moves into a game location (i.e., where crystals and possibly NPCs are), then he or she takes any available crystals and magical items if there are no other players or characters there. R61 tells us that there should be a duel if two players meet in a game location.

Looking at R38 first, the behavior node indicates an enter-location action, and the object nodes illustrate magical items, characters, crystals, location, and player objects. If we break down this requirement into logical steps, we have the following:

- Check the player's current location.

- Check the player's current location against the game locations.

- If in a game location, check if there are other players/characters in the location.

- If there are no players/characters, take the crystals and magic items.

The UML class diagram in Figure 5–9 illustrates the structural impact of design decisions made for each step. For example, one option for checking a mobile player's location is to have a thread periodically monitoring the player's GPS coordinates. This thread sends a `newLocation()` event if there is a "significant" change in the player's location. In this algorithm, the designer decides how often to perform the location check and when to consider a change significant enough to send the `newLocation()` event. This decision results in an active `Player` class that requires a relationship with the `GPSComponent`.

Also in this design, the `Game` class is given the responsibility of knowing about game locations, whether there are crystals or magic items in each location, and the locations of players and characters. We don't worry about how the `Game` class acquires this knowledge within this theme. All we decide is that it does, and that we can query that knowledge. This decision results in the `Game`, `Vector`, `Location`, `MagicItem`, and `Character` classes in the design.

Other decisions you might make here relate to whether an object node from the Theme/Doc individual theme view should be structurally represented in the design as a class or an attribute of a class. In this example, all are classes except the `crystal` element. When we think about crystals, we realize that there are no interesting characteristics relating to crystals other than how many a player has or how many there are in a location. Therefore, we decide that `crystal` does not merit more than a primitive type, and we make it an attribute of the `Player` and the `Location`. Though not illustrated by arrows on Figure 5–9, magical item and character map to corresponding classes in the structural design.

Moving on to requirement R61, we notice that the notation in the individual view highlights that a decision as to which theme should handle the dueling was postponed. On the one hand, we know that there is a different theme, **duel**, which handles the actual dueling. On the other hand, this

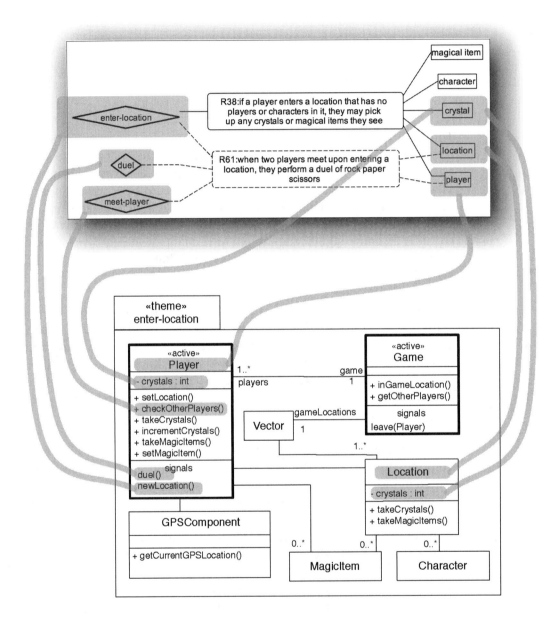

Figure 5–9 *Enter-location theme.*

enter-location theme knows a lot about when dueling should happen because, from R38, it checks where the player is in a location and whether there is already another player there. The **enter-location** theme has to provide a design for this event in order to know whether the player could pick up the crystals and magic items in a game location.

Recall that in Chapter 4, **duel** was examined to see whether it was actually an aspect of **enter-location**. **Enter-location** and **duel** shared an un-splittable requirement that described when dueling occurred. Additionally, **enter-location** triggered **duel**. However, since **duel** is only triggered in one situation (upon location entry), we could not justify making **duel** an aspect. Here, we see that because **duel** failed the final aspect-test, the trigger for the behavior in the **duel** theme must be placed within the **enter-location** theme explicitly.

We therefore decide that it makes sense for the **enter-location** theme to "mark" when dueling should happen by adding a `duel()` method signature that is not designed any further. As the designer of the **enter-location** theme, you don't have to worry about what it means to duel. In a sense, this is equivalent to considering `duel()` as an abstract element, where instead of it being concretized using a generalization relationship, it is concretized during composition, as specified by a composition relationship.

Chapter 6 talks more about this decision from the perspective of reconciling the likely appearance of a `duel()` method in both themes during composition. See Figure 5–9 for the resulting structural design of the **enter-location** theme.

Start Theme

In the **start** theme, a player has chosen to start a new game. The grouped requirements for this theme are listed in Table 5–1.

As we can ascertain from the requirements, the **start** theme is responsible for initializing the game, and therefore, in the design, for instantiating game and location objects. There may be many active games in a game boundary at the same time, and so we decide that we should have a `GameAdmin` class that handles the initial `newGame()` request and initializes the required game and location instances. Each game must hold

Table 5–1 *Start Theme Requirements*

R No.	Requirement Text
R10	One player is chosen to create a new game.
R11	To create a new game, a player chooses *Begin New* from the Options menu.
R14	Multiple games may be created in the same location at the same time and not interfere with one another.
R16	The host player's location at the time the game is created becomes the throne room.
R36	If a player's game device fails, as may happen in a power failure, the player can rejoin the game with the same number of crystals and the same game state as long as he or she restarts before the end of the game.
R94	Players can start a new game.

instances of its own location objects, since pertinent game state (such as number of crystals) is attached to location.

An interesting point to note is that two requirements are boxed in gray in the table. This denotes that the decision of where the design for the requirement should reside was postponed during the Theme/Doc process. When we look at R36, we notice that there are rules and checks associated with joining a game, so we decide to leave the whole joining process to the **join** theme. R11 (shown boxed in gray in Table 5–1) relates to the user interface, so we decide to leave the details of that with the **display** theme and assume that this theme receives a `newGame()` request. See Figure 5–10 for a structural design of the theme.

Though not included here, you can also expect Theme/Doc's individual theme view to highlight the behavioral and structural entities that must be accommodated, as we saw in detail for the **enter-location** theme. For example, classes such as `Player`, `Location`, and `Game` appear in the individual theme view. There are likely to be classes that emerge from decisions you make independent of the requirements text—for example, the use of a `Vector` (or some other kind of collection) to hold the game locations. Your behavioral models for this theme are influenced, of course, by the requirements that are grouped for it in the theme views.

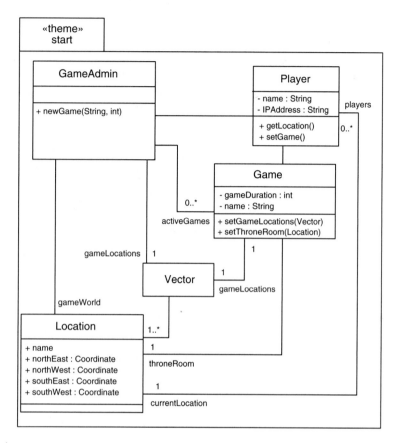

Figure 5–10   *Start theme.*

Distribute-Crystals Theme

The **distribute-crystals** theme is responsible for the distribution of a random number of crystals (up to ten) to a random number of random locations. See Table 5–2 for the list of requirements and Figure 5–11 for a structural design of the theme.

The requirements for **distribute-crystals** (and an individual theme view) result in structural entities such as game, location, and crystal. Of course, as the designer, you have to decide whether these elements should be classes or attributes of classes. Game seems like a good class because it has

Table 5–2 *Distribute Crystals Requirements*

R No.	Requirement Text
R17	The new game randomly distributes crystals throughout the game area.
R18	When the game environment is initially populated with crystals, a random number of random locations are populated with a random number of crystals up to 10.
R35	Dropped crystals are rescattered throughout the game area.

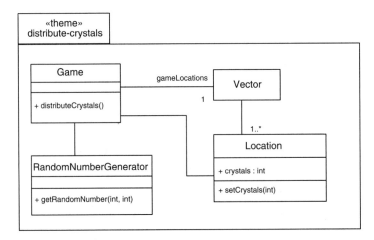

Figure 5–11   *Distribute-crystals theme.*

behavior related to distributing the crystals and knows about the game locations. `Location` seems like a good class because it contains crystals. Crystal is an interesting entity. Should it be a class or an attribute of `Location`? Similar to the decision when we came across crystals in the **enter-location** theme, we decide to make it as attribute of `Location`, as there is no interesting state or behavior for it. Finally, how you handle random-number generation to satisfy the requirements is a detailed design decision. We've encapsulated the responsibility for this into a `RandomNumberGenerator` class. You'll notice that R35 is shown boxed in gray in the table. This indicates that the requirement is shared between **drop** and **distribute-crystals**, and was postponed in the "Postpone Some Decisions" section of Chapter 4. We will not include the design for this requirement in this theme, but instead we leave it to the **drop** theme.

Setup-NPC Theme

The **setup-NPC** theme is responsible for distributing NPCs around the game environment. See Table 5–3 for the list of requirements and Figure 5–12 for a structural design of the theme. Each location may have, at most, one NPC, and there are a random number of different kinds of NPCs. As before, the choice of design elements is influenced by a combination of the Theme/Doc theme view's grouping of requirements, its object and behavior nodes, and detailed design decisions that you make.

Table 5–3 *Setup-NPC Requirements*

R No.	Requirement Text
R23	Not more than one NPC is sent to any one location.
R24	NPCs are randomly sent to locations.

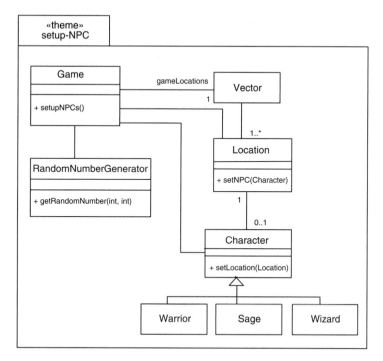

Figure 5–12 *Setup-NPC theme.*

Duel Theme

The **duel** theme handles wagering prior to the duel and the duel itself. See Table 5–4 for the list of requirements and Figure 5–13 for a structural design of the theme.

Table 5–4 *Duel Requirements*

R No.	Requirement Text
R31	Crystals can be collected by discovering them in a location in the world, interacting with characters, or dueling other players for them.
R61	When two players meet upon entering a location, they perform a duel of rock, paper, scissors.
R62	Each player wagers a crystal on the outcome of the duel.
R63	If one player has no crystals they will wager the promise of the first crystal they find on the duel outcome, or they may wager two magical items in their possession.
R70	Players may be involved in only one duel at a time.
R71	If there are both another player and an NPC in a location when a player arrives, the other player takes precedence over the NPC, and a duel occurs, followed by the challenge from the NPC.
R72	Duel losers pay their debts immediately, or, if they cannot, their debts are automatically repaid when they become able.
R87	If more than one player has the same number of crystals and energy, then they must duel to decide which wins.

This design is inherently event-based, and the negotiation between the players as to what will be wagered is handled with events. Each player in the duel reveals his choice of rock, paper, or scissors by sending a `duelRevealRPS(String, String)` event with his name and the choice as parameters. A `Player` object will only evaluate this event after an event declaring its own choice has been multicast. The duel loser gives the winner whatever was on wager, or if he does not have what was wagered, records this fact for future reference. Handling old debts is outside this theme, as the Theme/Doc process has identified a **pay** theme. See Figure 5–6 for a structural design of the **duel** theme.

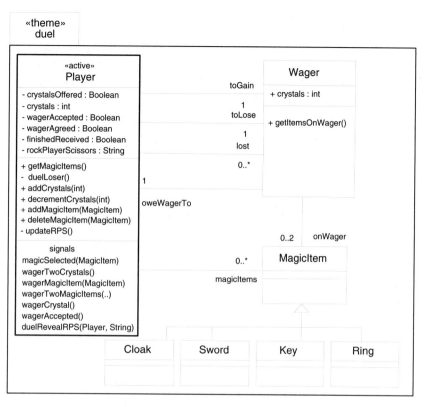

Figure 5–13 *Duel theme.*

Designing Crosscutting Themes

A theme is crosscutting (or an aspect) when at least some of its behavior is triggered by behavior in one or more other themes. In other words, there is behavior in the crosscutting theme that occurs only relative to the behavior in the theme(s) it crosscuts. When you're designing such a theme, you want to be able to refer to that outside behavior without explicitly naming it. Imagine a crosscutting theme that is designed to have multiple collaborating classes. The crosscut behavior (in the base theme) might occur at any stage in the collaboration between the classes—indeed, at more than one stage. Theme/UML uses an extension of UML's notion of templates that lets you refer to outside elements in a parameterized way. Given that there may be multiple behaviors (within multiple classes) that may be crosscut, then a crosscutting theme may have multiple templates. These templates may be parameters for different kinds of design elements, such as classes, operations, or attributes. At composition time, the "real" elements in the theme to be crosscut replace the templates in the design. Where the template is a class, the design elements in the crosscutting theme are added to the existing elements in the real class. Where the template is an operation, execution of the real operation occurs as specified in the collaboration diagram of the crosscutting theme. Where the template is an attribute, the real attribute is used where the template is referred to in the crosscutting theme. We describe the implications at composition time in more detail in Chapter 6. Here, we look at what the designer of a crosscutting theme has to do.

Changes to the UML

Before we look at some crosscutting theme designs, let's first discuss working with templates from a notational perspective.

Crosscutting Behavior and Templates

Crosscutting behavior is triggered by the behavior it crosscuts. Standard UML has useful models for specifying collaborative behavior, which can be used in Theme/UML. In particular, you will find sequence diagrams a useful means for specifying when crosscutting behavior should occur relative to the crosscut behavior. With a sequence diagram, you can supplement the real behavior by defining other behavior in a sequence around it. In essence, what you are saying is, "When the real behavior happens, do all this other behavior as well as the real behavior." In the sequence diagram, you will refer to the real behavior with a template that, from a notational perspective, looks like every other operation call. You will distinguish it as a template separately.

Of course, the real behavior has to happen at some point, and you need some way to distinguish between the operation that replaces the template (and therefore triggers the combination of its own behavior and the crosscutting behavior) and the actual execution of the replacing operation. For the latter, add _do_ to the beginning of the operation name in the sequence diagram. This is one hint that the operation is a template in the sequence diagram. As we describe in more detail in Chapter 6, this triggers, during the composition process, a renaming of the real operation (and setting its visibility to *private*) so that the original operation's name can trigger all appropriate behavior defined in the sequence diagram. For example, Figure 5–14 illustrates a sequence diagram for the `moveLocation(..)` template of the **track-energy** theme. When a player moves location, she may have entered a location where the energy loss is different, which must be checked by the **track-energy** theme. Energy is lost at either two units or one unit every five minutes, depending on where the player is located (R37 and R41 from Theme/Doc's individual theme view). This sequence diagram specifies that *after* the actual move-location operation is performed (`_do_moveLocation(..)`), the crosscutting behavior relates to finding out whether the player's current location is in a game location and setting the amount of energy to lose to either 1 or 2 appropriately.

Control Flow Restrictions on Triggers

In the `moveLocation(..)` example illustrated in Figure 5-14, any execution of real behavior that replaces the `moveLocation(..)` template will trigger the crosscutting behavior. In some cases, however, you may want to restrict when the real behavior becomes a trigger. In particular, you may

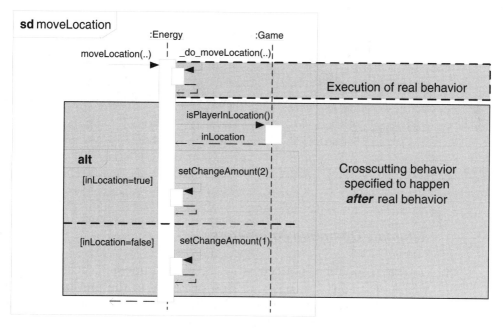

Figure 5–14   *Crosscutting behavior notation.*

want to say that the real behavior becomes a trigger only when it is executing within the control flow of other behavior. Again, sequence diagrams provide us with the means to express this. For example, as illustrated in Figure 5-15, crosscutting behavior is defined for an op2(..) trigger. However, it is defined within the flow of control of _do_op1(..), which means that op2(..) becomes a trigger for the crosscutting behavior before() and after() *only* when it occurs within _do_op1(..)'s flow of control.

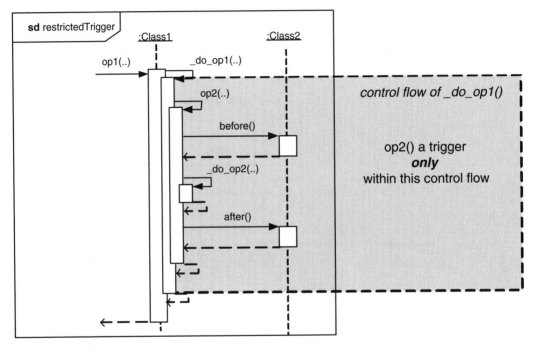

Figure 5–15   *Trigger within a specified flow of control.*

Template Operation Parameters

You've probably noticed the ".." parameter specification of moveLocation(..), op1(..) and op2(..) in the previous examples This indicates that an operation of any signature may replace the template. Possible parameter specifications relate to the scope within which the replacing operation is executed. For example, in Figure 5–14, the active period of the execution of `moveLocation(..)` defines the scope for this operation, and any parameters defined may be used within this scope. The parameter possibilities are defined in Table 5–5.

Table 5–5 *Parameter Specification*

Parameter	Usage
`op()`	The replacing operation must have no parameters.
`op(..)`	The replacing operation may have any signatures.
`op(.., Type, ..)`	The replacing operation must have a parameter of type `Type` in its parameter list, as it is required by the crosscutting sequence of behavior. Other than that, there may be any other parameter(s) of any type.

Listing the Templates for a Theme

UML's templates are parameterized model elements that are contained in a class that is then called a *template class*. These templates are ordered in a dotted box on the class box notation. In Theme/UML, a theme may have templates that are class types and therefore are placeholders to be replaced by real class elements. Here's a rule: *every template operation or template attribute must be defined as part of a template class.* In other words, if you have a class in your crosscutting-theme design that contains a template operation or parameter, then the class itself is also considered to be a template, and all its nontemplate elements are added to a real class at composition. This makes sense, because the replacing real operation or attribute already has a containing class, with potentially other elements that it needs or other elements that use it, and therefore should be merged with the template class. We describe this in more detail in Chapter 6, "Theme Composition."

Since template classes are contained in the crosscutting theme, Theme/UML (in the spirit of standard UML) places all the templates for the theme in a dotted box on the theme box notation. Within this box, templates are grouped by sequence diagram. The templates defined in each sequence diagram (or *behavioral group*) are grouped within < > brackets. There is one important rule here: *the first operation in the group must be the one that triggers the crosscutting behavior.* Remember we are specifying crosscutting behavior here that is triggered by behavior in a base theme. It would not make sense for the first operation of the sequence of behavior *not* to be the triggering operation. There may also, of course, be more templates defined within the sequence of behavior, and ordering within this group is important. These triggers may or may not be restricted by the control flow of others.

Figure 5–16 illustrates the templates for the **track-energy** theme. There are three behavioral groups, each with one template operation: `moveLocation(..)` (behavior illustrated in Figure 5–14), `energy Action(..)`, which supports the game requirement that a player may gain some energy after performing some action, and `joinGame(..)`, which supports the game requirement that a player periodically loses energy throughout the game.

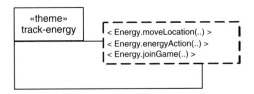

Figure 5–16   *Template notation.*

There is no limit (other than common sense!) to the number of behavioral groups you can have or the number of template operations/attributes you can define within a behavioral group. There must, however, be a corresponding behavioral group of templates for every sequence diagram that uses templates in the theme. In addition, every named template within the sequence diagram must be listed in the < > list, comma-separated.

Within a single < > behavioral group, you might have a number of template operations and attributes in the same template class. For convenience, you may qualify these with a list notation { }. For example, the following template group has six template operations, three in `ClassA` and three in `ClassB`.

`< ClassA{op1(), op2(), op3()}, ClassB{op1(), op3(), op4()} >`

Don't forget that the first operation is the one that triggers the crosscutting behavior in the corresponding sequence diagram—in this case, `ClassA.op1()`. A template class qualifies template operations and attributes, which means, for this example, that there is no conflict between `ClassA.op1()` and `ClassB.op1()`.

Referencing Template Structure and Behavior

Like base themes, an aspect theme design provides a design specification for all the requirements for which it is responsible. As such, it will contain structural and behavioral models appropriate to capture that specification. Structural models will specify the classes, attributes, and relationships of the theme. At least some, but probably not all, of the behavioral models will be triggered by operations outside the theme. In the base themes, operations that trigger a sequence of crosscutting behavior are likely to appear in different classes, but the corresponding template is captured in a single template class in the aspect theme. Such a template class will have additional elements defined to capture the crosscutting behavior. As we'll describe in Chapter 6, at composition, these additional elements will be added to the triggering class. Looking forward to any possible composed design, it may have many different classes that were composed with the template class because those classes have operations that trigger the relevant crosscutting behavior.

This has implications for using the template class as a reference type within the aspect theme design. Let's say we have a class called `ClassA` in the aspect design that is not a template class—in other words, has no crosscutting behavior to be triggered outside the aspect. We would expect `ClassA`, nonetheless, to be added to a composed design. Let's further say that `ClassA` has an attribute called `att1`. If we say that `att1`'s type is a template class, which of the many possible types will it be in a composed design? It is ambiguous because there may be many classes composed with the template class. To avoid such confusion, Theme/UML *does not allow external references to a template class.*

The same problem also applies to invoking methods within a template class from a different class in the aspect theme—let's say our `ClassA` again. If a method in `ClassA` invokes a method in a template class, which method should be executed when the aspect theme is composed with base themes? Again, it is ambiguous and to avoid confusion, Theme/UML *does not allow external method invocations on a template class.* Figure 5–17 summarizes what you can and can't do. In the figure, ClassB is a template class, and ClassA and ClassC are not.

These rules do not restrict you from invoking methods that you expect to be provided by a base theme. Recall the invocation of Player.duel() in

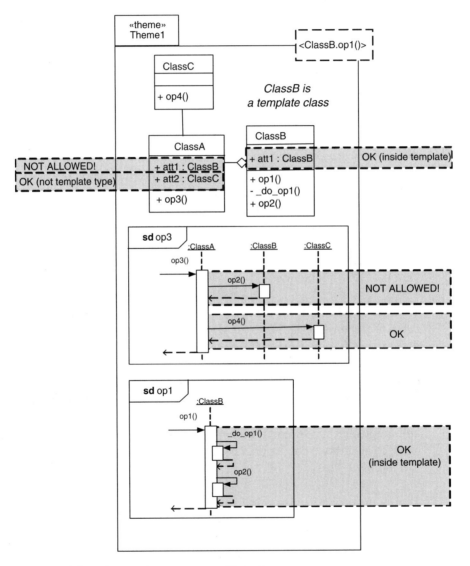

Figure 5–17   *Referencing template structure and behavior*

the **enter-location** base theme. There may be many such situations where you invoke a method you expect to be in another theme, and therefore don't provide any other specification for it. What do you do in an aspect theme if that method is in a class that you expect to have a trigger for cross-cutting behavior and therefore will be merged with a template class containing that crosscutting behavior? Theme/UML's rule says you can't invoke a method in a template class outside that class. However, you can still include in the aspect theme a class (such as `Player` from the example above) that you expect to have the behavior you need. The **P2PCommunication** aspect theme that we describe later in this section has good examples of how to handle adding aspect theme-specific behavior to `Player` that you explicitly want to be merged with the `Player` class from the base, while also working with triggers that are likely to come from the `Player` class. In Chapter 6, we describe compositions of aspect and base themes that sort out such situations.

Track-Energy Theme

Chapter 4 illustrated how the use of Theme/Doc can help you figure out which themes in the requirements crosscut other themes. One such theme is the **track-energy** theme, which is responsible for managing a player's energy. Requirements for the **track-energy** theme are listed in Table 5–6.

Table 5–6 *Track Energy Requirements*

R No.	Requirement Text
R21	If players do not reach their initial location within the specified time, they lose 1 energy point.
R37	Players lose energy faster while in a location: they lose two units per five-minute period.
R40	Players gain 10 units of energy when the game begins.
R41	As players proceed throughout the game, their energy dissipates by one unit for each five-minute period.
R42	Energy is gained by two units when they find a crystal upon entering a location.
R77	Completing an errand successfully provides four units of energy to the player.
R80	When players complete a physical test challenge successfully, they gain three units of energy and win a crystal.

The triggered behavior in the theme is illustrated in the individual aspect-theme view. Figure 5–18 illustrates a snippet of **track-energy**'s individual theme view that shows the crosscutting relationships between the actions. These relationships indicate that there are three triggers expected in base themes that will have crosscutting behavior here. They map to the Theme/UML templates for the theme, as these capture the triggers that initiate crosscutting behavior. Mappings are indicated by gray shadows in the figure.

On to the design, when we look at the group of requirements, we see that there is a lot of game-play decision making related to how much energy is gained or lost on various activities. We make the decision to encapsulate this knowledge into a class called Game that the Energy class can use to find out the information it needs to determine how to change state.

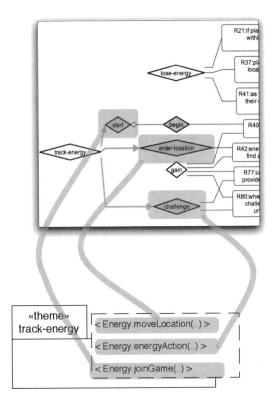

Figure 5–18   *Mapping templates from individual aspect-theme view.*

Let's look at the `lose-energy` behavior node from the individual theme view snippet in Figure 5–19. This action does not have a crosscutting relationship to other behavior in the theme view, and its sequence diagram simply changes the energy amount when it's triggered, as handled in the state diagram. However, crosscutting behavior is required to change the amount of energy units that are lost every five minutes. This behavior

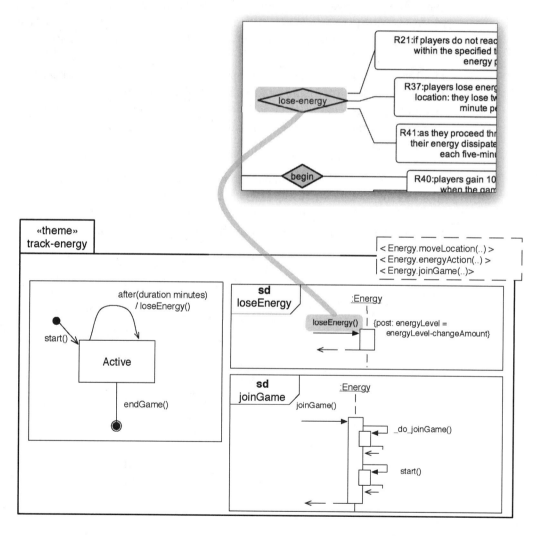

Figure 5–19   *Lose energy behavior.*

crosscuts moving location, which gave us the template operation
`moveLocation(..)` and its corresponding sequence diagram, as illustrated in Figure 5–14. Figure 5–19 illustrates how loss of energy works. The state
machine for the `Energy` class specifies that after a certain number of minutes (number defined in the duration attribute), a `loseEnergy()` event is
sent. Figure 5–19 also illustrates how the `Energy` class responds to the
`loseEnergy()` event—it decrements the `energyUnit` attribute by the
value in the `changeAmount` attribute. The response to the `loseEnergy()`
event does not crosscut any other behavior. Note that it is perfectly normal
in a crosscutting theme to have some behavior that is part of the responsibility of the theme that does not crosscut behavior outside the theme.

Figure 5–19 also illustrates some crosscutting behavior that specifies when
the thread to kick off losing energy should be started. In this case, as soon
as a player joins a game, energy is depleted after a specified duration. The
template operation is `joinGame(..)`, and after this has completed, the
thread is started.

Figure 5–20 illustrates the behavior that crosscuts some actions in the game
(denoted by the `energyAction(..)` template operation). The `Game` class is
responsible for knowing the game rules regarding how much energy a player
wins or loses after a particular action. These rules are defined in requirements

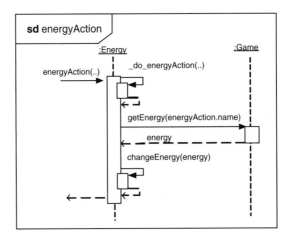

Figure 5–20   *Change energy after action.*

R42, R80, R77, and R21. This design uses the `name` metaproperty of the `energyAction(..)` model element[1] to get a `String` representation of the name so that the `Game` class can tell it by how much energy to change the current value. This behavior crosscuts the particular action, which is executed beforehand, as illustrated by `_do_energyAction(..)` in the sequence. The `changeEnergy(int)` operation either increases or decreases the energy levels, depending on the guidance of the `Game` object. This encapsulates both the `gain` and `lose` behavior nodes from the individual theme view.

As with all designs, there is likely to be a structural diagram that illustrates the structure of the classes in play in the behavior. Figure 5–21 illustrates

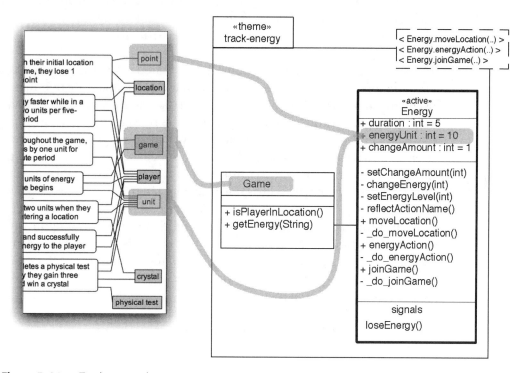

Figure 5–21   *Track-energy theme structure.*

---

[1] In general, Theme/UML allows a designer to refer to the metaproperties of any model element (i.e., the properties defined for the particular model element construct in the UML metamodel).

the class structure for the **track-energy** theme. Notice that requirement R40 is handled structurally by setting the initial value of the `energyUnit` attribute to 10.

There are a couple of interesting things to note here. In the Theme/Doc individual theme view snippet, there are two shadowed white object nodes (`point` and `unit`) and five shadowed gray object nodes (`location`, `game`, `player`, `crystal`, and `physical test`). As described in Chapter 4's, "Planning for Design" section, the white nodes indicate that the objects wholly belong to the theme. After looking at the requirements that refer to `point` (R41) and `unit` (all five other requirements), we consider them to be synonyms and map them to an attribute (`energyUnit`) in the `Energy` class. Again, the decision whether this should be a class or an attribute is a standard object-oriented one—at this stage, we don't see that unit has any interesting properties or behavior, so we make it an attribute.

The gray nodes indicate that the objects are shared with other themes. On examination of each one, we determine that `Game` is the only one that is useful to model for tracking energy. We need `Game` to tell us whether a player is in a game location and also to handle the rules related to changing a player's energy as a result of some action. We can also imagine that there is likely to be a `Game` class in other themes. This means that the **track-energy** theme is an example of a crosscutting theme that also shares concepts with other themes, which we address during composition.

Note also that the template operations and their corresponding private, renamed operations all appear in the `Energy` class. This makes sense because the template operation and the renamed operation each denote different behavior—one denotes the triggering of crosscutting behavior, and one denotes the real operation.

Finally, `Energy` is an active class because it responds to the `loseEnergy()` event.

P2P Communication Theme

The **track-energy** theme we just described was one of the crosscutting themes identified during the Theme/Doc analysis process. Of course, during detailed design of a system, you are concerned with architectural, system questions that may not directly manifest in the requirements. As a result of such detailed design, more technical kinds of behavior may crosscut the application logic. Indeed, many of the aspect examples you've seen probably describe such technical behavior. One example of crosscutting behavior that arises because of the chosen P2P architecture for the Crystal Game is the event-based communication between player peers. To handle this communication, we defined a theme called **P2PCommunication**.

In essence, the **P2PCommunication** theme monitors the game state that all players (or potential players) are interested in, gathers up (or *marshals*) that game state, and broadcasts or multicasts (as appropriate) an event containing it. This theme is also responsible for listening for such events and for unmarshaling the game state information for its player. Recall that we assume a total-order, atomic broadcast/multicast, so this theme may assume that for all events any player sees, every other player sees those events in the same order.

The **P2PCommunication** theme has a combination of behavior that directly crosscuts game-logic behavior and behavior that occurs either on receipt of an event or periodically and therefore does not directly crosscut game-logic behavior. We need to treat the design of these two (crosscutting behavior *vs.* noncrosscutting behavior) differently, as you'll see in how `Player`, `Location`, and `GamesAdmin` are handled. Taking `Player` as an example, we are trying to do two things here. First, we're creating behavior that we know we want to be merged with the `Player` class in the base. Second, we want to capture a trigger to tell us when a player changes state —triggers that, coincidentally, are highly likely to come from the `Player` class.

As we've described previously, the crosscutting theme model allows for multiple triggers from potentially multiple different base classes. We therefore need to conform to the rules that help to avoid referencing confusion described in the section "Referencing Template Structure and Behavior." To achieve both our objectives for the `Player` class, we separate them by having a `Player` class that holds behavior we want to be merged with a base `Player` class, and separately having a `TPlayer` template class, to capture the behavior that crosscuts a trigger. This approach is also taken for the design of behavior for `Location` and `GamesAdmin`. How these are composed is sorted out later.

Two examples of crosscutting behavior are illustrated in Figure 5–22. Game state that all players are interested in relates to state associated with a location (e.g., any change to the number of crystals or magic items there) and also state associated with a player (e.g., when a player finds crystals or magic items, or duels another player, or has an encounter with an NPC).

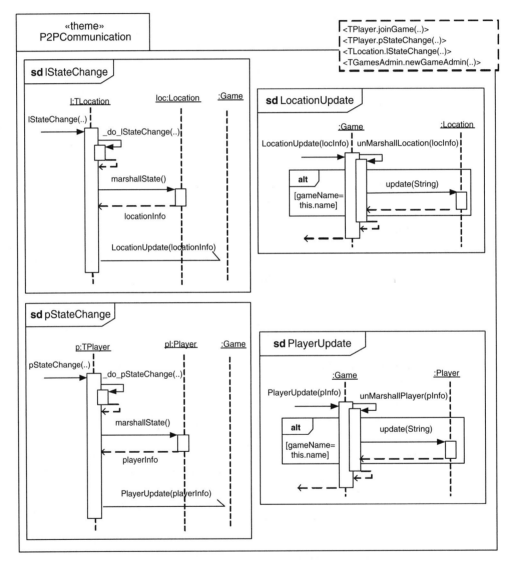

Figure 5–22 *Behavior crosscutting player and location changes.*

Any changes to location or player state are of interest to every player and so need to be multicast to all the players in the game.

The `lStateChange()` and `pStateChange()` template operation sequence diagrams first indicate that the real operations are executed (with `_do_lStateChange()` and `_do_pStateChange()` (respectively), and then the location or player state is marshaled into `LocationUpdate()` and `PlayerUpdate()` events that are multicast for the attention of each player's `Game` object. On receipt of these events, the `Game` objects unmarshal the location or player information and update the corresponding objects with the new information.

Crosscutting behavior is also illustrated in Figure 5–23. When a player joins a game, he needs the complete game state and so broadcasts an event called `FullGameStateRequest(gameName)` intended for the attention of game objects. When a `Game` object receives this event, it marshals all relevant game state relating to game locations and other players, and multicasts this information in a `FullGameState(state)` event also intended for the attention of `Game` objects. When a `Game` object receives a `FullGameState(state)` event, it unmarshals and updates the player and location information.

Other behavior in the **P2PCommunication** theme is time triggered and does not crosscut game behavior. For example, Figure 5–24 illustrates how potential players are informed of ongoing games in the region that they might be interested in joining. After a time period (currently 30 seconds), each `GamesAdmin` object broadcasts an event called `CrystalGamesAvailable(games)`, containing the games it knows about, that is intended for other `GamesAdmin` objects. On receipt of this event, a `GamesAdmin` object updates the games it knows about. Figure 5–24 also illustrates some crosscutting behavior in which the thread to kick off the time-triggered behavior is started. The template operation `newGamesAdmin(..)` is defined to capture the instantiation of the `GamesAdmin` object, after which it should broadcast games it knows about.

Figure 5–25 illustrates the class structure for the **P2PCommunication** theme. As you can see, the `Games` and `GamesAdmin` classes are active classes and respond to events received. They are not template classes, though it is likely that these concepts will appear in other themes in the Crystal Game. As with the **track-energy** theme, you do not have to concern yourself with this now—we sort it out at composition time. Also, note that the `TPlayer`

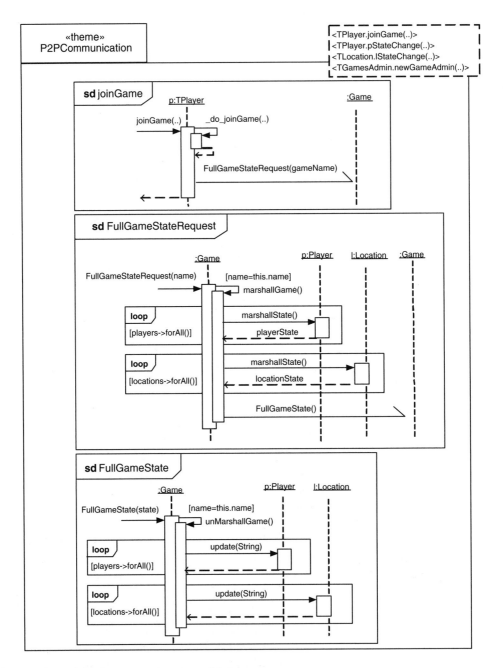

Figure 5–23   *Behavior crosscutting players joining a game*

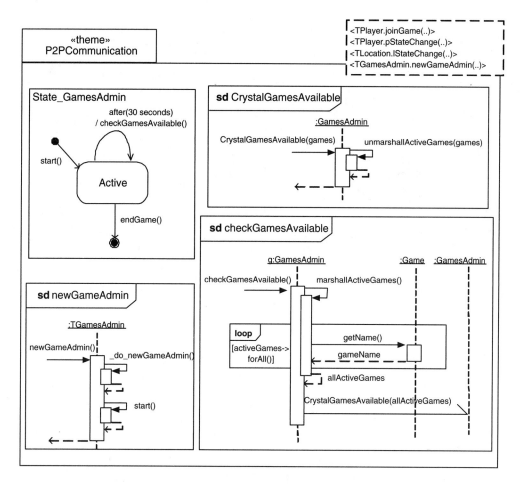

Figure 5–24   *Behavior for broadcasting game information.*

class has both a `pStateChange()` template operation and corresponding private `_do_pStateChange()` operation, and also a `joinGame()` template operation and corresponding private `_do_joinGame()` operation. Also, the `TLocation` class has an `lStateChange()` template operation and corresponding private `_do_lStateChange()`. As before, these relate to the need to distinguish between the operation that triggers all crosscutting behavior and the execution of the replacing operation itself.

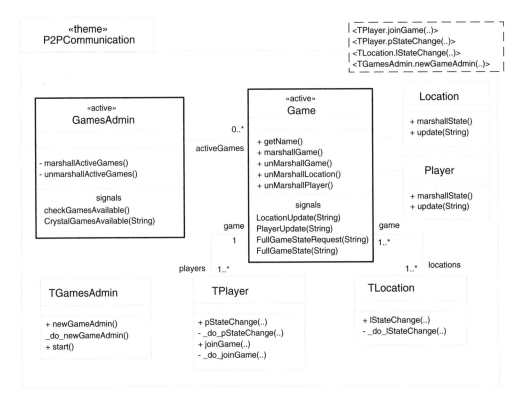

Figure 5–25   *P2PCommunications theme structure.*

The **P2PCommunication** theme has demonstrated a good range of the possibilities for specifying crosscutting themes. There are a number of templates with different behavior in play under different circumstances. In addition, there is noncrosscutting behavior related to the responsibilities of the theme. Two small capabilities of Theme/UML are not covered in either this theme or the **track-energy** theme. Table 5–5 illustrates three parameter specification possibilities, one of which (..) is widely used in our two example themes. This is probably the most common one you will encounter, where you are saying that the template operation can have any signature. Sometimes, however, your sequence of actions may need to use an object of some type, which is when you use the (.., Type, ..) parameter specification. In this case, the parameter of type Type is named in the sequence diagram and can be used by name by later operations. The restricted parameter specification () is included for completeness. We have not encountered a situation where you must limit the template operation to no parameters, as we expect a real operation to occur independently of any defined crosscutting behavior (or not at all, if that is what is defined in the sequence diagram).

Summary

In this chapter, we looked at how to design separate base and aspect themes with Theme/UML. For base themes, standard UML is all you need. For aspect themes, we looked at minor extensions to standard UML to handle the need to reason about design elements in other themes for the purposes of crosscutting behavioral specification. These primarily relate to extensions to UML's templates. We described how, in aspect themes, you can use templates to represent the triggers for crosscutting behavior that happen outside the aspect themes. You can express the crosscutting behavior that you want to happen before, after, or around the trigger templates using sequence diagrams. We also described how you can indicate that a trigger will become a trigger only within a particular flow of control in the execution of the system.

Along the way in this chapter, we provided designs for many Crystal Game base and aspect themes. Next, we look at what to do now that we have all these themes designed. How do they relate to each other? The answers to this question (and more) are in the next chapter.

6

Theme Composition

Up to this point in the design of our game, we concentrated on ensuring that we have modularized the designs for each of the concerns (themes) of the game. Most of these themes were identified during the Theme/Doc process (Chapter 4), with some arising from detailed design (Chapter 5). We then designed each theme individually without including direct reference to any other theme. Just to remind you of why we did this, we revisit our rationale: we want to avoid scattering and tangling properties that negatively impact modularization and wreak corresponding havoc on good software engineering.

In this chapter, we look at specifying how all your themes relate to each other and how they should be composed into a single, coherent application.

Overview of Composing Themes

With Theme's symmetric approach to separation, there is a theme for each concern in a domain. In order to specify a coherent application, you must compose the themes that address the needs of the application. The set of themes to be composed for an application may include all the themes you have designed, or different applications may require only different subsets of those themes. In all cases, Theme/UML provides a means to specify how

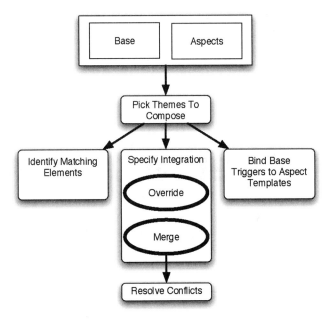

Figure 6–1   *General view of the composition process.*

the themes you select should be composed. Figure 6-1 illustrates the steps to follow when you are composing themes.

In general, the steps are these:

1. Pick the themes to be composed. Composition in Theme/UML is at the theme level of granularity.

2. Identify the design elements within the themes that match. Up to now, we have described themes that may have specifications for the same domain concepts. Now is the time to work through matching up those concepts.

3. Specify how the themes should be integrated. Theme/UML provides two kinds of integration—merge and override.

4. Specify how conflicts should be resolved between matching design elements. When themes are merged, resolving conflicts may be needed.

5. Identify triggering behavior in a base theme to bind to templates in an aspect theme.

In this section, we give you a very brief introduction to the concepts and notations for these steps, and do not allow ourselves to get sidetracked in describing all the finer points. In the remainder of the chapter, we go through the steps again in the context of the Crystal Game application, presenting the full set of rules and features.

Pick Themes

The first thing you need to do is pick the themes to be composed for your application and draw a *composition relationship* between the themes you've picked. A composition relationship is a new kind of relationship defined within Theme/UML that provides you with the means to specify all the steps for composition identified above. In Figure 6–2, you can see how different compositions are possible from a pool of theme designs.

The notation for a composition relationship is a curved, dashed line between the design elements to be composed. In Figure 6–2, there are three examples,—one for each application. As we go through the steps, we describe more notations to the line, such as arrowheads and tags, to denote further composition choices.

In Theme/UML, composition happens at the theme level of granularity, and you must first pick the themes to be composed. You can use further composition relationships between design elements inside the themes, denoting that those design elements should themselves be composed within the context of the theme composition, which we see in the next section.

There is no upper limit to the number of themes that you can compose at once.

Identify Matching Design Elements

In the Theme approach, you modularize themes based on encapsulating related requirements to handle a particular concern. As a result, you are likely to have multiple design themes with design elements that represent

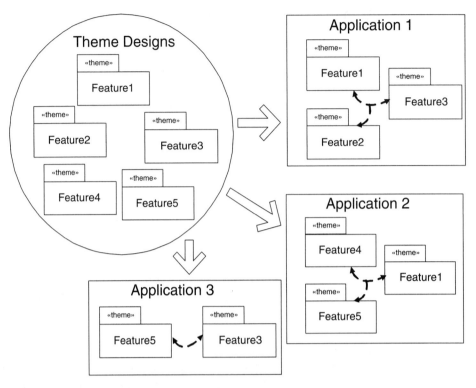

Figure 6–2   *Pick themes to compose.*

the same core concepts in the domain. An example of a core-concept might be the concept of a player in the Crystal Game. This might appear as a `Player` class in one theme, and as `Participant` class in another theme, but they would refer to the same concept. When you're designing an individual theme, it's useful to have a design from the perspective of the requirement(s) of that theme. When you compose themes, however, you want to be able to identify those concept-sharing elements and ensure that they are composed together. This is because when you compose themes, you are essentially taking every element from each of the input themes and putting them together into a new theme—you therefore want to ensure that the concept-sharing elements are put together in the new theme.

The simplest kind of composition occurs when there have been no common concepts designed within the themes. For example, in Figure 6–3, classes in

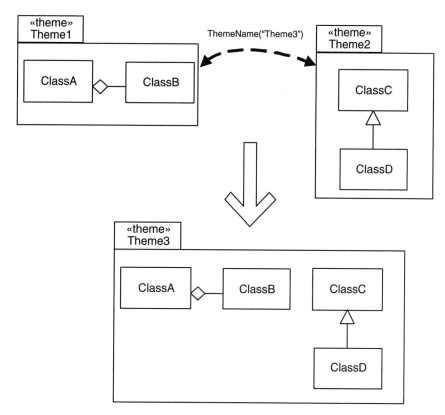

Figure 6–3   *No common concepts.*

the input themes represent different concepts in the domain and so appear separately in the composed theme. Notice also in Figure 6–3 that you can specify a name for the composed theme with a `ThemeName("Name")` tag on the composition relationship.

It is likely, however, that your input themes do provide designs for common concepts, each from its own perspective. In a composed design, common concepts should themselves be "composed." In other words, if you have a design for `ClassA` with its own attributes and methods in one theme, and a design for `ClassA` in another theme with different attributes and methods, and both `ClassA`s represent the same domain concept, then there should be one `ClassA` in a composed design that contains all the relevant attributes and methods. You must specify a matching for such design elements, which can be done with composition relationships.

Figure 6–4 shows two ways to specify what design elements within input themes match, giving the same result. On the left side, the composition between `Theme1` and `Theme2` is specified with two composition relationships. The first is, as always, a composition relationship between the themes to be composed. The second composition relationship is between `ClassB` in `Theme1` and `ClassB` in `Theme2`. This relationship identifies these two classes as matching concepts, and so `ClassB` appears once in the composed design. On the right side of Figure 6–4, there is only one composition relationship between the themes to be composed. However, notice that there is an additional tag on the relationship that reads `match[name]`. This tag indicates that classes in the themes with the same name match and should be composed. You must take the former approach, with explicit composition relationships, when classes don't have the same

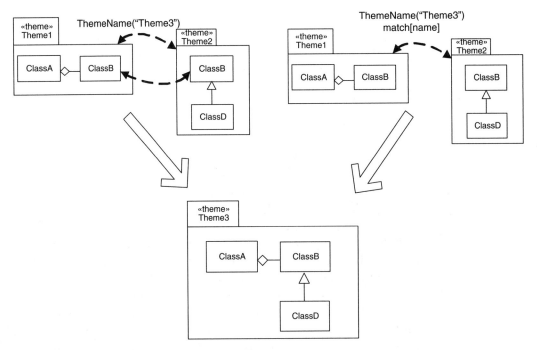

Figure 6–4   *Common concepts in themes.*

name but yet do represent the same concept. The latter approach is convenient when the classes have the same name.

You can have further composition relationships between design elements of any type that make sense to compose, but each composition relationship must be between design elements of the same type. In other words, you can only compose a theme with a theme, a class with a class, an operation with an operation, and so on. A composition relationship between design elements within the input themes indicates that the elements represent the same concept and should be composed.

Design elements other than classes can be matched with a `match[name]` tag like the one illustrated in Figure 6–4. Indeed, any elements of the same type with the same name that are contained in matching classes will be matched for composition purposes. For example, in Figure 6–5, attributes

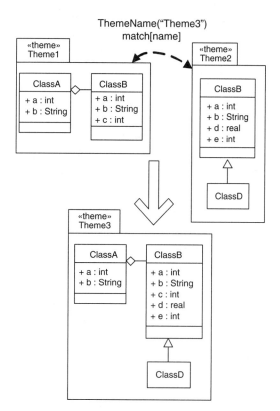

Figure 6–5   *Matching with match[name].*

a and b in `ClassB` are matched and appear once in the composed `ClassB` class. Notice that attributes a and b in `ClassA` are not deemed to match with any attributes in `ClassB`, because `ClassA` itself does not match with `ClassB`.

What happens with matching behaviors (i.e., with operations that "match") is dependent on the kind of integration you define, which we look at next.

Specify Integration

Theme/UML defines two different kinds of integration policies to determine the composition choices to be made for input elements in the composed result. *Merge* integration is useful when you have multiple themes that were each designed to capture its own concern (as represented by the different set of requirements for which the theme is responsible) and you want to compose these themes for the required application. If we merge themes, then all the structure and the behavior defined within each theme should exist in the composed result.

Override integration is useful when you have a new version of a theme that provides a more up-to-date specification of the requirements than an existing theme. With override integration, you can specify that one theme overrides another theme such that elements in the overriding theme replace *matched* elements in the overridden theme. Unmatched elements are treated in the same way as in merge integration—in other words, they are simply added to the composed result.

Merge Integration

In general, the composed result of merging themes is the union of the models in the input themes. Behavioral models such as state machines, sequence diagrams, and activity diagrams are all added to the composed result. Class models are merged into a single class model for the composed result. When composing class models, unmatched structural elements are all added to the composed class model. Matched structural elements appear once in the design. Matched operations are merged in the sense that the execution of one of the matching operations triggers the execution of all matching operations. Figure 6–6 illustrates the output of merging two simple themes.

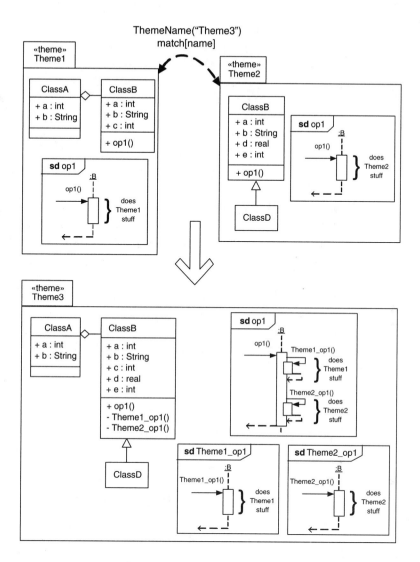

Figure 6–6   *Merge integration.*

The op1() operations in the two input ClassB classes match. To indicate that the behaviors are merged, a sequence diagram is generated to specify that when a request is made to op1(), the two operations are called. Note that the input operations have been renamed to avoid a name clash both in their class model representation and in their sequence diagram specifications.

Matching classes (i.e., the two ClassB classes) and their matching attributes (a and b) appear once in the composed model. All other elements are added unchanged to the composed model.

A final interesting point to note is the arrowheads on the composition relationship. You denote merge integration with an arrowhead at all ends of the composition relationship.

Override Integration

With override integration, you are replacing matched elements in the overridden theme with their matching elements from the overriding theme. Elements from both themes that are not matched are added unchanged to the composed theme. Figure 6–7 illustrates an example.

The match[name] tag on the composition relationship results in a match for the ClassBs from the input themes, their attributes a, b, and their operations op1(). Notice that the specification of a in the result is public, as defined in the overriding theme (Theme1). In addition, the behavior of op1() in the result is as defined in Theme1—the sequence diagram for op1() from Theme2 has been replaced with the sequence diagram for op1() from Theme1.

Notice again the arrowhead on the composition relationship. You denote override integration with an arrowhead at the overridden theme end of the composition relationship.

Finally, we have defined the following rule for override integration:

> A composition relationship with override integration must be one-to-one. In other words, one design element overrides another design element.

This rule ensures that there is no conflict as to which specification the result should have for the overridden element. See later in this chapter for some more detailed rules when we specify overriding in the Crystal Game.

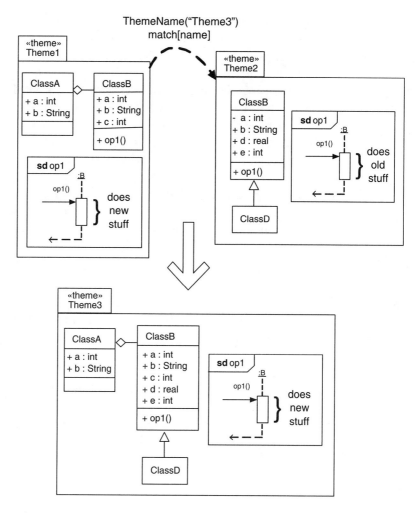

Figure 6–7   *Override integration.*

Specify Resolution of Conflicts

In Figure 6–7, matching elements had different specifications in the input themes—for example, attribute a is defined as `public` in `Theme1` (the overriding theme) and as `private` in `Theme2` (the overridden theme). This is fine when one theme overrides another, but what happens if we are merging themes and such a conflict exists in the input themes? With merge integration, matched elements such as attributes and classes appear in the result once. We therefore need a means to specify how to resolve conflicts in the specifications of matched elements.

Theme/UML provides three different mechanisms to allow you to state what should happen when a conflict arises: explicitly specifying values for a specific conflict; specifying default values for particular design constructs; and defining theme precedence. If a conflict arises during composition, Theme/UML first determines whether that conflict has been explicitly resolved, then searches for default values for the relevant construct, and finally selects the specification from the theme with the highest precedence. Each of these mechanisms is specified by means of a tag on the composition relationship, as follows.

Explicit Values

The most basic way to resolve a conflict between two design elements is to explicitly state what the specification should be in the result. Figure 6–8 illustrates an explicit resolution for attribute a in ClassB.

In this example, the conflict arises because of a difference in the visibility specification—ClassB in Theme1 deems the attribute a to be public, while ClassB in Theme2 deems the attribute a to be private. In the resolve tag on the composition relationship, we explicitly state that ClassB.a's visibility should be private.

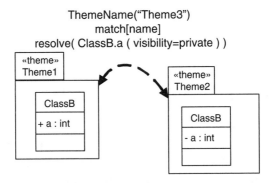

Figure 6–8   *Conflict resolution with explicit values.*

There is potential for any of a construct's properties[1] to conflict—for example, attributes also have a name, type, initial value, multiplicity, and so on. You can state the required values for all of these on the tag if necessary.

You can imagine that explicitly specifying a lot of conflict resolutions for individual conflicts might become rather tedious. The next two conflict resolution mechanisms allow you to provide a more general statement of what should happen when a conflict arises.

Default Values

Instead of picking out individual design elements and specifying what their values should be in the composed result, you can specify default values for all elements of a particular type to be used only in the event of a conflict. For example, you can say that when there's a conflict in an attribute's visibility, then specify it as `private`, or that when there's a conflict in a class's visibility, then specify it as `public`, and so on. Figure 6–9 illustrates an example that captures the conflict in attribute a in `ClassB`.

In the `resolve` tag on the composition relationship, we state that in the event of a conflict in any attribute's visibility, then specify it as `private`. In this case, `ClassB.a`'s visibility in the composed result is therefore `private`.

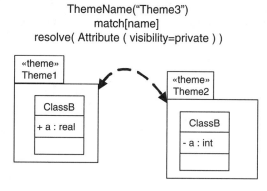

Figure 6–9   *Conflict resolution with default values.*

---

[1] See the UML specification for general UML constructs' properties.

While you can, as with the explicit value specification, specify defaults for all properties of a construct, you are not likely to specify defaults for properties such as name or type, for example. Default values are useful only in the kinds of properties that don't identify a design element or otherwise describe the element in a material way. If you need to resolve a conflict in such properties, then explicit values (or theme precedence, coming up next) are the way to go.

Theme Precedence

The final means to resolve a conflict between elements is to say which theme's specification should have precedence. If one theme has precedence over another, then when a conflict arises between matching elements, the specification as defined in the theme with precedence is used in the result. Figure 6–10 illustrates an example.

In the 1.prec tag on the composition relationship, we state that in the event of a conflict between the specifications of matching elements, the specification as defined in Theme2 should be used in the composed result. This makes ClassB.a's visibility private.

The number in the prec tag indicates an ordering for precedence. Where you are composing multiple themes, you can indicate which themes have higher precedence than others, with 1 being the highest. The specification from the theme with the highest precedence (that contains a specification for the matching element in conflict) will be used in the composed result.

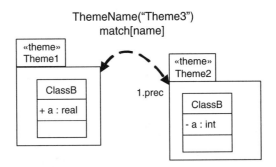

Figure 6–10   *Conflict resolution with theme precedence.*

Specify Binding to Aspect Themes

When you compose base themes with an aspect theme, the themes are composed with merge integration semantics. You have an additional task, though, when one of the themes is an aspect theme. An aspect theme is one where (some of) the behavior of the aspect is triggered by behavior in a base. When you are composing base themes with an aspect, you must identify what those triggers in the base are. You can achieve this with our final tag on Theme/UML's relationship—the `bind[]` tag. With the `bind[]` tag, you essentially list all the triggers that match each of the templates in the aspect theme. Figure 6–11 illustrates a simple example.

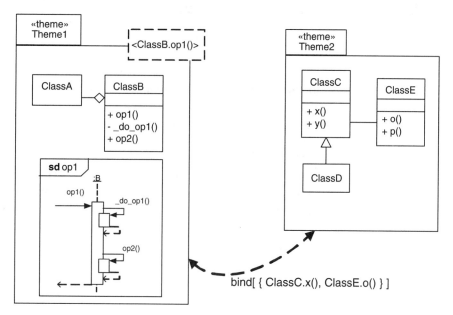

Figure 6–11   *Binding triggers to aspect templates.*

`Theme1` in Figure 6–11 has one piece of crosscutting behavior (`op2()`) that executes after any trigger. The triggers are represented in the design with a template operation called `op1()`. The bind attachment identifies two triggers in the `Theme2` base theme—`x()` from `ClassC` and `o()` from `ClassE`. This design now specifies that when either `ClassC.x()` or `ClassE.o()` happens, `op2()` from the aspect theme should be executed afterwards.

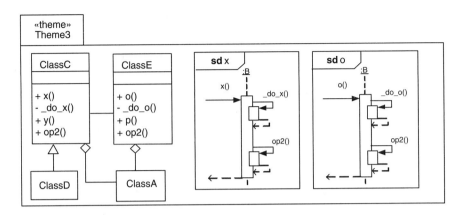

Figure 6–12   *Base operations trigger aspect behavior.*

Figure 6–12 illustrates how Theme/UML models this in the result. A sequence diagram is generated indicating the behavior that now occurs as a result of the base theme's triggers.

There is another interesting point to note here. When you specify that an operation in a base theme matches a template operation in the aspect theme, you are implicitly matching the corresponding classes. As a result of this matching, the classes are merged and named from the base theme. From the example in Figures 6–11 and 6–12, `ClassB` has been merged with both `ClassC` and `ClassE`, separately. Because only elements within a class with templates can refer to other elements in the class (see Chapter 5), there is no confusion over which of the merged classes is intended by a reference. This means that from the example aspect, because only methods in `ClassB` can call methods in `ClassB` and refer to attributes in `ClassB`, then all references map to `ClassC` and `ClassE` appropriately in the result. Methods in `ClassB` can, of course, execute other methods in other classes in the aspect, provided that the other classes are not themselves potentially merged with multiple other classes.

Finally, you don't always have to explicitly list all the triggers in the base theme. Theme/UML provides the following means (see Table 6–1) to specify multiple replacing elements without explicit naming, including some compound operators.

Table 6–1 *Multiple Element Specification*

Construct	Resolution
*	All elements of this construct resolve as a replacing element. For example, ClassName.*() resolves to all operations in ClassName. Using *.* (to replace a template operation) resolves to every operation in every class in the base theme.
cc*	Similar to *, only the first characters of the replacing element must be the characters specified before the *. For example, Player.set* (to replace a template operation) resolves to every operation that starts with set in the Player class.
*cc	Similar to cc*, only the last characters of the replacing element must be the characters specified after the *.
meta:property=value	Using the metatag, you can query the values of metaproperties of the construct to determine the replacing elements. For example, meta:visibility=public resolves to every public operation.
() AND ()	All elements resolved in the operands replace the template.
() AND NOT ()	The AND NOT operator includes the set of operations that are resolved in the first operand and excludes the set of operations that are resolved in the second operand.

Composing Game Themes

The overview we've just been through gives a high-level view of how you compose themes. We now go through each step again with our Crystal Game example, reiterating some rules and pointing out some more detailed features that we didn't mention in the overview.

The first thing you have to do is pick the themes to be composed. This gives a context for the composition as a whole. You will be able to specify more composition relationships between elements within the context of the selected themes, which will be about matching particular design elements for a more fine-grained composition.

Figure 6–13 illustrates a composition relationship between some of our game concept-sharing (or base) themes: **start**, **distribute-crystals**, and **enter-location**.

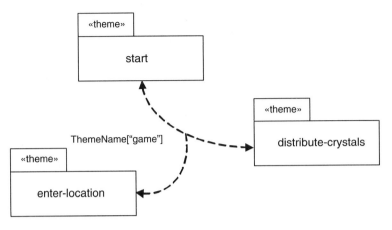

Figure 6–13   *Composing themes.*

There are a few things to note here.

First, while this particular composition is between three themes, there is no upper limit to the number of themes that can be composed with a single composition relationship.[2] There is, of course, a lower limit of two.

Second, notice the `ThemeName["game"]` text tag on the relationship. The result of every composition is contained in a new theme, which you can name here. In this example, the name of the composed theme is `game`. If you do not specify a name, the name of the composed theme defaults to a concatenation of the names of the themes that were composed.

Finally, notice that there is an arrowhead at each end of the relationship. This means the kind of integration required is a *merge* of the elements. In this case, all themes have designs relevant to the application, so all their design elements must be included. Another integration possibility is *override*, where matching elements in one theme are essentially replaced by the overriding theme. We'll be using both merge and override integration for the game later.

---

[2] When we talk about overriding themes and about composing crosscutting themes later, we see refinements to this level of flexibility.

Matching Design Elements

The game design has multiple base themes that share many of the same game concepts. For example, *player, location,* and *game* appear in many of the base themes, each with specifications from the perspective of the requirements for which the theme is responsible. We now need to identify those shared concepts so that they will be composed together.

The composition relationship specification in Figure 6–13 does not indicate that any of the themes share concepts, and so it specifies that all elements in each of the three input themes will appear separately in the composed `Game` theme. Because we have not said otherwise, the composition therefore considers any elements with the same name as a clash, which it resolves through renaming. For example, recall from Chapter 5 that each of these three themes has a class called `Player`. As specified in Figure 6–13, the composition does not recognize these as the same concept and so considers these class names as clashing. Therefore, in the composed **game** theme, the three classes in the input themes will correspond to three classes that are renamed to `start.Player`, `enter-location.Player`, and `distribute-crystals.Player`. This clearly is not satisfactory. Fundamentally, the class `Player` represents the same core concept in each of the themes and should be a single class in the output. Stating this can be achieved in one of two ways: explicitly with an additional composition relationship or implicitly by adding another tag to the main composition relationship.

Explicit Matching

One way you can identify elements that provide designs for the same domain concepts is by explicitly drawing a composition relationship between them. Composition relationships can be defined between design elements of the same type to state that those elements match and therefore should be composed. Figure 6–14 illustrates using multiple composition relationships to specify matching of concepts.

In Figure 6–14, a subset of the **duel** and **enter-location** themes is shown, both of which have a class called `Player`. There are three composition relation-

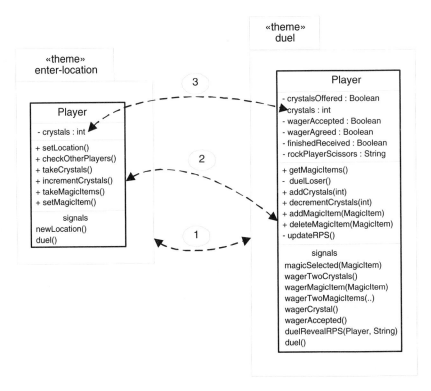

Figure 6–14   *Explicit matching of design elements.*

ships here. The one marked 1[3] is the obligatory composition relationship that specifies the themes to be composed. The composition relationship marked 2 is between the matching classes in Figure 6–14 and indicates that they should be composed. Each element of the matched classes will be added to the composed result, with name clashes resolved through renaming. If this is not what you want—for example, if there are elements at a smaller level of granularity (like attributes) that represent the same concept—then you draw more composition relationships. For example, the `Player` classes in Figure 6–14 both have an attribute `crystal`, which should be matched in the composition. The composition relationship marked 3 captures this matching.

Another example in Figure 6–15 illustrates a subset of the **start, distribute-crystals**, and **setup-NPC** themes, all of which have classes called `Location`,

[3]The numbering in Figures 6–14, 6–15, and 6–16 is for illustration, and is not part of the Theme/UML notation.

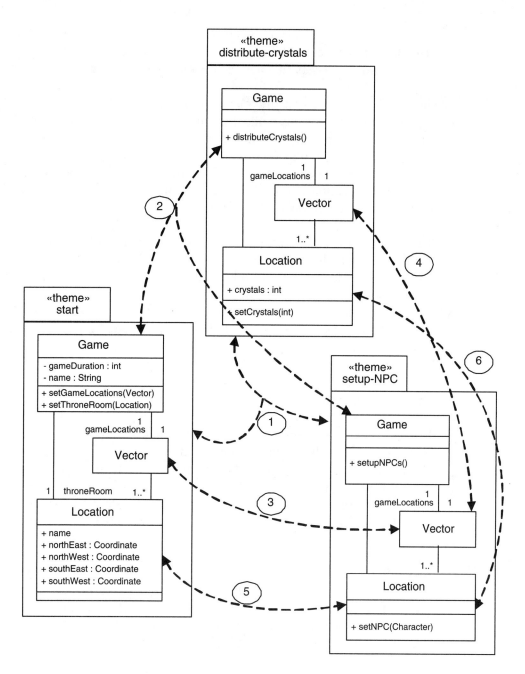

Figure 6–15 *Elements with more than one relationship.*

Game, and Vector. There are six composition relationships here! As you can see, the more explicit matching to be done, the more difficult it is to read what is happening—a problem we address in the next section.

First, though, notice that the relationship (marked 2) between the Game classes is a three-way one, while there are two relationships each between the Vector classes (relationships 3 and 4) and the Location classes (relationships 5 and 6). The effect of composition in both these styles is the same. In all cases, because we have drawn these composition relationships, the three classes match (one from each theme) with the three matching classes composed in the result.

This leads us to an important rule. A design element may compose to only one result, so using multiple composition relationships in the manner of Vector and Location is transitive. In other words, if start.Location matches distribute-crystals.Location, and distribute-crystals.Location matches setup-NPC.Location, then start.Location also matches SetupNPCs.Location. All three classes therefore match and will be composed.

Implicit Matching

Explicitly matching elements with a composition relationship for every match is particularly useful when elements do not have the same name. However, as you can imagine (and is illustrated in Figure 6–15), it is likely to get laborious (and messy!) quite quickly. You can also define a rule for the composition relationship that specifies that identically named elements should match. You can do this by adding a match[name] tag to a composition relationship.

By adding a match[name] tag, you can state that any elements within matching elements that have the same name should also be considered to match. In effect, you are saying that classes within themes that have the same name should be matched; attributes within matching classes that have the same name should be matched; and so on.

Figure 6–16 illustrates this tag for the composition relationship previously shown in Figure 6–13.

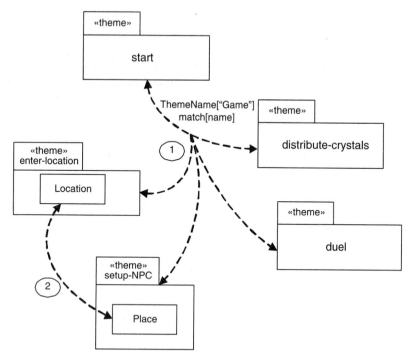

Figure 6–16   *Implicit matching of design elements.*

The composition relationship marked 1 is the obligatory composition relationship that specifies the themes to be composed. We have attached the `match[name]` tag here, indicating that identically named elements (and which are of the same type) match. In Figure 6–15, a `match[name]` tag on the composition relationship between the themes would remove the need for all the other composition relationships and also cover all other elements that match by name that are not illustrated.

You can still use an explicit composition relationship between elements you want to match that are not captured by the `match[name]` tag. For example, from Figure 6–16, if the designer of the **setup-NPC** theme had decided to name the class to handle locations `Place`,[4] then you could

---

[4] The design in Chapter 5 does not have location information in a class called `Place`—we just use it here as an example.

explicitly draw a relationship between them that indicates that these should match, as illustrated in the composition relationship marked 2.

Of course, it is also possible that, by coincidence, there are elements that have the same name that should not be matched. In a manner similar to explicitly matching elements, you can also explicitly unmatch elements. This is achieved with a composition relationship with a `dontMatch` tag between the elements that you don't want matched. Automatic renaming of the elements will occur in the composed design.

Rules for Concept Matching with Composition Relationships

One of the most important characteristics of a design element to think about when considering the syntactic validity of a composition relationship is whether it is a container for other elements and/or a component of another element. For example, attributes and operations are contained in a class; classes are contained in a theme; and so on. The container/component relationships between design elements are important to the composition process in determining what elements match and also in determining what the namespace of composed elements should be. On now to the rules, the first two of which we have already stated:

- A composition relationship may only be drawn between elements of the same type.

- In order to match design elements, it is first necessary to draw a composition relationship between two or more of the themes in which they are contained.

- Two (or more) design elements may be matched (either implicitly or explicitly) only if their containers are matched. Every composed element must have a namespace, and this rule ensures that there is no confusion over to which container a composed element belongs.

- Each design element may be matched in only one set of matching elements. This means that every design element may be composed into only one result in the composed design. This rule is defined so that there is no confusion with references in the composed result. For example, recall that the setup-NPC.Location class in Figure 6–15 was involved in two composition relationships with other Location classes. Let's say that there is an attribute of type Location somewhere in the **setup-NPC** theme design. In the composed theme, this attribute's type will be the Location type that is composed of all three Location classes.

- Aspect themes are allowed an exception to the "match-once" rule. Behavior defined in a crosscutting theme may be composed with many different elements specified to replace templates used in the crosscutting behavior. See Chapter 5, "Theme Design," for different rules for aspect themes that avoid reference confusion.

Integration Options

Theme/UML supports two different kinds of integration—merge and override. Merging themes is probably what you will use the most often, as it ensures that all structure and behavior defined in individual themes is incorporated into the composed design. You may find override integration useful, though, in later versions of the design. With override, you can have a new theme that has a more up-to-date design for an application and specify that it should replace a previous version.

In this section, we restrict our discussion to the integration of only concept-sharing (or base) themes. Many of the principles are relevant for composing crosscutting themes with base themes, but as there are additional policies for crosscutting themes, we deal with them together later.

Merge Integration

As we've said, there is no upper limit to the number of themes that can be merged. The underlying principle is that each theme involved contains a design that is relevant in the composed design and should be added. In a sense, a merged theme is the union of all the input themes. At the simplest level, this means that every design element from every participating theme will be added separately to the composed result.

However, we spent some time talking about how concepts may be shared across base themes, and therefore match, and we saw how we can specify matching between elements. When matching elements are container types, all the component elements for each of the matched containers are merged into the composed container. For example, Figure 6–17 shows a

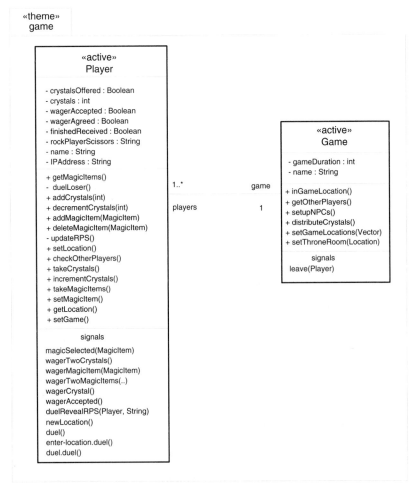

Figure 6–17   *Merged container classes.*

subset of the composed result of the composition relationship in Figure 6–16. All the attributes and operations in the `Player` and `Game` classes appear in the corresponding composed classes.

Figure 6–17 also illustrates an example of matching elements that are components (and that do not contain other elements). In general, matched component elements appear only once in the composed design. For example, the `crystal` attribute in the `Player` classes need appear in the composed `Player` class only once.

Merging Operations

Merging design elements works this way for structural elements such as containers and attributes. However, operations work a little differently. Bearing in mind that different behavior is generally modularized into separate themes, we think it's useful to be able to specify that some set of operations match in that they should be executed together. A classic example here is when you have matching classes with different attributes and each has a `print()` method that prints attribute values. When such classes are composed, you would like all the information printed, and therefore, when `print()` is executed on the composed class, all `print()` operations from the matching classes should be executed.

This is the basis for the semantics of merging matching operations in Theme/UML. When operations with the same name match, the input operations are renamed (prepended with their theme name) to avoid confusion, and the original name is used to generate a sequence diagram that executes each of the operations in sequence. This is the default behavior for matched operations.

However, this default behavior may not always be what is required. Indeed, in our `Game` example, we need to change this default for the `duel()` operations. Notice operations `duel()`, `enter-location.duel()`, and `duel.duel()` in the composed design in Figure 6–17. Matching could have been avoided with an explicit composition relationship between the two `duel()` operations with a `dontMatch` tag, but in fact, we don't need `enter-location.duel()` at all. This `duel()` method was just a placeholder; it contained no real functionality. It was simply how the designer of **enter-location** indicated when a duel should happen. Here's an example of where override integration is useful, and we discuss it in more detail in the "Combining Integration Policies" section later.

The semantics for merging operations does come in handy for us in the Crystal Game for some operations that don't have the same name. Consider, for example, the **start**, **setup-NPC**, and **distribute-crystals** themes. From the requirements, you can see that there is a lot of work to be done when a game is started, much of which we have modularized into separate themes. Here is where you can say, "Group these operations together, and execute them sequentially," or, in Theme/UML shorthand, "Merge these operations."

Figure 6–18 illustrates a specification of matching operations. When operations are merged (whether or not they have the same name), the order of execution of the sequence of matching operations is generated randomly. If the order of operation is important to you, you can specify a sequence diagram defining the order that can be attached to the composition relationship, as illustrated in Figure 6–18.

Another example from the game relates to the order in which dueling between players or a challenge from an NPC to a player happens. Though we did not provide a design for the **challenge** theme identified in Chapter 5, you may recall from Figure 4–13 in Chapter 4 that at the end of our analysis stage, R71 was not associated with any particular theme. R71 related equally to two themes, **duel** and **challenge**, and described which operation came first: dueling or the challenge. Assuming a **challenge** Theme/UML design, you could merge `duel()` and `challenge()` operations, and attach a sequence diagram (similar to the one in Figure 6–18) that specifies that the duel should precede the challenge.

You're probably wondering by now what happens when there are conflicting parameters in merged operations, or what happens if one or more of the operations returns a value. In the first instance, the general rule for matching operations is that they must have the same signature (not just match by name). On execution, values input to the composed operation may be used in the calls to each of the matching, renamed operations. We've made one exception to this rule. Where one of the matching operations has parameters whose values may be used in other matching operations with *a subset*

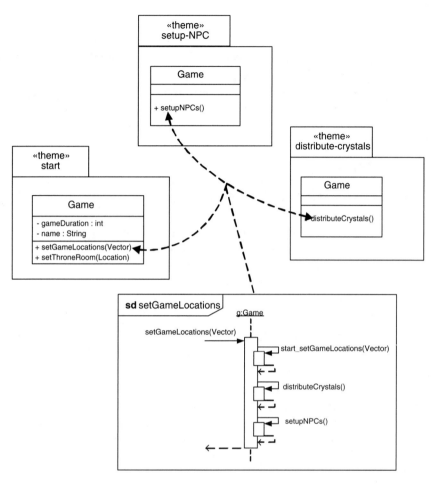

Figure 6-18   *Merging operations.*

of the parameters in the called operations, these operations may be defined as matching. In this case, you *must* attach a sequence diagram to the composition relationship indicating how the operations are called. If you don't do this, the operations won't be matched.

As for operations with return values, the default behavior is that the value from the last operation executed is returned. If you want different behavior, you must specify that in a sequence diagram on the composition relationship.

Elements That Don't Have a Match

In general, design elements that don't match other design elements are simply added to the composed design in the appropriate namespace. For example, classes that do not match any other classes appear, with all their components unchanged, in the composed theme; attributes that do not match any other attributes in their matching classes are simply added to the composed class; and so on.

Override Integration

Override integration means that the elements in one theme (the overridden theme) are replaced by the elements in another theme (the overriding theme). This is very straightforward for elements that are not containers. For such elements, think of it as a simple deletion of the overridden element and an insertion of the overriding element.

For container elements, it's a little more complicated. Matching becomes important here, and overriding happens to matched elements only. Any elements contained in an overridden container that don't have a matching element in the overriding container are added to the composed design. Of course, such elements are inserted into the overriding container (as the overridden container is deleted). Other than that, you can think of all overridden elements as deleted with the overriding elements inserted.

The notation is a single arrowhead at the end of the composition relationship that denotes the element to be overridden.

See Figure 6–19 for a contrived example from the game. Let's say we have a Version 2 design of the **duel** theme. As it turned out in Version 1, players spent so long haggling over their wagers that game progress was too slow. Therefore, we want to change wagering to be a simple wager of crystals. This means that everything to do with wagering magic items is no longer needed, and the behavior for `duel()` and `wagerAccepted()` that contained some reference to magic items is changed. In keeping with the principles of Theme/UML, the **duel-V2** theme contains the fully redesigned wagering process (including the attributes it needs).

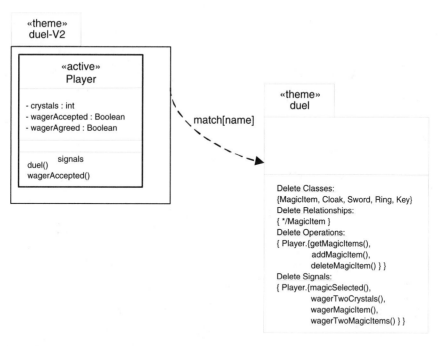

Figure 6–19   *Override integration.*

The composition relationship in Figure 6–19 specifies that every matching element in the **duel** theme should be overridden by its matching element in the **duel-V2** theme. Any behavioral specifications for the signals will override matching behavioral specifications so that there is no behavior that deals with magic items for wagering. However, if you look at the **duel** theme design in Chapter 5, there are a lot of design elements (classes, relationships, operations, and signals) that will remain when the matched elements are overridden. Recall that elements that don't have an overriding match are added to the composed design. This is not what we want in this case, as wagering is no longer a required part of the design. Theme/UML allows you to explicitly say that unwanted elements should be deleted. These elements can be listed in a new section at the bottom of the package box, as illustrated in Figure 6–19.

Figure 6–20 illustrates the composed result of the specification in Figure 6–19. As you can see, any design element not matched appears in the output, and all elements listed for deletion are no longer included.

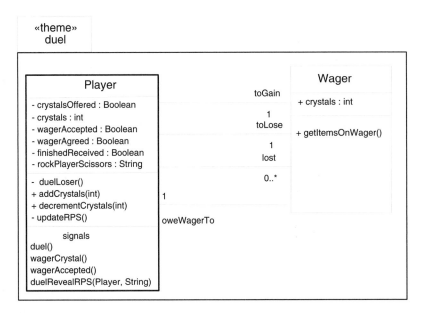

Figure 6–20   *Overridden duel theme.*

Override Rules

Rules for specifying composition relationships with override integration are a little more restrictive than for merge integration. The first of which we have already stated, the rules are as follows:

- A composition relationship with override integration must be one-to-one. In other words, one design element overrides another design element.

- A design element may be overridden only once in a single composition specification.

- Overriding and overridden design elements may not participate in any other merge or override composition. This rule is defined so that there is no confusion with references in the composed result.

Combining Integration Policies

Different integration policies can be used within the same composition specification. Recall our rule that for any composition: you first have to define a composition relationship between the themes to be composed. Then, you may further refine matching and integration with additional composition relationships between the components of the theme container. A composition relationship specified between container elements applies to all components within that container unless a further composition relationship is defined at a lower level. Therefore, the integration specification of the composition relationships does not have to be the same, since application of either merge or override is unambiguous.

For example, in Figure 6–21, the composition relationship between themes **enter-location**, **duel**, and **start** defines merge integration, with a `match[name]` matching policy. Any elements that have the same name (within same-name matching containers) will be merged. However, recall our difficulty with the default semantics for merging operations—we do not want both the `duel()` operations from the **enter-location** and **duel** themes. From the design in Chapter 5, `enter-location.Player.duel()` was defined to

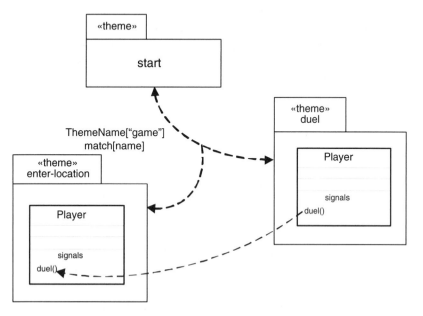

Figure 6–21   *Combining integration policies.*

allow the designer to state where the dueling should happen when a player enters a location. We described this as analogous to referencing an abstract method whose detailed specification is provided using a composition relationship, instead of the usual generalization relationship. We therefore would like that specification to be overridden by the real duel behavior as specified in `duel.Player.duel()`. This is defined by the composition relationship between them. If the **start** theme had a `duel()` operation in its `Player` class in this example (hard to imagine, we know, as that would probably be a very poor theme design!), then it would not match with the other `duel()` operations in `enter-location.Player` or `duel.Player` because their composition relationship takes precedence over the higher level merge composition relationship that matches `Player` classes. As always, renaming would occur to avoid a name clash.

Where the theme-level composition relationship is specified with override integration, only two themes participate in the composition. Any further composition relationships with merge integration must be defined between elements from only those two themes. This is an implication of our rule that states that you must first select the themes to participate in the composition. To remind you, this gives a context for the composition process to indicate the namespace for composed elements. Where you have more than two themes that you want to be composed with a combination of integration strategies, you should define the theme-level composition relationship with merge integration, and then define the override integration requirements at a finer level of granularity.

Resolving Conflicts

With merge integration, matched elements appear once in the composed design.[5] This worked smoothly in Figure 6–16 and its output illustrated in Figure 6–17, where, for example, the `crystals` attribute was declared `private` and as type `int` in every input theme where it was specified. However, there is considerable potential for matching elements to have different values for any of the properties of their respective constructs. For example, what visibility should the `crystals` attribute have if any one of

---

[5] We exclude the single exception, operations, from the discussion here, as managing conflict does not arise in the same way.

the input themes had defined it as `protected` or `public`? What if the **duel** theme had defined the `Player` class as a `leaf` class while each of the others said it was a `root`? Clearly, you need a means to specify how to resolve such conflicts. Theme/UML supports three different mechanisms to allow you to state what should happen when a conflict arises: defining theme precedence, specifying default values, and explicitly specifying values for a specific conflict.

Theme Precedence

You may indicate an order of precedence for the participating themes by adding an `n.prec` tag to the composition relationship ends, where n indicates precedence in ascending order. For example, in Figure 6–22, the **duel** theme has the highest precedence, and the **distribute-crystals** theme has the lowest precedence. Where a conflict arises, the specification from the highest order precedence theme is chosen. Of course, this precedence

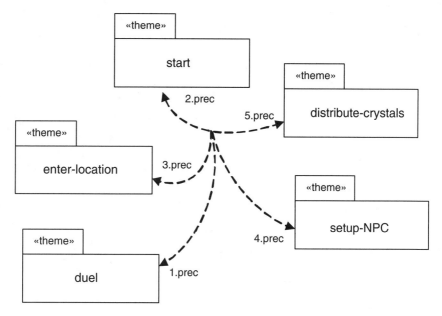

Figure 6–22   *Resolving conflict with theme precedence.*

order could be further refined with precedence specifications on composition relationships between lower level components of the themes.

Default Values

With another tag on a composition relationship, you can also give default values for any UML construct's properties. For example, you can say that for attributes, the default value for visibility is `private`; for multiplicity it is `*`; and so on. The following tag gives defaults for select properties from attributes and can be attached to a composition relationship. The properties are named as they are in the construct's UML metamodel description. All of the properties of all kinds of constructs can be added to this tag, defining a default value for each.

```
resolve ( Construct ( property=value; property=value; ..)
          Construct ( property=value; property=value; ..)
          ....)
```

If there are any properties *not* listed in the tag that result in conflict, a further attempt to reconcile the conflict is made from any precedence tags.

Explicit Values

If you are aware of a specific conflict between two elements that match, and you have a preference for how the element should look in the composed design, you may attach a further tag to the composition relationship so indicating. For example, the following tag resolves an assumed conflict between the `crystals` attribute in the `Player` classes and indicates what values `crystals` should have in the composed design. Again, properties are named as they are in the construct's UML metamodel description.

```
resolve ( Player.crystals (visibility=private;
                           multiplicity=*; ..)
          Element_name ( property=value;
                         property=value; ..)
          ....)
```

If there are no explicit listings for a conflict, further attempts to reconcile a conflict are in the order of a search for a default-value specification for that construct, followed by precedence tags.

Binding to Crosscutting Themes

A Theme/UML-based design for a system is likely to be made up of multiple base and multiple crosscutting themes. Up to now, we've looked at specifying how base themes should be composed. Here, we address composing crosscutting themes with your base themes.

The principles behind composing a crosscutting theme with a base theme are based on the principles of merge integration we've already met. Assuming merge integration, this section describes *additional* facilities within Theme/UML for binding real elements from a base theme to the templates defined in a crosscutting theme. Recall how the templates in the design of a crosscutting theme look with the example in Figure 6–23. This shows us the **track-energy** theme from the game, as also illustrated in Chapter 5.

As you can see, there are three sets of crosscutting behavior here, as indicated by three sets of templates in < > brackets. For the first, we need to identify base operations to match `moveLocation(..)`; for the second, base operations to match `energyAction(..)`; and for the third, base operations to match `joinGame(..)`. In order to figure out what operations should match, you'll probably find it useful to go back to the Theme/Doc views of the requirements to see where the **track-energy** theme crosscut other themes and also to look at those crosscutting theme views and their corresponding

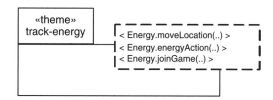

Figure 6–23   *Track-energy templates.*

Theme/UML designs. From the requirements and Theme/Doc views, energy is depleted at different rates depending on whether or not the player is in a game location. This behavior can be triggered each time a new location is registered, as designed in the **enter-location** theme. This is achieved with the `setLocation()` operation in the `Player` class, as illustrated in the Theme/UML design from Chapter 5. There is no other place in the game design that registers a change in location. The Theme/Doc views illustrate more instances of actions that trigger a change in energy levels: when a player gets crystals and also when a player completes some NPC-assigned tasks, for example a physical test. From the Theme/UML designs, the operations that denote a player obtaining crystals are in `Player.incrementCrystals` from the **enter-location** theme and `Player.addCrystals(int)` from the **duel** theme. We did not include Theme/UML designs for completing tasks from NPCs, but we can assume here that the operations `Player.completeWizardErrand()` and `Player.completeWarriorTest()` indicate when these actions are completed. Finally, from the Theme/UML designs, the operation that denotes a player joining a game is `Player.joinGame()`.

Now that you've identified the operations that will bind to the templates in the **track-energy** theme, it's time to indicate this with a composition relationship and a `bind[ ]` tag. For each set of templates denoting different sequences of behavior within the < > brackets, you may define one or more "real" elements to bind to those templates, also in matching < > brackets. As illustrated in Figure 6–24, the first < > bracket has just a single real operation to indicate a move in location, while the second < > bracket includes a set of operations that correspond to an action requiring a change in energy. Note that where there is more than one real operation to be bound to the template, the set of operations is bound in { } brackets. We also compose with the **game** theme that is the result of the composition specified in Figure 6–16. Indeed, we advise you to compose base themes first, and then compose with crosscutting themes. We should also point out an important rule here—only one crosscutting theme may be composed at a time. This forces you to consider the ordering of execution of multiple crosscutting behaviors, thereby reducing the potential for conflict.

Adding a `bind[]` attachment to the composition relationship has the effect that a sequence diagram is generated for each of the replacing operations. Each generated sequence diagram indicates how the crosscutting behavior

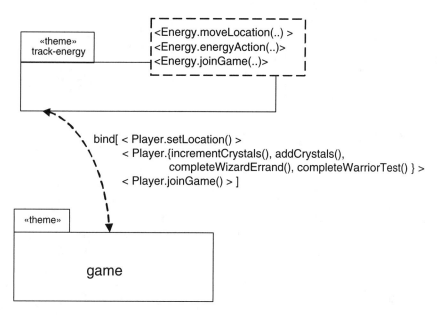

Figure 6–24   *Binding to the track-energy crosscutting theme.*

impacts the replacing operation. In addition, there are now two operations in the design for each of the replacing operations. One is an operation of the same name as the replacing operation. This operation triggers all behavior, as defined in the sequence diagram. The second operation is the real operation renamed with a prepended _do_ to indicate the original behavior.

For the remaining elements in the crosscutting theme and the base theme, elements are merged as described previously. When a crosscutting theme is being composed, a `match[name]` tag is assumed, which means that elements with the same name will be matched and merged. In the **track-energy** theme (refer to Figure 5–21), there is a class called Game, which will be merged with the Game class in the **game** theme.

Let's look at another example—the **P2PCommunications** crosscutting theme. Recall the template specification from the Theme/UML design from Chapter 5, as copied here in Figure 6–25. As you can see, there are four different sequences of crosscutting behavior: when a player joins a game, when a player's state changes, when a location's state changes, and when the game application starts.

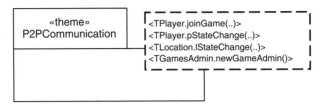

Figure 6–25   *P2PCommunication templates.*

As you can see in Figure 6–26, one operation, `Player.join(..)`, replaces the `TPlayer.joinGame(..)` template. In addition, state of interest for locations relates to the crystals they have, and state of interest for players relates to the crystals and magic items they have. By replacing the templates with methods that effect these states, we say that the relevant crosscutting behavior should also occur. Notice that we specify the composition relationship with the composed **game** theme and corresponding composed

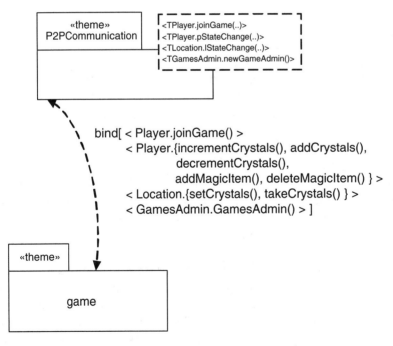

Figure 6–26   *Binding to the P2PCommunication crosscutting theme.*

`Player` and `Location` classes. As before, the other elements in both themes are merged, with elements matched by name. This has the effect that the `GameAdmin`, `Game`, `Player`, and `Location` classes in the **P2PCommunication** theme illustrated in Figure 5–25 will be merged with the classes of the same name in the **game** theme. Since `Player`, `Location`, and `GamesAdmin` have the methods that replace the templates, then this, in effect, means that the crosscutting behavior is also merged with the matching classes.

In all of the examples of crosscutting behavior in our game, there is only one template for each sequence of behavior defined in a sequence diagram. Of course, this may not always be the case. There is no limit to the number of templates that can be specified within a single sequence of behavior. However, there is one important rule here: the *first* template in the < > sequence group in the template box *must* represent the replacing operation that triggers the sequence of behavior. Correspondingly, the first replacing operation in the `bind[]` attachment will be the one that triggers the behavior.

The Observer design pattern is a good example of when more than one template is required within a single sequence of events. In the Observer pattern, there are subjects and observers. Observers register an interest in being notified of changes in state in subjects. When a change in state happens in the subject (sounds like a good Theme/UML template!), an event is sent to observers (again, another good template!). Figure 6–27 illustrates the template box of an observer crosscutting-theme design that includes templates for three sequences of behavior. Crosscutting behavior is also illustrated for changes in state in the subject. There is also crosscutting behavior in the **observer** theme for when an observer initiates or terminates its interest in a subject, which is not illustrated.

As you can see, the state change sequence of behavior has two templates, `aStateChange(..)` and `update()`, and a single sequence diagram captures the combination of behaviors. This brings us to a refinement of a statement made previously: we said that a sequence diagram is generated for each replacing operation in a composed design. We now need to clarify this and state that a sequence diagram is generated for *each set of* replacing operations related by a single sequence of behavior (i.e., for groupings within < > brackets in the template box).

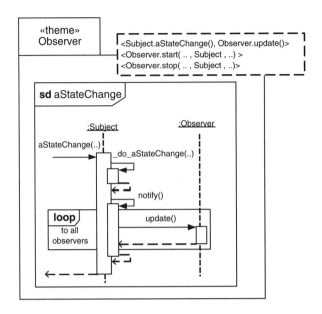

Figure 6–27 *Observer templates.*

Let's look at the simple case where we have instances of a `Location` class (subjects) being observed by instances of a `Player` class (observers). In particular, the state-change operation (`takeCrystals()`) in `Location` is observed by the `Player`, who is to be notified using the `crystalsTouched()` operation. In this case, the `bind[]` attachment on the composition relationship between the **observer** theme, and the **game** theme would be[6]

```
bind[ < Location.takeCrystals(),
      Player.crystalsTouched() >
    < .. >
    < .. > ]
```

---

[6] We do not illustrate the binding to the other two sequences initiated by `start()` and `stop()`, as these are the simple case, and specifying their bindings has the same syntax as the previous examples from the game.

In this example, a single sequence diagram is generated that sends a `crystalsTouched()` event to an instance of the `Player` class when the instance of the `Location` class it has expressed interest in executes `takeCrystals()`.

What if there are multiple state changes to be observed? The { } bracketing can be used here to group the operations that replace a template. For example,

```
bind[ < { Location.takeCrystals(),
          Location.addCrystals()} ,
        Player.crystalsTouched() >
      < .. >
      < .. > ]
```

In this example, two sequence diagrams are generated to indicate what happens when `takeCrystals()` and `addCrystals()` are executed. In both cases, `crystalsTouched()` from the `Player` class is also executed. A further syntactical refinement is possible here with additional { } brackets to group operations from the same class. For example, since `takeCrystals()` and `addCrystals()` are both in the `Location` class, we can also group them together in that context, as follows:

```
bind[ < { Location.{takeCrystals(), addCrystals()}} ,
        Player.crystalsTouched() >
      < .. >
      < .. > ]
```

In general, when multiple operations replace the *first* template (i.e., the template that represents triggering of the crosscutting behavior), a sequence diagram is generated for each.

What if you did not want `Player.crystalsTouched()` to be executed in every instance of a state change? We do not allow multiple replacements for any template following the triggering template, so in this case, you must specify the groupings explicitly. You need to specify multiple nested bindings within a < > set, with further < > sets. Let's say we want `crystalsTouched()` from `Player` to be called any time `takeCrystals()` or `stealCrystals()` is executed in `Location`. We also want players to observe when crystals are added to a location, but instead of calling `crystalsTouched()`, we want `newCrystals()` to be executed.

In the following example, all operations that start with `add` in the `Location` class trigger behavior that results in the execution of `Player.newCrystals()` (enclosed in nested `<>` brackets), while `takeCrystals()` and `stealCrystals()` result in the execution of `Player.crystalsTouched()` (also enclosed in nested `<>` brackets).

```
bind[ < < {Location.add*()}, Player.newCrystals() >
        < {Location.{takeCrystals(), stealCrystals()}},
            Player.crystalsTouched() > >
      < .. >
      < .. > ]
```

Within each `<>` grouping, the first template in a sequence group that triggers the crosscutting behavior may have multiple bindings, but subsequent templates may not.

Some Comments on Process

If you are the person who plans and tracks the activities for your development project, you will want to know who does the individual theme design, who specifies the compositions, and when it should all happen. You will also want to know how complicated the composition specifications are likely to get and what can be done to minimize potential complexity.

The designs for the individual base themes are straightforward and require standard object-oriented design skills. Indeed, it is probably easier to design a single base theme than standard object-oriented projects, as the designer has to consider only a single concern. The complexity of the design is relative to the complexity of that single concern. Therefore, it is likely that a relatively junior designer could design an individual base theme. Crosscutting themes are a little more complicated and may require a designer with a little more experience. Again, however, this designer has less to worry about with a single concern.

As for when these can happen—in theory, separated themes can be designed separately, since they have been selected to be independent.

However, this brings us to the question relating to the complexity of the composition specification. The more independent theme design teams are, the more likely there will be significant differences in structure and naming within the designs, and therefore the more complicated composition will be. We advise that where the design themes share a lot of concepts, the designers should meet at the start and agree on general policies, such as naming conventions and similar issues. For example, if the design problem has a notion of containers and components, then perhaps each theme that encounters these should design them with the Composite pattern. As another example, perhaps every design theme in the Crystal Game that has the notion of a player should name the corresponding class `Player`, and so on. You need to find a balance between, on the one hand, avoiding a situation in which everyone designs all the themes at once in this initial meeting and, on the other hand, reaping the benefits of concurrent team design where each team can design each theme separately.

So, who should specify the composition? The composer needs an overall understanding of the system and is therefore likely to be a more senior, experienced designer or software architect. This person must be able to make decisions relating to the resolution of conflicts and understand the impact of combining potentially multiple crosscutting themes with multiple base themes. With the Theme/UML approach, fewer people of this level are required than might be the case with standard object-oriented design, as it is only at the composition stage that the overall picture requires understanding. It is likely that the composer will need to examine the output of the composition process to ensure that the overall structure and behavior of the game integrate correctly and to rework theme designs or composition specifications if necessary.

Summary

In this chapter, we explained how to specify how themes should be composed. We described a new kind of relationship called a composition relationship that is an extension to UML. We saw how, with a composition relationship, you can decide what themes should be composed; what design elements in the themes match each other and should be integrated; how themes should be integrated; how to resolve conflicts between matching elements; and how to bind base design elements to templates in crosscutting themes. Of course, a composed design will have all the scattering and tangling properties that Theme/UML is designed to avoid, but designers need only work with the individual themes, which are cleanly modularized. In the next chapter, we look at how to move forward to implementation with the theme designs.

7

Map to Implementation

In this chapter, we look at some different possibilities for implementing your Theme/UML designs. Up to now, we have focused on modularizing design models into themes and specifying how themes should be composed. Moving on to the coding phase, you have a number of options. You can use a standard object-oriented programming language such as Java or C++, but if you go this route, you must work with composed designs. This means, of course, that you will lose the separation of your code artifacts into base modules and crosscutting modules. Alternatively, a number of aspect-oriented programming (AOP) languages can be used. In general, most AOP languages support similar separations as manifest in the Theme/UML designs, which means that you can maintain some level of traceability between your designs and your code. In this chapter, we focus on using AOP languages and consider the steps required to map the Theme/UML designs to a selection of them. We work through the implementation task, using the Crystal Game themes as examples.

There are a growing number of AOP languages in existence. While some languages are based on different programming languages, such as Java, C++, and Smalltalk, the most mature of these, at the time of writing, are based on Java. We have selected three representative approaches to describe in this chapter—AspectJ,[1] AspectWerkz,[2] and the Concern Manipulation Environment (CME).[3] AspectJ and AspectWerkz have similar philosophies in that they follow the asymmetric composition model in which aspects are separate from the core functionality. Theme/UML evolved more directly from the CME approach in which the focus is a more symmetric model and core functionality is further separated into concerns in addition to the aspects. See Chapter 1, "Introduction," for a discussion on the difference between the asymmetric and symmetric models. This chapter demonstrates that the Theme approach allows you to move to either approach in the implementation phase.

You should not consider this chapter a tutorial on any of the AOP languages discussed—there are more appropriate sources that provide detailed information on these languages. Our intent is to examine the mapping of Theme/UML constructs to corresponding code constructs and to illustrate how code can be derived. In addition, our intent is to describe mapping in such a way that if you are using a different AOP language than one discussed here, you will be able to relate our discussions to whatever other AOP language you are using.

AspectJ

AspectJ is the most mature AOP language and currently the most widely used. It is an aspect-oriented extension to the Java language that supports the implementation of crosscutting code (i.e., aspects) as separate aspect modules. At a high level, AspectJ adds four kinds of program elements to Java: *aspects, pointcuts, advice,* and *intertype declarations.* Table 7–1 describes these elements and maps them to the corresponding design elements in Theme/UML. Of course, we look later at many details of AspectJ within these four constructs.

From the perspective of mapping your Theme/UML models to AspectJ, you must consider the base themes and crosscutting themes somewhat differently. The AspectJ model for aspects is primarily concerned with separating

---

[1] http://www.eclipse.org/aspectj.

[2] http://aspectwerkz.codehaus.org/.

[3] http://www.eclipse.org/cme.

Table 7–1 *High-Level Mapping of AspectJ Programming Elements to Theme/UML*

Element	AspectJ	Theme/UML
Aspect	An aspect is a type that contains language elements that specify crosscutting structure and behavior. It may be instantiated, and it can be reasoned about at compile time. Keyword: `aspect`	A crosscutting theme is a design equivalent to an aspect, though it may also contain behavior that is not crosscutting.
Pointcut	During the execution of a program, and as part of that execution's scope, there are points in the execution where behavior can be joined. These points are *joinpoints*. A pointcut is a predicate that can determine, for a given joinpoint, whether it is matched by the predicate. Keyword: `pointcut`	Operation template parameters may be defined and referenced within sequence diagrams representing points in the execution of the sequence of behavior where behavior can be joined. These templates are replaced by (possibly multiple) actual operations as specified in the `bind[]` attachment. Template specifications and their matching `bind[]` specifications are therefore equivalent to pointcuts.
Advice	A piece of advice is code that executes at a joinpoint, using some of the execution scope. Keywords: `before`, `after`, `around`	Within a sequence diagram, crosscutting behavior may be specified to execute when a template operation is called. This behavior is equivalent to advice code.
Intertype declarations	An intertype declaration is a programming element, such as an attribute, constructor, or method, that is added to a type that may add to or extend that type's structure.	Design elements that are not template elements may be defined within crosscutting themes. These may be classes, attributes, operations, or relationships and are equivalent to elements that are added to (merged with) base theme elements.

and weaving crosscutting behavior onto a single base. It is, however, possible to maintain a separation of the base themes in AspectJ (discussed later) but first, we examine mapping the crosscutting themes to AspectJ's aspects.

In general, we advise you to define an abstract aspect for each of your crosscutting themes and a corresponding concrete aspect to capture the binding specification to the base themes. Figure 7–1 illustrates Table 7–1 in a little more detail (though still at a high level) and shows the general approach we take to mapping Theme/UML design models to AspectJ constructs. It especially illustrates a separation into abstract and concrete aspects. As in previous chapters, shadows are used to indicate mapping between elements.

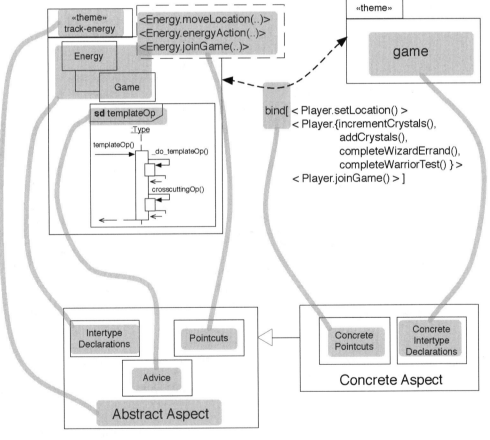

Figure 7–1   *Map to implementation.*

Overview of Steps

In this section, we provide general principles for mapping the main Theme/UML design constructs to the main AspectJ constructs. Following is a set of guidelines for deriving an abstract aspect. Don't worry if some of the steps aren't immediately clear—we work through them in detail next.

1. Declare an abstract aspect to represent the crosscutting theme.

2. For each class with templates in the crosscutting theme:

    2.1. Declare an interface in the abstract aspect.

    2.2. For each template operation that initiates a sequence diagram:

       2.2.1. Declare a corresponding abstract pointcut.

       2.2.2. The abstract pointcut should have the following formal parameters:

          One to capture the target object.

          One for each of the specified formal parameters on the template operation.

       2.2.3. Declare before, after, and around advice relative to the sequence of behavior defined in the sequence diagram.

    2.3. For each template operation listed after the template operation that initiates the sequence diagram:

       2.3.1. Declare a corresponding abstract method on the class's interface.

    2.4. For each operation in the class that is not defined as a template:

       2.4.1. Implement as an intertype declaration against the class's interface.

    2.5. Each attribute maps to an intertype declaration on the class's interface.

    2.6. Each association from the class to another class maps to an intertype declaration on the class's interface.

3. Any other class (i.e., those without template operations) should be implemented directly if not already present. If a class already exists in the base with which the crosscutting theme's specification is intended

to merge, then the crosscutting theme's specification should be implemented as intertype declarations on that class.

Mapping to a concrete aspect is straightforward—you extend the abstract aspect and provide concrete pointcuts from the `bind[]` specifications (watching out for control flow restrictions) and concrete implementations for the intertype declarations. We now demonstrate the general policies useful for implementing your system using AspectJ by working through mapping the **track-energy** and **P2PCommunication** crosscutting themes.

Track-energy

The **track-energy** crosscutting theme[4] provides a design for three crosscutting behavior specifications and some additional time-related behavior. This specification yields an abstract aspect with a combination of interfaces, aspect attributes and methods, abstract pointcuts, and advice. We also look at how we can define a concrete aspect that extends the abstract aspect, and map the `bind[]` specification of base operations to the pointcuts.

Abstract Aspect

As defined in the AspectJ documentation, an aspect is a new kind of type for crosscutting behavior that encapsulates all the elements required by an aspect—that is, pointcuts, advice, and intertype declarations. An abstract aspect allows you to provide as much of the code needed by the aspect as is possible without directly referring to the base code that it will crosscut. This is directly analogous to what a crosscutting theme does in that a crosscutting theme provides the design of crosscutting behavior without direct reference to the base theme(s) it will crosscut. AspectJ provides the keyword `aspect` to allow you to define your aspect, which you can qualify with the `abstract` keyword. From the **track-energy** crosscutting theme, we can therefore declare an abstract aspect as follows:

```
abstract aspect TrackEnergy {
}
```

---

[4] Refer to Chapter 5 for the design and Chapter 6 for the composition specification

Note that we have changed the style of the theme name for the aspect to naming conventions more common to classes than to packages. Aspects in AspectJ are more closely related to classes than to packages, and so we move to the appropriate convention. We recommend that the name you give the abstract aspect be strongly related to the name of the Theme/UML design theme for traceability purposes.

Interfaces

Within the **track-energy** theme design, two classes are defined and used to achieve the theme's goals: these classes are the Energy class and the Game class. In essence, these classes are placeholder classes to be merged with base classes, supplementing the base classes with additional structure and behavior. In AspectJ, there are two possible options to handle this—we could define a class or an interface for each. If we use a class, an inheritance relationship must be defined for the concrete class, because the crosscutting theme's class may name operations that are essentially abstract in the aspect. However, a base class may already have a superclass, which would cause us difficulties as multiple inheritance is not possible in Java. Defining an interface for each class is therefore a better idea, and we can add a specification of which base classes implement these interfaces to the concrete aspect later. For the **track-energy** theme, the AspectJ code for defining interfaces for the Energy and Game classes follows.

```
interface EnergyEntityI{Game getGame();}
interface GameI{boolean isPlayerInLocation();
              boolean isActive();}
```

Notice that each interface also has an operation defined. If you use operations that you expect to be implemented in a base class, then you can list them in the interface, giving a context for the compilation of your aspects. For the **track-energy** theme, we need a reference to the relevant game object (obtained using getGame()), because the Game class is responsible for figuring out the amount of energy loss or gain as a result of a particular action. In addition, the Game knows about game locations, and so we assume it provides us with the implementation of isPlayerInLocation() that is referenced in the design (refer to Figure 5–14 in Chapter 5, "Theme Design"), used to tell us whether a player is in a game location. We have also added an isActive() method interface that we can query to determine whether the game is still running (used later by a thread that manages the time-based loss of energy).

Your crosscutting theme's classes may also require additional interfaces not explicitly defined in the design. For example, the `Energy` class responds to a signal `loseEnergy()` that is sent periodically. If you implement this using threads (which seems like a good idea), this means that the `Energy` class should implement Java's `Runnable` interface for handling threads. We can declare this in the aspect using the standard Java `extends` keyword:

```
interface EnergyEntityI
        extends Runnable {Game getGame();}
```

Aspect Attributes

From the design of the **track-energy** theme, we can see that the `Energy` class is specified as having three attributes, which we can define on the interface. The initialization values are taken from the class model in the theme design.

```
// aspect attributes
int EnergyEntityI.duration = 5;
int EnergyEntityI.energyUnit = 10;
int EnergyEntityI.changeAmount = 1;
```

In the crosscutting theme design, the `Energy` class also has a relationship to the `Game` class. It looks as if we've ignored it, as it might have been mapped to an aspect attribute. If you're trying to decide whether an attribute or a relationship such as this should be defined as an aspect attribute, you should consider your expectations of the base class. If you think that it is reasonable to expect, for example, that base entities in the game will have references to a game object, then we can exclude game as an aspect attribute for `TrackEnergy`. In this implementation, we assume there is a `getGame()` method in the class that implements the `EnergyEntityI` interface that we can use when we need a reference to the game. Consequently, we do not need to define it as an aspect attribute here.

Aspect Methods

In general, the process of moving from method designs to method code in AspectJ is no different than how you would move to any Java implementation from a standard UML design, with one exception. Each method should be defined in the context of the particular interface to which it is attached.

Remember from the design that we intend the classes in the crosscutting theme to be merged with classes in the base themes. We can achieve this by attaching the methods to the relevant interfaces, causing any base classes that implement the interface to implicitly have the methods added to them.

The **track-energy** theme defines a number of methods that do the work of tracking energy: setChangeAmount(), changeEnergy(), loseEnergy(), and getEnergy(). Each method may be implemented in the abstract aspect as follows:

```
private void EnergyEntityI.setChangeAmount(int a)
{ changeAmount = a; }

private void EnergyEntityI.changeEnergy(int e)
{ energyUnit += e; }

private void EnergyEntityI.loseEnergy()
{ energyUnit -= changeAmount; }

private void GameI.getEnergy(String name,
                            EnergyEntityI energyEntity)
{
    if(name.equals("completeWizardErrand"))
    { energyEntity.changeEnergy(4); }
    else if(name.equals("completeWarriorTest"))
    { energyEntity.changeEnergy(3); }
    //... and so on
}
```

You must also consider whether there are further methods that the aspect requires as a result of particular implementation decisions you've made. An example is a run() method, which is required because we declared that the EnergyEntityI interface extends Runnable. While the game is active, we want an energy entity to periodically lose energy. The run() method is implemented as follows:

```
public void EnergyEntityI.run()
{
    GameI game = getGame();
    while(game.isActive())
    {
        try {
```

```
                    loseEnergy();
                    Thread.sleep(5000);
              } catch (InterruptedException e) {
                    // Log or notify exception occurred
                    e.printStackTrace();
              }
         }
}
```

Abstract Pointcuts

In AspectJ, a pointcut describes points of execution in a program where crosscutting behavior is required. In Theme/UML, template operations initiate a sequence of behavior defined in a sequence diagram. These template operations represent a placeholder for base operations where crosscutting behavior is required. The two concepts are analogous for operations, making AspectJ's pointcuts a good match to represent such template operations. The **track-energy** theme has three examples: moveLocation, energyAction, and joinGame. As the pointcuts are being used in an abstract aspect, we choose to also define the pointcuts as abstract:

```
public abstract pointcut moveLocation(EnergyEntityI energyEntity);
public abstract pointcut energyAction(EnergyEntityI energyEntity);
public abstract pointcut joinGame(EnergyEntityI energyEntity);
```

We can override these pointcuts in the concrete aspect later. Note that each pointcut has one parameter of type EnergyEntityI. When pointcuts have a parameter, any advice (described in the next section) that uses this pointcut can reference this parameter, which is read from the context of the currently executing joinpoint. A reference to an instance that implements EnergyEntityI is required for the implementation of crosscutting behavior for each pointcut, as you will see later.

Advice

In AspectJ, advice is the implementation of behavior that crosscuts the set of execution points defined by the pointcut. This makes advice an obvious construct to use to implement the sequence of behaviors defined in sequence diagrams in the crosscutting themes. Advice can be defined to execute before, after, or around the execution points defined by pointcuts.

From the Theme/UML designs, you may remember that in some cases, we added _do_ to the front of the names of the template operations that initiate a sequence of behavior. We did this within the sequence of execution to indicate the execution of the base operation to which the crosscutting behavior is to be applied. This is analogous to the execution points defined by operation pointcuts and so we can examine the sequence diagrams to assess whether the crosscutting behavior happens before, after, or around the template operation starting with _do_. When to choose before or after is clear from the timeline of the sequence of operations. Around advice, which essentially replaces the base operation, will be obvious from any conditional specifications of operation execution defined within the sequence diagram.

From the **track-energy** theme, the sequence diagram for the moveLocation template operation indicates that after the base operation is executed, the game object is asked whether the energy entity is in a game location and, depending on a true or false answer, sets the amount that affects the periodic energy loss to 1 or 2 energy units. This behavior is captured in the following after advice. Notice that this code requires a reference to the energy entity, which is why we needed to define energyEntity as a parameter in the abstract pointcut.

```
after(EnergyEntityI energyEntity) returning:
                        moveLocation(energyEntity)
{
    GameI game = energyEntity.getGame();
    if(game.isPlayerInLocation())
    {   energyEntity.setChangeAmount(2);        }
    else
    {   energyEntity.setChangeAmount(1);        }
}
```

The sequence diagram for the energyAction template operation indicates that after the base operation is executed, the game object is asked to figure out the impact on the energy entity's energy as a result of the execution of the template operation. We can use AspectJ's thisJoinPoint construct to obtain a String representation of the name of the base method being crosscut, which the getEnergy() method uses to determine the energy impact, as follows.

```
after(EnergyEntityI energyEntity) returning:
                                energyAction(energyEntity)
{
    String currentActionName =
            thisJoinPoint.getSignature().getName();
    GameI game = energyEntity.getGame();
    game.getEnergy(currentActionName, energyEntity);
}
```

The sequence diagram for the `joinGame` template operation (refer to Figure 5–19) indicates that after the base operation is executed, the thread to handle the loss of energy should be started. You saw the corresponding `run()` method earlier.

```
after(EnergyEntityI energyEntity) returning:
                    joinGame(energyEntity)
{
    Thread energyLossThread = new Thread(energyEntity);
    energyLossThread.start();
}
```

We now have the full abstract aspect code to implement the **track-energy** theme, as illustrated in its entirety in Listing 7–1.

Listing 7–1 *Abstract Aspect*

```
abstract aspect TrackEnergy {

  // interfaces
  interface EnergyEntityI extends Runnable {Game getGame();}
  interface GameI{boolean isPlayerInLocation();
                boolean isActive();}

  // aspect attributes
  int EnergyEntityI.duration = 5;
  int EnergyEntityI.energyUnit = 10;
  int EnergyEntityI.changeAmount = 1;

  // aspect methods
  private void EnergyEntityI.setChangeAmount(int a)
  { changeAmount = a; }
```

```
private void EnergyEntityI.changeEnergy(int e)
{ energyUnit += e; }

private void EnergyEntityI.loseEnergy()
{ energyUnit -= changeAmount; }

private void GameI.getEnergy(String name,
                             EnergyEntityI energyEntity)
{
   if(name.equals("completeWizardErrand"))
   {  energyEntity.changeEnergy(4); }
   else if(name.equals("completeWarriorTest"))
   { energyEntity.changeEnergy(3); }
   //... and so on
}

public void EnergyEntityI.run()
{
GameI game = getGame();
   while(game.isActive())
   {
      try {
         loseEnergy();
         Thread.sleep(5000);
      } catch (InterruptedException e) {
         // Log or notify exception occured
         e.printStackTrace();
      }
   }
}

// abstract pointcuts
public abstract pointcut moveLocation(
                         EnergyEntityI energyEntity);
public abstract pointcut energyAction(
                         EnergyEntityI energyEntity);
public abstract pointcut joinGame(
                         EnergyEntityI energyEntity);

// advice
after(EnergyEntityI energyEntity) returning:
                         moveLocation(energyEntity)
```

```
{
    GameI game = energyEntity.getGame();
    if(game.isPlayerInLocation())
    {   energyEntity.setChangeAmount(2);    }
    else
    {   energyEntity.setChangeAmount(1);    }
}
after(EnergyEntityI energyEntity) returning:
                    energyAction(energyEntity)
{
    String currentActionName =
            thisJoinPoint.getSignature().getName();
    GameI game = energyEntity.getGame();
    game.getEnergy(currentActionName, energyEntity);
}
after(EnergyEntityI energyEntity) returning:
                    joinGame(energyEntity)
{
    Thread energyLossThread = new Thread(energyEntity);
    energyLossThread.start();
}
}
```

Concrete Aspect

Now that we've implemented the abstract aspect, we need to think about how we implement the binding specification of the composition relationship's bind[] attachment. In AspectJ, concrete aspects extend an abstract aspect in a manner similar to Java classes, and so we can use them to implement the base operations to be bound to the template operations (or, the pointcuts, in AspectJ parlance). As it turns out, mapping to a concrete aspect is relatively straightforward, and we work through the steps with the **track-energy** theme and its binding illustrated in Figure 7–1 and copied here:

```
bind[ < Player.setLocation()>
        < Player.{incrementCrystals(), addCrystals(),
                completeWizardErrand(), completeWarriorTest() } >
        < Player.joinGame() > ]
```

Extending Abstract Aspect

AspectJ uses the same `extends` construct as Java to extend an abstract aspect. For the `TrackEnergy` aspect, this looks as follows:

```
public aspect ConcreteTrackEnergy extends TrackEnergy {

}
```

Binding to the Aspect's Interfaces

The crosscutting theme's classes, `Energy` and `Game`, are represented through interfaces declared on the abstract aspect. As we described in Chapter 6, we want to merge the base classes with the classes defined using interfaces in the aspect. The intertype declarations mechanism we used in the abstract aspect effectively merges the methods and attributes defined in the aspect's interface with a base class that implements that interface, which is what we need. We can code this using the `declare parents` construct from AspectJ as follows:

```
declare parents: Player implements EnergyEntityI;
declare parents: Game implements GameI;
```

So, how do you decide which base classes implement `EnergyEntityI` and `GameI` from the theme design? Deciding on `Player` for `EnergyEntityI` was easy. When we look at the `bind[]` attachment, we see that the `Player` class contains all the methods that replace both the `moveLocation` and the `energyAction` templates. Both these templates initiate behavior on the `Energy` class in the theme, which we mapped to the `EnergyEntityI` interface. As such, it makes sense that the `Player` class implements `EnergyEntityI`. Deciding on `Game` for `GameI` appears, on the surface, to be straightforward because they have the same name, and Theme/UML defaults to same-name merge for crosscutting theme composition (refer to Chapter 6). However, it is possible that a base theme's class and a crosscutting theme's class have the same name but should not be merged, as we discussed in Chapter 6. In this case, the designer so indicates in the Theme/UML models with further composition relationships that indicate which base classes should be merged with the classes in the crosscutting theme.

Binding to Concrete Pointcuts

The abstract aspect declared abstract pointcuts that also must be made concrete. Each abstract pointcut corresponds to a template operation in the design model, and you can tell which base operations replace the templates (and therefore should be concrete pointcuts) from the bind[] attachment. As follows, the concrete pointcuts capture the execution of the concrete operations and expose the target object and arguments of each. The sequence diagrams did not indicate any control flow restrictions, so we do not have to consider cflow or cflowbelow here.

```
pointcut moveLocation(EnergyEntityI energyEntity):
        this(energyEntity) &&
        execution (* Player.setLocation(..));

pointcut energyAction(EnergyEntityI energyEntity):
        this(energyEntity) &&
        (execution (* Player.incrementCrystals(..)) ||
        execution (* Player.addCrystals(..)) ||
        execution (* Player.completeWarriorTest(..)) ||
        execution (* Player.completeWizardErrand(..)));

pointcut joinGame(EnergyEntityI energyEntity):
        this(energyEntity) &&
        execution (* Player.joinGame(..));
```

Other Concrete Implementations

You may also need to consider whether it is necessary to provide concrete methods or advice, some of which may override methods/advice in the abstract aspect. Though we don't have any examples in the **track-energy** theme, it is supported by AspectJ and may be required for some implementation reason. In general though, we think it's better to, where possible, keep the aspect code in the abstract aspect and the concrete mappings to the interfaces and pointcuts in the concrete aspect.

We now have the full concrete aspect code to implement the bindings to the **track-energy** theme, as illustrated in its entirety in Listing 7–2.

Listing 7–2 *Concrete Aspect*

```
public aspect ConcreteTrackEnergy extends TrackEnergy {

  declare parents: Player implements EnergyEntityI;
  declare parents: Game implements GameI;

  pointcut moveLocation(EnergyEntityI energyEntity):
          this(energyEntity) &&
          execution (* Player.setLocation(..));


  pointcut energyAction(EnergyEntityI energyEntity):
          this(energyEntity) &&
          (execution (* Player.incrementCrystals(..)) ||
          execution (* Player.addCrystals(..)) ||
          execution (* Player.completeWarriorTest(..)) ||
          execution (* Player.completeWizardErrand(..)));

  pointcut joinGame(Player player):
          this(player) &&
          execution (* Player.joinGame(..));
}
```

P2PCommunication

The **P2PCommunication** crosscutting theme provides a design for four crosscutting behavior specifications and, similarly to the **track-energy** theme, some additional time-related behavior to be implemented in a separate thread. Again, we can define an abstract aspect for the **P2Pcommunication** behavior designed in Theme/UML, and a concrete aspect to capture the bind[] specification, and other concrete code.

Abstract Aspect

After following the same steps as we did for the **track-energy** theme, we get the abstract aspect illustrated in Listing 7–3. There are some interesting details to point out here. First, Line 8 uses the AspectJ declare precedence construct that we have not met previously. When you are applying more than one aspect to your base code, you may state which should be executed first with this construct. If we look at the design of both the **P2PCommunication** theme and the **track-energy** theme, we can see that both have a joinGame pointcut. If the concrete aspects for both name the same concrete pointcuts that capture the same points of execution (as is likely), then both advices will be executed. We have decided that it makes more sense to ensure that a player requests the full game state prior to starting the clock on losing energy. Though not illustrated in Chapter 6, it is likely that the ordering of this composition would be clear as **track-energy** would be composed with the result of the composition of the base game with the **P2PCommunication** theme.

Another interesting difference with this aspect is that some of the behavior that belongs in this theme has been encapsulated in another class. See Line 11, which references a GameComms class. At a general level, Theme/UML does not prescribe any minimum or maximum size (in terms of number of classes, methods, etc.) for a theme—it should be whatever size is necessary to handle the requirement(s) it supports. At the design level, this is not an issue, as we can use multiple classes to provide sensible modularizations. If you think that the aspect is getting too large, it might be possible to further modularize some functionality into a separate class (or indeed aspect). We illustrate this approach with the GameComms class—everything to do with the actual broadcasting of events has been removed from the aspect into this class. Indeed, the P2PCommunication aspect has turned out to be quite large, and so it is a good candidate for further refactoring into differ-ent classes or aspects. For example, you could have multiple concrete aspects: one to handle changes to the game, one to handle player-state change, one to handle location-state change, and so on.

The remainder of the P2PCommunication abstract aspect code follows in a straightforward manner from the steps described in detail for the **track-energy** theme. Lines 17 to 127 provide the methods for the aspect, includ-ing an implementation of the run() method (17–25). Marshalling and unmarshalling the game state is illustrated in some detail in lines 38 to 103, while only skeleton code is illustrated for marshalling and unmarshalling player and location state in lines 105 to 121. Abstract pointcuts to map to the four template operations are in lines 130 to 133, with corresponding after advice from lines 136 to 161.

Listing 7–3 *P2PCommunication Abstract Aspect*

```
1     import java.util.Collection;
2     import java.util.Iterator;
3
4     abstract aspect P2PCommunication {
5
6     // Inter-type declarations
7     declare parents: GameAdmin implements Runnable;
8     declare precedence: P2PCommunication, TrackEnergy;
9
10    // aspect attributes
11    private GameComms Game.gameComms = GameComms.getInstance();
12
13    // aspect methods
14    public GameComms Game.getGameComms()
15    {   return gameComms;  }
16
17    public void GameAdmin.run()
18    {
19       while (true) {
20          try { checkAvailableGames();
21                Thread.sleep(5000);
22          } catch (InterruptedException e) {
23                // Log or notify exception occured }
24       }
25    }
26
27    public void Game.fullGameStateRequest(String gameName)
28    {
29       GameState gameState = marshallGame();
30       GameComms gameComms = getGameComms();
31       gameComms.publishGameState(gameState);
32    }
33
34    public void Game.fullGameState(GameState gameState)
35    {   unMarshallGame(gameState);    }
36
37
38    public GameState Game.marshallGame()
39    {
40       GameState gameState = new GameState();
41       // get game location states and add them to game state
```

```
42      Collection gameLocations = getLocations();
43      Iterator gameLocationsIteration = gameLocations.iterator();
44      while(gameLocationsIteration.hasNext())
45      {
46          Location location = (Location)gameLocationsIteration.next();
47          LocationState locationState = location.marshallState();
48          gameState.addLocationState(locationState);
49      }
50      // get game player states and add them to game state
51      Collection gamePlayers = getPlayers();
52      Iterator gamePlayersIteration = gamePlayers.iterator();
53      while(gamePlayersIteration.hasNext())
54      {
55          Player player = (Player)gamePlayersIteration.next();
56          PlayerState playerState = player.marshallState();
57          gameState.addPlayerState(playerState);
58      }
59      // set the duration remaining in the game
60      gameState.setDuration(getGameDuration());
61      // set the throne room
62      Location throneRoom = getThroneRoom();
63      gameState.setThroneRoom(new LocationState(throneRoom));
64      //........
65      return gameState;
66  }
67
68  public synchronized void Game.unMarshallGame(
                              GameState gameState)
69  {
70      Collection gameLocations = getLocations();
71      Collection locationsStates = gameState.getPlayersStates();
72      Iterator gameLocationsIterator = gameLocations.iterator();
73      Iterator locationsStatesIterator =
                locationsStates.iterator();
74
75      while(gameLocationsIterator.hasNext())
76      {
77          Location location = (Location)gameLocationsIterator.next();
78          while(locationsStatesIterator.hasNext())
79          {
80          LocationState locationState =
81              (LocationState)locationsStatesIterator.next();
```

```
82          if(location.getName().equals(locationState.getName()))
83             {  location.unMarshallState(locationState);      }
84          }
85       }
86
87       Collection gamePlayers = getPlayers();
88       Collection playerStates = gameState.getLocationsStates();
89       Iterator gamePlayersIterator = gamePlayers.iterator();
90       Iterator playerStatesIterator = playerStates.iterator();
91
92       while(gamePlayersIterator.hasNext())
93       {
94          Player player = (Player)gameLocationsIterator.next();
95          while(playerStatesIterator.hasNext())
96          {
97             PlayerState playerState =
98                   (PlayerState)playerStatesIterator.next();
99             if(player.getName().equals(playerState.getName()))
100            {  player.unMarshallState(playerState); }
101         }
102      }
103 }
104
105 public PlayerState Player.marshallState()
106 {
107    PlayerState playerState = new PlayerState(this);
108    return playerState;
109 }
110
111 public void Player.unMarshallState(PlayerState playerState)
112 { update(playerState); }
113
114 public LocationState Location.marshallState()
115 {
116    LocationState locationState = new LocationState(this);
117    return locationState;
118 }
119
120 public void Location.unMarshallState(
121              LocationState locationState)
121 { update(locationState); }
122
```

```
123  public synchronized void GameAdmin.checkGamesAvailable()
124  {
125      Collection activeGames = marshallActiveGames();
126      crystalGamesAvailable(activeGames);
127  }
128
129  // Pointcuts
130  abstract pointcut newGameAdmin(GameAdmin gameAdmin);
131  abstract pointcut joinGame(Player player);
132  abstract pointcut pStateChange(Player player);
133  abstract pointcut lStateChange(Location location);
134
135  // Advice
136  after(Player player) returning: joinGame(player)
137  {
138      Game gamePlayerIsPlaying = player.getGame();
139      gamePlayerIsPlaying.fullGameStateRequest(
140                          gamePlayerIsPlaying.getName());
141  }
142  after(Player player)returning: pStateChange(player)
143  {
144      PlayerState playerState = player.marshallState();
145      Game game = player.getGame();
146      GameComms gameComms = game.getGameComms();
147      gameComms.publishPlayerState(playerState);
148  }
149  after(Location location)returning: lStateChange(location)
150  {
151      LocationState locationState = location.marshallState();
152      Game game = location.getGame();
153      GameComms gameComms = game.getGameComms();
154      gameComms.publishLocationState(locationState);
155
156  }
157  after(GameAdmin gameAdmin)returning: newGameAdmin(gameAdmin)
158  {
159      Thread checkAvailableGameThread = new Thread(gameAdmin);
160      checkAvailableGameThread.start();
161  }
162  }
```

Concrete Aspect

Abstract aspects must be specified concretely to be instantiated and to operate. Part of specifying the concrete aspect is defining the joinpoints where the advice should happen. To do this, each abstract pointcut declared in the aspect must be made concrete. Since each abstract point-cut corresponds to a template operation in the design model, you can tell which base operations should become concrete pointcuts from the matching specification in the bind[] attachment, ordered in the same way as the template box on the crosscutting theme. Mapping the bind[] specification for the **P2PCommunication** crosscutting theme to a concrete aspect is, again, similar to that described for **track-energy**. Referring back to Figure 6-26, the bind[] specification was:

```
bind[ < Player.joinGame()>
       < Player.{incrementCrystals(), addCrystals(),
                 decrementCrystals(), addMagicItem(),
                 deleteMagicItem() } >
       < Location.{setCrystals(), takeCrystals() } >
       < GameAdmin.GameAdmin()> ]
```

As shown in Listing 7–4, the concrete pointcuts capture the execution of the concrete operations and expose the target object and arguments of each.

Listing 7–4 *P2PCommunication Concrete Aspect*

```
1    public aspect ConcreteP2PCommunication extends
                  P2PCommunication {
2
3        pointcut newGameAdmin(GameAdmin gameAdmin):
                  this(gameAdmin) &&
4                 execution(GameAdmin.new(..));
5
6        pointcut joinGame(Player player): this(player) &&
7                 execution(* Player.joinGame(..));
8
9        pointcut pStateChange(Player player): this(player) &&
10               (execution(* Player.incrementCrystals(..)) ||
11                execution(* Player.decrementCrystals(..)) ||
```

```
12                 execution(* Player.addCrystals(..)) ||
13                 execution(* Player.addMagicItem(..)) ||
14                 execution(* Player.deleteMagicItem(..))) ;
15
16      pointcut lStateChange(Location location): this(location) &&
17                 (execution(* Location.setCrystals(..)) ||
18                 execution(* Location.takeCrystals(..)));
19    }
```

Base Themes

In the Crystal Game design, we have multiple themes that are base themes, in addition to the crosscutting themes. This appears to contrast somewhat with the AspectJ model of a single base. However, it is possible to maintain the symmetrical base-theme separation using AspectJ's intertype declaration facilities. To achieve this, for each base theme, you implement aspects that contain intertype declarations for the structure and behavior defined in the theme. Each such aspect will be different from the aspects we've looked at so far in that it will not contain any pointcuts or advice, as there is no crosscutting behavior. You then specify a "base" program with skeleton definitions of the relevant classes, and specify concrete classes to which the intertype declarations in the aspects will be added. See Figure 7–2 for an illustration for the **start**, **enter-location** and **duel** themes.

Each theme is modularized into its own namespace, with an aspect for each class's intertype declarations. Themes that work with the same classes each have an aspect for that class's intertype declaration in its corresponding namespace. Listings 7–5, 7–6, and 7–7 illustrate the methods' signatures[5] and attributes that are relevant for the `Player` class in the **start**, **enter-location** and **duel** themes, with Listing 7–8 illustrating the stub `Game.Player` class.

---

[5] Method code excluded for brevity.

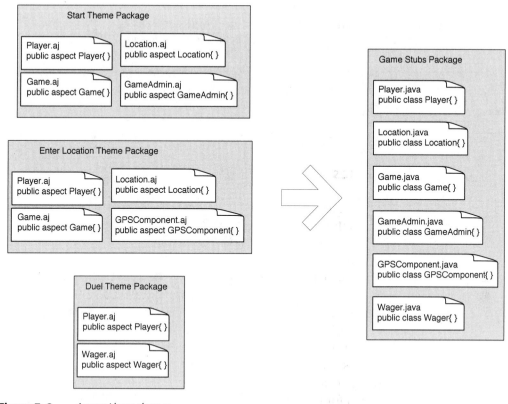

Figure 7–2   *AspectJ base themes.*

Listing 7–5 *Start Theme Player*

```
1    public aspect Player
2    {
4        private String Game.Player.name;
5        private String Game.Player.ipAddress;
6        private Location Game.Player.location;
7        private Game Game.Player.game;
8
9        public void Game.Player.setPlayerslocation(
                    Location location)
10       public Game.Player.new(String name)
11       public String Game.Player.getName()
```

```
12      public Game Game.Player.getGame()
13      public Location Game.Player.getLocation()
14      public void Game.Player.joinGame(Game game)
15  }
```

Listing 7–6 *Enter-Location Theme Player*

```
1   public aspect Player {
2       private GPSComponent Game.Player.gpsComponent;
3
4       public void Game.Player.setLocation(Location location)
5       public Collection Game.Player.checkOtherPlayers()
6       public void Game.Player.takeCrystals()
7       public void Game.Player.takeMagicItems()
8       public void Game.Player.setMagicItem(MagicItem item)
9       public void Game.Player.setMagicItems(Collection magicItems)
10      public void Game.Player.newLocation(Location location)
11  }
```

Listing 7–7 *Duel Theme Player*

```
1   public aspect Player
2   {
3       private int Game.Player.crystals;
4       private boolean Game.Player.crystalsOffered;
5       private boolean Game.Player.wagerAccepted;
6       private boolean Game.Player.wagerAgreed;
7       private boolean Game.Player.finishedRecieved;
8       private String Game.Player.rockPaperScissors;
9       private Collection Game.Player.magicItems =
                new LinkedList();
10
11      public void Game.Player.getMagicItems()
12      public String Game.Player.getRockPaperScissors()
13      public int Game.Player.getCrystals()
14      public void Game.Player.duel()
15      public void Game.Player.duelLoser()
```

```
16       public void Game.Player.addCrystals(int numberOfCrystals)
17       public void Game.Player.decrementCrystals()
18       public void Game.Player.incrementCrystals()
19       public void Game.Player.addMagicItem(MagicItem magicItem)
20       public void Game.Player.deleteMagicItem(MagicItem magicItem)
21       public void Game.Player.updateRPS(String rockPaperScissors)
22       public void Game.Player.magicSelected(MagicItem magicItem)
23       public void Game.Player.wagerTwoCrystals()
24       public void Game.Player.wagerMagicItem(MagicItem magicItem)
25       public void Game.Player.wagerTwoMagicItems
26          (MagicItem firstMagicItem, MagicItem firstMagicItem)
27       public Wager Game.Player.wagerCrystal()
28       public boolean Game.Player.wagerAccepted(Wager wager)
29       public String Game.Player.duelRevealRPS
30          (Player player, String rpsSelection)
31   }
```

Listing 7–8 *Player (in Game Project)*

```
1    public class Player
2    {
4        // empty stub class into which the aspect intertype
5        // declarations are woven
6    }
```

You cannot have clashing method or attribute names in the different aspects to be woven with the same base class. We had one example in the game: the `duel()` method, which was defined in both the **enter-location** and the **duel** themes. If this occurs, then you must decide whether the methods are actually different and therefore could be renamed to avoid a clash or whether the method is really the same and therefore should be implemented in only one theme's namespace. The Theme/UML design guides us in the decision here, as the composition specification that includes **duel** and **enter-location** (refer to Figure 6–21) states that the `duel()` method in the **duel** theme should override the one in the **enter-location** theme. Because of this, we provide the implementation of the `duel()` method in the `Duel` project.

Taking this approach to intertype declarations for themes, you will have a different namespace for every theme in your design. This has the advantage of giving you traceability from your requirements to your Theme/Doc and Theme/UML models through to your code.

Alternatively, you could work with a design made up of the composition of base themes, and apply standard object-oriented programming techniques. In this case, you end up with a set of standard object-oriented classes that have the different themes tangled together. This is the base to which the crosscutting aspects will be applied as we have already seen.

AspectWerkz

AspectWerkz[6] describes itself as a "dynamic, lightweight, and high-performant AOP framework for Java." Its AOP model is deeply based on the AspectJ model. It provides capabilities for runtime weaving through bytecode manipulation. Though the general model is similar to AspectJ's, aspect expression is different in that aspects, advice, and intertype declarations are written in plain Java, with aspect definitions defined using either XML or annotations. Here, we go the annotations route for two reasons. First, at the time of writing, it seems that annotations in Java are increasing in popularity (as manifest by their introduction to the Java language in Version 1.5), and second, we think that they are more accessible than the XML representations of aspects.

If you've dipped directly into this section without reading about how to get to AspectJ from Theme/UML, then we recommend that you review the AspectJ section. From the perspective of mapping Theme/UML to AspectWerkz, the similarities between the two models are such that the basic steps turn out to be correspondingly similar, with similar reasons for making the various implementation choices. For this reason, we take the approach of illustrating AspectWerkz's syntax here and also highlighting the interesting differences between it and AspectJ.

---

[6] http://aspectwerkz.codehaus.org/.

As we did with AspectJ, we look at the AspectWerkz approach by examining the implementation of a crosscutting theme from the Crystal Game, **track-energy**.

Track-energy

As a general policy for mapping to code from Theme/UML, we make an effort to provide the same kinds of encapsulations as were illustrated in the designs. As such, we like the idea of making the crosscutting theme code reusable by making it an abstract aspect and using a concrete aspect to represent the bindings to the base code. This worked well for us with AspectJ, and we take the same approach with AspectWerkz.

In general, plain Java is used to write code in AspectWerkz. In addition, a library of classes is provided that implements the AOP model that you can use primarily for introspection purposes.

Abstract Aspect

An abstract aspect is written as an abstract class, as follows:

```
import org.codehaus.aspectwerkz.joinpoint.JoinPoint;
abstract class TrackEnergy {
// aspect code goes here.
}
```

Intertype Declarations

Intertype declarations in AspectWerkz are dealt with as inner classes and interfaces. The EnergyEntityI and GameI interfaces to match the classes in the **track-energy** theme are illustrated in Listing 7–9, lines 1 to 8 and 10 to 15, respectively. The Energy class in the **track-energy** theme is an active class that periodically responds to an event to lose energy, which is implemented as a thread. This means that the corresponding interface, EnergyEntityI, should extend Java's Runnable interface.

Listing 7–9 *Interfaces for Track-Energy*

```
1    package ie.tcd.cs.dsg.aosd.theme.game;
2
3    public interface EnergyEntityI extends Runnable {
4       public void setChangeAmount(int changeAmount);
5       public void changeEnergy(int changeAmount);
6       public void loseEnergy();
7       public GameI getGame();
8    }
9
10   package ie.tcd.cs.dsg.aosd.theme.game;
11
12   public interface GameI {
13      boolean isPlayerInLocation();
14      void getEnergy(String name, EnergyEntityI energyEntity);
15   }
```

Listing 7–10 illustrates the abstract inner classes to capture the structure and behavior defined for the Energy class (lines 1–42) and the Game class (lines 43–61) in the **track-energy** theme. These classes implement the relevant interfaces previously defined, with EnergyAbstract also implementing a run() method for threads. Notice, in particular, that both classes have a variable m_info of type CrossCuttingInfo (lines 3 and 45). In AspectWerkz, the CrossCuttingInfo class has a number of useful methods for introspection on the runtime execution of the system. Particularly for the **track-energy** theme, the concrete aspect classes need to use this object to obtain a reference to the currently executing object at runtime. We have two examples of this in Listing 7–10. The getGame() method in EnergyAbstract calls getMixinTargetInstance() (lines 28–29) to obtain the required instance, as does the isPlayerInLocation() method on line 58. In order to work with a CrossCuttingInfo object, AspectWerkz mandates a constructor that takes one CrossCuttingInfo as its only parameter (see lines 4–5 and 46–47).

Listing 7–10 *Inner Classes for Track-Energy*

```
1  public static abstract class EnergyAbstract implements
                               EnergyEntityI
2  {
```

```
3    protected final CrossCuttingInfo m_info;
4    public EnergyAbstract(final CrossCuttingInfo info) {
5        m_info = info;
6    }
7    // attributes
8    private int duration = 5;
9    private int energyUnit = 10;
10   private int changeAmount = 1;
11   GameI game;
12
13       // methods
14   public GameI getGame()
15   {   return game;  }
16
17   public void setChangeAmount(int a)
18   {   changeAmount = a;  }
19
20   public void changeEnergy(int e)
21   {   energyUnit = energyUnit + e;    }
22
23   public void loseEnergy()
24   {   energyUnit = energyUnit - changeAmount;  }
25
26   public GameI getGame()
27   {
28      EnergyEntityI player =
29           EnergyEntityI)m_info.getMixinTargetInstance(this);
30      GameI game = (GameI)player.getGame();
31      return game;
32   }
33   public void run()
34   {
35      try {
36         loseEnergy();
37         Thread.sleep(5000);
38      } catch (InterruptedException e) {
39         // Log or notify exception occured
40      }
41   }
42 }
43 public static abstract class GameAbstract implements GameI
44 {
45     protected final CrossCuttingInfo m_info;
```

```
46   public GameAbstract(final CrossCuttingInfo info) {
47      m_info = info;
48   }
49   public void getEnergy(String name, EnergyEntityI energyEntity)
50   {
51      if(name.equals("completeWizardErrand"))
52      {  energyEntity.changeEnergy(4);    }
53      else if(name.equals("completeWarriorTest"))
54      {  energyEntity.changeEnergy(3);    }
55      //. . . and so on
56   }
57   public boolean isPlayerInLocation() {
58      GameI game = (GameI)m_info.getMixinTargetInstance(this);
59      return game.isPlayerInLocation();
60   }
61   }
```

Pointcuts and Advice

In AspectWerkz, pointcuts and advice are defined using a combination of annotations for pointcut naming and by enforcing that a JoinPoint object is passed to the advice. The JoinPoint class is part of AspectWerkz and implements the specification of particular points of execution in the code (or joinpoints). Using this instance, you can get static information and runtime type information about the current joinpoint.

The following code illustrates the moveLocation pointcut and the after advice. The annotation @After indicates that the code should be executed after execution of the joinpoint. The pointcut is named as moveLocation directly following the @After annotation. We also see an example of runtime information being requested from the joinPoint instance in the call to getTarget(), which returns the object in which the joinpoint is executing.

```
@After moveLocation
   public void moveLocation(JoinPoint joinPoint)
   {
      EnergyEntityI energyEntity =
      (EnergyEntityI)joinPoint.getTarget();
      GameI game = energyEntity.getGame();
```

```
        if(game.isPlayerInLocation())
        {   energyEntity.setChangeAmount(2);    }
        else
        {   energyEntity.setChangeAmount(1);    }
    }
```

The following code illustrates the remaining two pointcuts and advice for **track-energy**: energyAction and joinGame. These are similar in form to the moveLocation pointcut. You can see how the joinPoint object was used again to get the name of the currently executing method with a call to getSignature().getName().

```
@After energyAction
public void energyAction(JoinPoint joinPoint)
{

    String currentActionName = joinPoint.getSignature().getName();
    EnergyEntityI energyEntity =
                (EnergyEntityI)joinPoint.getTarget();
    GameI game = energyEntity.getGame();
    game.getEnergy(currentActionName, energyEntity);
}

@After joinGame
 public void joinGame(JoinPoint joinPoint)
{
    EnergyEntityI energyEntity =
                (EnergyEntityI)joinPoint.getTarget();
    Thread energyLossThread = new Thread(energyEntity);
    energyLossThread.start();
}
```

Concrete Aspect

Now that we've implemented an abstract class that represents the abstract aspect, we need to provide concrete implementations to capture the bindings defined in the bind[] attachment to the crosscutting theme. In addition to a standard extension of the abstract class, we implement concrete pointcuts, and concrete inner classes.

Concrete Pointcuts

Concrete pointcuts are defined using the @Expression annotation followed directly by a declaration of the pointcut as AspectWerkz type Pointcut. The @Expression annotation has expressiveness similar to AspectJ's in terms of the types of joinpoints that can be defined—in this case, we use the execution of bound methods for each of our concrete pointcuts, as follows:

```
@Expression execution (* Player.joinGame(..))
Pointcut joinGame;

@Expression execution (* Player.setLocation(..))
Pointcut moveLocation;

@Expression execution (* Player.incrementCrystals(..)) ||
      execution (* Player.addCrystals(..)) ||
      execution (* Player.completeWarriorTest(..)) ||
      execution (* Player.completeWizardErrand(..))
Pointcut energyAction;
```

The bind[] attachment on the composition relationship to Theme/UML's **track-energy** theme tells you which concrete methods to use.

Concrete Intertype Declarations

You now need to provide concrete implementations for the abstract inner classes that AspectWerkz uses to provide intertype declarations. The following code shows an implementation of EnergyIntroduction that extends EnergyAbstract and of GameIntroduction that extends GameAbstract. Notice that an @Introduce within annotation specifies that the EnergyIntroduction class should be "introduced" to the base Player class—in other words, EnergyIntroduction's methods and variables are added to the Player class. Another annotation specifies that the GameIntroduction class should be introduced to the base Game class. As they do with AspectJ, the Theme/UML designs help you decide which classes these are by looking at the bind[] attachment (in the case of Player), or by using the class with the same name in the base program (in the case of Game), or by looking at other explicit a composition relationships that indicate matching.

```
@Introduce within(ie.tcd.cs.dsg.aosd.theme.game.Player)
           deploymentModel=perInstance
public static class EnergyIntroduction extends EnergyAbstract {

    public EnergyIntroduction(final CrossCuttingInfo info) {
        super(info);
    }
}
@Introduce within(ie.tcd.cs.dsg.aosd.theme.game.Game)
           deploymentModel=perInstance
public static class GameIntroduction extends GameAbstract {

    public GameIntroduction(final CrossCuttingInfo info) {
        super(info);
    }
}
```

We now have all we need to provide concrete implementations for the aspect's abstract class, as illustrated in its entirety in Listing 7–11.

Listing 7–11 *Concrete Aspect for Track-Energy*

```
package ie.tcd.cs.dsg.aosd.theme.game;
import org.codehaus.aspectwerkz.CrossCuttingInfo;
import org.codehaus.aspectwerkz.Pointcut;

public class ConcreteTrackEnergy extends TrackEnergy {

 @Expression execution (* Player.joinGame(..))
 Pointcut joinGame;

 @Expression execution (* Player.setLocation(..))
 Pointcut moveLocation;

 @Expression execution (* Player.incrementCrystals(..)) ||
        execution (* Player.addCrystals(..)) ||
        execution (* Player.completeWarriorTest(..)) ||
        execution (* Player.completeWizardErrand(..))
 Pointcut energyAction;

 @Introduce within(ie.tcd.cs.dsg.aosd.theme.game.Player)
        deploymentModel=perInstance
```

```
public static class EnergyIntroduction extends EnergyAbstract {

    public EnergyIntroduction(final CrossCuttingInfo info) {
        super(info);
    }
}

@Introduce within(ie.tcd.cs.dsg.aosd.theme.game.Game)
         deploymentModel=perInstance
public static class GameIntroduction extends GameAbstract {

    public GameIntroduction(final CrossCuttingInfo info) {
        super(info);
    }
}
}
```

Deployment Descriptor

Finally, an XML deployment descriptor is required to deploy the aspect classes into your system. Following is an example for the Crystal Game. Notice the order in which aspects are specified—this is similar to AspectJ's declare precedence list in that crosscutting behavior from ConcreteP2PCommunication is executed before any from ConcreteTrackEnergy.

```
<!DOCTYPE aspectwerkz PUBLIC
"-//AspectWerkz//DTD 1.0//EN"
"http://aspectwerkz.codehaus.org/dtd/aspectwerkz.dtd">
<aspectwerkz>
<system id="CrystalGame">
    <package name="ie.tcd.cs.dsg.aosd.theme.game">
        <aspect class="ConcreteP2PCommunication"
                        deployment-model="perClass"/>
        <aspect class="ConcreteTrackEnergy"
                        deployment-model="perClass"/>
    </package>
</system>
</aspectwerkz>
```

Concern Manipulation Environment

The CME[7] provides a set of open, extensible components and a set of tools that promote aspect-oriented software development throughout the software lifecycle. It has two main goals. The first goal is to provide an open, integrated development environment (IDE) for those using AOSD across the lifecycle and to allow developers to use different AOSD approaches in an integrated manner. The second goal is to promote the rapid development of new tools supporting AOSD at any stage of the software lifecycle.

For our purposes in this section, we are interested in the first goal—that which includes support for an applications programmer in the separation of the code for different pieces of functionality and the specification of how to compose them. The CME's open framework provides support for both the asymmetric and symmetric schools of AOSD. In this section, we look at mapping Theme/UML to the CME's symmetric AOSD model. Theme/UML was based on the origins of the CME, and so it is no surprise that mapping to the CME is very straightforward.

For all themes, whether they are base or aspect, you implement the structure and behavior defined in the theme in standard Java. You then specify the composition requirements in a separate file that captures the specifications in the Theme/UML composition relationships. We look first at composing base themes and then at composing aspect themes.

Base Themes

Figure 7–3 illustrates the CME mappings for base themes. As with both base and aspect themes, the structure and behavior of each theme is captured separately. In our implementation of these examples, we used the Eclipse[8] IDE, and put each theme in a different Eclipse project. Each project contains classes to support the design. The CME composition specification file cap-

---

[7] http://www.eclipse.org/cme.

[8] http://www.eclipse.org/.

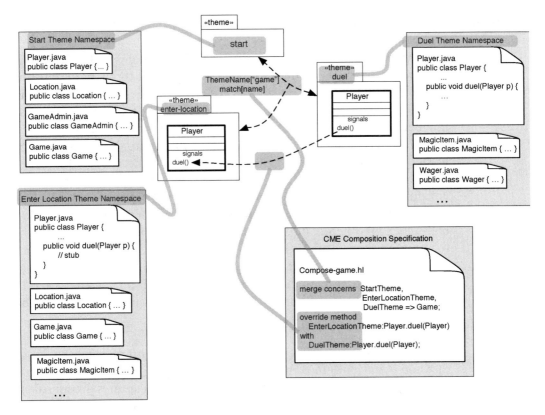

Figure 7–3 *The CME and base themes.*

tures the composition relationships from Theme/UML, with `merge` and `override` keywords capturing the integration possibilities.[9]

Figure 7–3 uses the Theme composition design from Chapter 6. We also use this Theme composition design to illustrate the CME in more detail with a subset of the code.

---

[9] CME can work with themes separated into either packages or projects. Projects provide a stronger separation, making it easier for CME to identify composition namespaces.

Standard Java for Base Themes

In the composition design represented in Figure 7–3, three game themes are composed—**start**, **enter-location**, and **duel**. Each design theme should be implemented in a different Java namespace. In general, the process of moving from designs to code in the CME is no different than how you would move to any Java implementation from a standard UML design. Here, we illustrate the structure of the Player class for each of the themes.[10] Note that you can call all the classes Player, since they are in their own namespaces. Listing 7–12 shows the structure of the Player class from the Start project, Listing 7–13 shows the structure of the Player class from the EnterLocation project, and Listing 7–14 shows the structure of the Player class from the Duel project.

Listing 7–12 *Project Start Game.Player*

```
public class Player
{
  private String name;
  private String ipAddress;
  private Location location;
  private Game game;

  public Player (String name) { ... }
  public String getName() { ... }
  public Game getGame() { ... }
  public Location getLocation() { ... }
  public void joinGame(Game game) { ... }
}
```

Listing 7–13 *Project Enter-Location Game.Player*

```
public class Player {
  private GPSComponent gpsComponent;
  private Game game;
```

---

[10] You will have similar class implementations for all the classes in the theme designs contained within the theme namespaces.

```
   private Location location;
   private Collection magicItems;
   private MagicItem magicItem;

   public void setLocation(Location location)  { ... }
   public Collection checkOtherPlayers()  { ... }
   public void duel() {
      throw new ImplementationNotProvidedError(); }
   public void takeCrystals()  { ... }
   public void takeMagicItems()  { ... }
   public void setMagicItem(MagicItem item)  { ... }
   public void setMagicItems(Collection magicItems)  { ... }
   public void newLocation(Location location) { ... }
}
```

Listing 7–14 *Project Duel Game.Player*

```
public class Player
{
  private int crystals;
  private boolean crystalsOffered;
  private boolean wagerAccepted;
  private boolean wagerAgreed;
  private boolean finishedRecieved;
  private String rockPaperScissors;
  private Collection magicItems = new LinkedList();

  public void getMagicItems() { ... }
  public String getRockPaperScissors() { ... }
  public int getCrystals() { ... }
  public void duel() { ... }
  public void duelLoser() { ... }
  public void addCrystals(int numberOfCrystals) { ... }
  public void decrementCrystals() { ... }
  public void incrementCrystals() { ... }
  public void addMagicItem(MagicItem magicItem) { ... }
  public void deleteMagicItem(MagicItem magicItem) { ... }
  public void updateRPS(String rockPaperScissors) { ... }
  public void magicSelected(MagicItem magicItem) { ... }
  public void wagerTwoCrystals() { ... }
```

```
public void wagerMagicItem(MagicItem magicItem) { ... }
public void wagerTwoMagicItems(MagicItem firstMagicItem,
    MagicItem secondMagicItem) { ... }
public Wager Player.wagerCrystal() { ... }
public boolean Player.wagerAccepted(Wager wager) { ... }
public String Player.duelRevealRPS (Player player,
                                String rpsSelection) { ... }

}
```

There is one interesting point to note when implementing base themes separately. There may have been some operations in the Theme/UML designs whose structures were included to allow the individual theme designer to reason about them without actually providing a detailed design for such operations. The designer of the theme would have known that the operation was to be provided in a separate theme. The duel() operation in the **enter-location** theme is a good example of this. As we discussed in Chapter 5, the **enter-location** theme provides a design for knowing when a player is in a game location. This is important for knowing whether a player can pick up crystals and also whether a player should get involved in a duel. We decided in Chapter 5 that it made sense for the **enter-location** theme to "mark" when dueling should happen, but not provide a design for the actual dueling, since it appears in the **duel** theme. This results in a method signature for duel() in the Player class in the EnterLocation project.

This leaves us with a question of how you can work with the EnterLocation project separately. The CME treats a method whose body begins with throwing an ImplementationNotProvidedError as indicating that the real implementation will be provided by another concern (see Listing 7–13).

Composition Specification

Now that the base themes are implemented, each in its own Eclipse project, we address how to compose them. The two composition relationships in the Theme/UML design illustrated in Figure 7–3 indicate that

- the three themes should be merged into a theme called "**game**," and matching is by name.

- the duel() operation in **enter-location**'s Player class should be overridden by the duel() operation in **duel**'s Player class

The CME provides a merge concerns construct that can be used to specify merging themes. For our example, this results in:

merge concerns StartTheme, EnterLocationTheme, DuelTheme **=>** Game;

The default for this specification is to match code elements by name. Notice that you can name the composed result using =>.

Override integration is similarly directly supported by the CME with its override method with construct. For the duel() operation, the integration specification looks like this:

override method
    EnterLocationTheme:Player.duel(Player)
with
    DuelTheme:Player.duel(Player);

The full CME composition specification for the Theme/UML design is illustrated in Listing 7–15.

Listing 7–15 *Merge Start, Enter-Location, and Duel Themes*

```
1 merge concerns StartTheme, EnterLocationTheme, DuelTheme => Game;
2
3 override method
4       EnterLocationTheme:Player.duel(Player)
5 with
6       DuelTheme:Player.duel(Player);
```

Aspect Themes

Aspect themes are different than base themes from a composition perspective because some subset of their behavior is triggered by behavior in a different theme. The CME provides additional constructs that allow you to

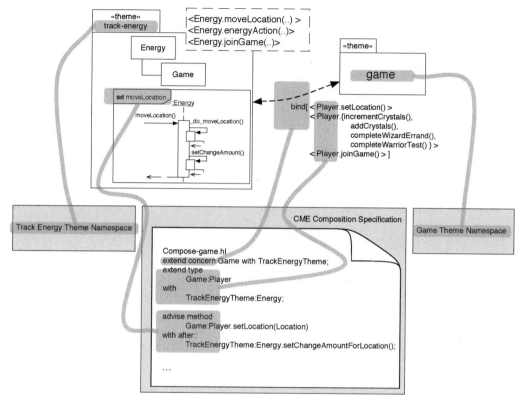

Figure 7–4   *The CME and aspect themes.*

specify the methods in a base theme that trigger the methods in an aspect theme. Figure 7–4 illustrates the mappings from a Theme/UML aspect theme to the CME's composition specification.

Standard Java for Aspect Themes

In the game, we identified two aspect themes—**track-energy** and **P2PCommunication**. As with base themes, these themes should be implemented with standard Java in their own namespaces, using the standard process of moving to any Java implementation from a standard UML design. Listing 7–16 illustrates the code for the `Energy` class from the `TrackEnergy` project. As you can see from the first line, `Energy` is implemented as an abstract class because it is expected that it will be composed with a class in a base theme that triggers behavior here. It also implements the Runnable interface to handle the energy tracking thread. The remainder of the code provides implementations for the rest of the design.

Listing 7–16 *Track-Energy Theme Energy Class*

```
public abstract class Energy implements Runnable
{
  // methods expected in base theme
  public abstract Game getGame();

  // attributes
  int duration = 5;
  int energyUnit = 10;
  int changeAmount = 1;

  public void setChangeAmount(int a)
  { changeAmount = a; }

  public void changeEnergy(int e)
  { energyUnit += e; }

  public void loseEnergy()
  { energyUnit -= changeAmount; }

  public void run()
  {
      Game game = getGame();
      while(game.isActive()) {
         try {
                   loseEnergy(); Thread.sleep(5000);
         } catch (InterruptedException e) {
         // Log or notify exception occurred
         }
      }
```

```
}
// advice methods
public void setChangeAmountForLocation()
{
  Game game = (Game)getGame();
  if(game.isPlayerInLocation())
  { setChangeAmount(2); }
  else
  { setChangeAmount(1); }
}
private void changeEnergyForIncrementCrystalsAction()
{ changeEnergy(1); }

private void changeEnergyForAddCrystalsAction()
{ changeEnergy(2); }

private void changeEnergyForCompleteWizardErrandAction()
{ changeEnergy(4); }

private void changeEnergyForCompleteWarriorTestAction()
{ changeEnergy(3); }

private void joinGame()
{
  // Starting new energy loss thread
  Thread energyLossThread = new Thread(this);
  energyLossThread.start();
}
}
```

Listing 7–17 illustrates some of the structure of the code for the **P2PCommunication** theme. The theme contains implementations (not illustrated) for each class used in the theme.

Listing 7–17 *P2PCommunicationTheme.Game*

```
public class Game
{
  private GameComms Game.gameComms = new GameComms();

  public GameComms getGameComms(Game game) { ... }
  public GameComms getGameComms() { ... }
  public void Game.fullGameState(GameState gameState) { ... }
  public void Game.fullGameStateRequest() { ... }
  public void update(State state) { ... }
  public void unmarshallGame() { ... }
  public GameState marshallGame() { ... }
}
public class Player
{
  public void playerJoinGame(Game) { ... }
  public void stateChange() { ... }
  public void update(State) { ... }
  public void unmarshallPlayer() { ... }
  public PlayerState marshallPlayer() { ... }
}
public class Location
{
  public void stateChange() { ... }
  public void update(State) { ... }
  public void unmarshallLocation() { ... }
  public LocationState marshallLocation() { ... }
}
public class GameAdmin implements Runnable
{
  public void run() { ... }
  public void checkAvailableGames() { ... }
  public void newGameAdmin() { ... }
}
```

Composition Specification

Again, now that the aspect themes are implemented, each in its own
Eclipse project, we address how to compose them with the base themes.
The composition relationship with bind[] attachment, illustrated in

Figure 7–4, indicates that the **game** theme should be composed with the **track-energy** theme. This is captured with the CME construct `extend concern with` as follows:

extend concern Game **with** TrackEnergyTheme;

The difference between the `extend concern with` construct and the `merge` construct (used for the base themes earlier) is equivalent to the difference between composing template classes with classes that contain triggers and merging nontemplate classes. In the former, the template class is merged with each triggering class separately, while in the latter, there is one merged class in the result (see Chapter 6). In the CME, the `extend concern with` construct provides for extending many different triggering classes with behavior, while the `merge` construct composes classes to a single result.

There is behavior in the `Energy` class that is triggered by behavior outside the **track-energy** theme as indicated by the templates in the template box. The `bind[]` attachment to the composition relationship lists the `Player` class in the **game** theme as containing all the triggers for the templates. In the CME, `Energy` is therefore seen as an extension to the base theme's class (i.e., **game**'s `Player` class) which is captured with its `extend type with` construct, as follows:

extend type
    Game:Player
with
    TrackEnergyTheme:Energy

You would add more of these constructs if there were other classes in the `bind[]` attachment that contained triggers for the templates in the template box.

Finally, we need to specify the methods that trigger the aspect's behavior, and indicate when that behavior should be executed. Again, we find a direct correlation to Theme/UML in the CME's constructs. The CME provides an `advise method` construct that you can use to capture the concrete method in the base theme that should replace the template, as specified in the `bind[]` attachment.

The first example for **track-energy** is specifying that the `setLocation()` method (first in the `bind[]` attachment) should trigger the `moveLocation` template implementation. From the implementation of the **track-energy** theme, the method that implements the actual behavior to be executed was named appropriately for that implementation and called `setChangeAmountForLocation()`. This naming is reasonable in the implementation, as there is no need to indicate a generic intent for appropriate kinds of triggers, as was the case in naming the `moveLocation` template in the design. The resulting CME specification is as follows:

advise method
```
        Game:Player.setLocation(Location)
```
with after:: TrackEnergyTheme:Energy.setChangeAmountForLocation();

Notice that the `with` part of the `advise method` construct indicates that the crosscutting behavior should be executed after the trigger method. This is as specified in the Theme/UML sequence diagram.

`TrackEnergy` defines two more template parameters: `energyAction()` and `joinGame()`, both of whose concrete bindings can be specified in a similar manner. For example, mapping to `energyAction()` is as follows:

advise method
```
        (Game:Player.incrementCrystals(..) ||
        Game:Player.addCrystals(..) ||
        Game:Player.completeWarriorTest(..) ||
        Game:Player.completeWizardErrand(..))
```
with after:: TrackEnergyTheme:Energy.changeEnergyForAction
```
        (String = $methodName);
```

There are two interesting points to note here. First, you can list multiple triggers to be advised, separated with || notation. Second, the CME allows you to reason about the metaproperties of an executing method—for example, a method's name with $methodName.

Listing 7–18 illustrates the full composition specification for the **TrackEnergy** theme.

Listing 7–18 *Track-Energy Theme Composition Specification*

```
extend concern Game with TrackEnergyTheme;

extend type
     Game:Player
with
     TrackEnergyTheme:Energy;

advise method
     Game:Player.setLocation(Location)
with after::TrackEnergyTheme:Energy.setChangeAmountForLocation();

advise method
     (Game:Player.incrementCrystals(..) ||
     Game:Player.addCrystals(..) ||
     Game:Player.completeWarriorTest(..) ||
     Game:Player.completeWizardErrand(..))
with after::TrackEnergyTheme:Energy.changeEnergyForAction
     (String = $methodName);

advise method
     Game:Player.joinGame(Game)
with after::TrackEnergyTheme:Energy.joinGame();
```

For your interest, Listing 7–19 illustrates the CME composition specification for the **P2PCommunication** theme. To remind you, the bind[] specification from Chapter 6 is as follows:

```
bind[ < Player.joinGame()>
      < Player.{incrementCrystals(), addCrystals(),
              decrementCrystals(), addMagicItem(),
              deleteMagicItem() } >
      < Location.{ setCrystals(), takeCrystals() } >
      < GameAdmin.GameAdmin()> ]
```

In this example, there are three different classes in the base theme that have triggers for the crosscutting behavior—Player, Location, and GameAdmin. Lines 3 to 6 illustrate an extend type with construct for the Game concern level. Each of the three lower level extensions required for `Player`, `Location`, and `GameAdmin` are implied by this concern-level one because the class names are the same in both concerns. This is equivalent to intertype declarations for these classes. Lines 8 to 26 list the advise method specifications that indicate when the crosscutting behavior should be executed, as specified by their respective sequence diagrams (see Chapter 5).

Listing 7-19 *P2PCommunication Theme Composition Specification*

```
1    extend concern Game with P2PCommunicationTheme;
2
3    extend type
4       Game:Game
5    with
6       P2PCommunicationTheme:Game;
7
8    advise method
9       Game:GameAdmin.new(..)
10   with after::P2PCommunicationTheme:GameAdmin.newGameAdmin();
11
12   advise method
13      Game:Player.joinGame(Game)
14   with after::P2PCommunicationTheme: Player.playerJoinGame();
15
16   advise method
17      Game:Location.setCrystals(..)
18   with after::P2PCommunicationTheme: Location.stateChange();
19
20   advise method
21      (Game:Player.incrementCrystals(..)) ||
22      Game:Player.decrementCrystals ||
23      Game:Player.addCrystals(..) ||
24      Game:Player.addMagicItem(..)) ||
25      Game:Player.deleteMagicItem(..)))
26   with after::P2PCommunicationTheme: Player.stateChange();
```

Summary

In this chapter, we explained how to map your Theme/UML designs to different AOP approaches. AspectJ and AspectWerkz demonstrate considerable similarity, and the same general approach applies to both. If you use a different AOP language whose principles are rooted in AspectJ, then you will find these useful, since it is likely that the general principles of mapping from Theme/UML also apply to the language you use. At a high level, the CME also demonstrates some similarity, though it is more straightforward to maintain the separation of the base themes because the Theme approach is modeled on the same principles as the CME.

In the next two chapters, we work through two case studies to further illustrate the Theme approach. For each, starting from a requirements specification, we work through aspect-oriented analysis with Theme/Doc and aspect-oriented design with Theme/UML.

8

Case Study: Phone Features

Up to this point in the book we've been primarily working off the main example of the Crystal Game. Now, we depart from the Crystal Game example for the sake of further illustration. This chapter and the next provide small case studies showing how the Theme approach can be applied in different situations. In this chapter, we look at a set of simple phone features and their composition. This is a scaled-down version of what you would find in the real world. Of course, telephony systems have many interacting features; here we have limited the number of interactions between features so that we can comprehensively describe the case study system. We've also chosen to focus not on features related to call-handling (like call waiting, call forwarding, etc.), but on broader features, specifically, voice call, short messaging service (SMS), a media player, and a game application, all provided on a mobile phone handset.

Analyzing Requirements and Identifying Initial Themes

Once again, we have a set of numbered requirements (given in Table 8–1). This time, the requirements are broken up explicitly by feature: menu, alerts and rings, voice call, SMS, game, and a media player feature. We've

Table 8–1 *List of Phone Feature Requirements*

Feature	Requirements
Menu	R1: The **menu** consists of several options: make a **voice call**, write an **SMS**, use the **media player**, play a **game**.
	R2: A user can **scroll** through the **menu** and select an item to **start**.
Alerts and Rings	R3: **Ring**ing is used to **signal** an incoming **voice call**.
	R4: **Alerts** are used to **signal** an incoming **SMS**.
	R5: When **alerts** and **rings** occur, other audio (**media player**, **voice call**, **game sounds**) is momentarily **muted** but not **paused**.
Voice Call	R6: When a **voice call** occurs, other activities (**media player**, **game**, **SMS edit**) are **paused**, and their state **saved**, to be **resumed** when the call ends.
SMS	R7: A user can **send** and **edit** an **SMS** from within the **SMS** application.
Game	R8: A user can **play**, **pause**, **save**, and **exit** a **game** session.
Media Player	R9: The **media player** has several functions: **play audio**, **record audio**, **radio**, **memo play**, and **memo record**.
	R10: The **media player** can **start, stop, pause,** and resume all those functions.

gone through these requirements and bolded the key concepts that we initially believe will be our themes.

A quick look at these theme names flags for us that some of them might be too general. For instance, there are two **save** themes, which are behaviorally quite different (saving a game, from R8, and saving the state of a preempted activity, from R6). It would be inappropriate to group requirements related to both senses of **save**. To remedy ambiguities such as these, you can split the themes to make them more specific. Table 8–2 lists the new theme names.

To complete the split, we also have to attach the requirements with the correct themes, since the lexical matching will not link the requirements to the new theme names. The requirement numbers in parentheses show the requirement attached to each new theme.

Table 8–2 *Themes Names Split into More Specific Names*

Original	Split Themes
save	**audio-save** (R6), **game-save** (R8)
pause	**audio-pause** (R6), **game-pause** (R8), **media-pause** (R10)
start	**media-start** (R10), **menu-start** (R2)
play	**media-play** (R10), **game-play** (R8)
signal	**signal call** (R3), **signal sms** (R4)

Refining the Themes

Now that we have an initial set of themes, we can look at the theme-relationship view.

Figure 8–1 shows the relationship view with the new theme names. You can see that the requirements are attached to the themes, as specified in Table 8–2. In Figure 8–1, you can also see that we've clustered and named likely groups of themes (shown with dashed outlines). There are also three requirements that are shared between the various clusters: R1, R5, and R6. These are expanded in Figure 8–1. Next, we make the clusters into groups. For instance, **menu-start** and **scroll** are both grouped under the **menu** theme. We also make the choice to group **ring** with **voice call** and **alert** with **sms**.

There are also four themes that didn't have an obvious group, and so weren't clustered in Figure 8–1: **mute, audio-pause, audio-save,** and **audio-resume**. These are all more or less related to the concept of preemption of audio activity when some other behavior occurs. After looking at R5 and R6 (which both discuss situations in which another activity is preempted based on a certain trigger), we decide to group the **audio-pause** theme with the other **audio** themes. Finally, as considered above, we introduce a new theme, **preempt**, which better captures the spirit of the **audio** requirements.

Looking at Figure 8–1, you'll notice that three of the clusters (Media Player, Game, and Menu) have only one main theme that relates to the other themes through shared requirements. The **game** theme, for instance, is the only theme in the Game cluster that is linked to any of the expanded requirements. The same holds true for the **media player** theme in the Media

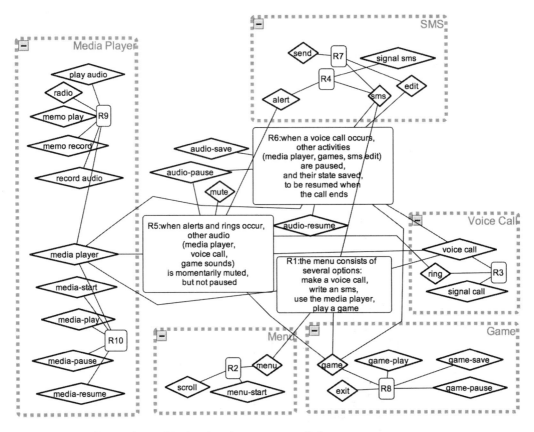

Figure 8–1   *Theme-relationship view (requirements expanded).*

Player cluster, and the **menu** theme in the Menu cluster. However, in the SMS and Voice Call clusters, there are two themes that relate to the expanded requirements. In the SMS cluster, **alert** is externally linked; in the Voice Call cluster, **ring** is also externally linked. **alert** and **ring** represent the triggers of the audio preemption behavior. When we were deciding how to group the themes, we simply translated the clusters into groups directly. However, we could have chosen to group **ring** and **alert** with **preempt** instead of with **voice call** and **sms**, respectively. This decision does have an impact on the design. When we go over the **preempt** theme design, we discuss other options for this grouping.

In the end, we arrive at six major themes, as detailed in Table 8–3.

Table 8–3 *Themes and Their Subthemes*

Main Theme Name	Subthemes
game	game-play, game-pause, game-save
media player	radio, play audio, record audio, memo play, memo record
menu	scroll, select, start
sms	send, edit, signal sms, alert
voice call	signal call, ring
preempt (new theme)	mute, audio-resume, audio-pause, audio-save

Identifying Crosscutting Themes

There are three shared requirements in the set: R1, R5, and R6. They are expanded in Figure 8–2. We now look at each requirement, applying the heuristics for deciding whether they reveal aspect behavior.

R1 reads, *The menu consists of several options: make a voice call, write an SMS, use the media player, play a game.* The first thing to consider is whether the requirement can be split. Since the requirement lists the components of a menu, there is no way to rewrite it to isolate the themes from one another. The second thing to determine is whether one theme dominates the requirement. In this case, the **menu** theme seems to be the dominant requirement, since the requirement lists a set of things that are contained in the menu. Next, we check to see whether the other themes (such as **voice call**) trigger action in the dominant theme, **menu**. This check fails—there is no trigger relationship described in the requirement. Instead, the relationship between **menu** and the other themes is more of a "has-a" relationship. So, we postpone the requirement and likely design the dominant theme, **menu**, as a concept shared theme.

R5 reads, *When alerts and rings occur, other audio (media player, voice call, game sounds) is momentarily muted, but not paused.* Once again, this requirement cannot be split, but in this case, it's dominated by the behavior related to the **preempt** theme. This requirement also passes the trigger test: **preempt** (actually its subtheme **mute**) is triggered by **alerts** and **rings**, and since this requirement describes more than one situation in which pre-

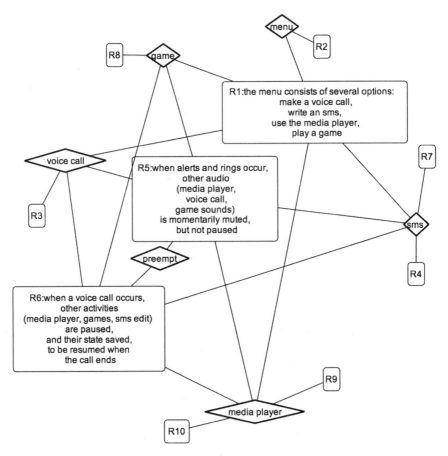

Figure 8–2   *Grouped themes, shared requirements expanded.*

emption is triggered (when both alerts and rings occur), we can conclude that **preempt** is an aspect.

R6 reads, *When a voice call occurs, other activities (media player, games, SMS edit) are paused, and their state saved, to be resumed when the call ends*. Once again, this requirement cannot be split and is dominated by preemption behavior, and also triggers preemption behavior. This requirement describes an additional situation in which preemption is triggered: when a voice call occurs. Once again, **preempt** is an aspect.

Figure 8–3 shows the crosscutting view of the system. You can see the five concept-sharing (or base) themes and the crosscutting theme **preempt**.

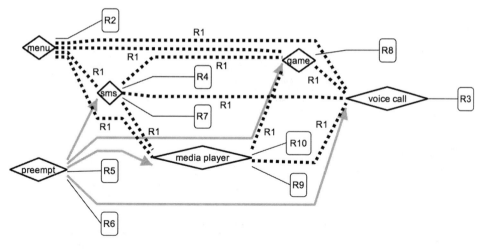

Figure 8–3   *Crosscutting view.*

Designing the Concept Sharing Themes

We can now design the base themes for **sms**, **game**, **voice call**, and **media player**. These themes are quite simple, so we don't need to investigate their individual-theme views to help clarify the structures that should be involved. It's enough just to read the requirements associated with each theme and move quickly to design from there. In straightforward cases like this, it's fine to skip specifying the structure at the Theme/Doc level altogether.

The only interesting base theme is **menu**, which dominated the postponed requirement, R1. The individual view for the **menu** theme is shown in Figure 8–4. R2 describes the main **menu** theme operation. R2's functionality will be modeled within the **menu** theme, whereas the implementation of R1 will likely be spread throughout all five themes. You'll notice that there are no structural nodes in this view—that's because here, too, we chose to skip the step of specifying structural elements this time around. You may have noticed by now that with the exception of the heuristics for aspect identification, the activities available in the Theme/Doc process should be used when convenient and helpful, but are not meant to be religiously adhered to.

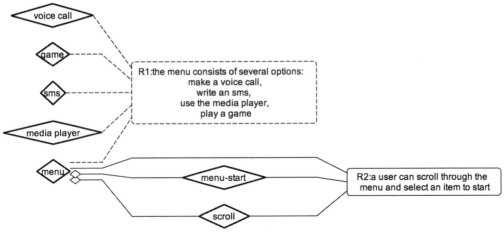

Figure 8–4   *Menu individual-theme view.*

The design for each of the base themes is displayed in Figure 8–5. You can see that we have added an **audible** theme to describe in detail the behavior related to volume. The Audible behavior and the class hierarchy in the **audible** theme could have been repeated in the other themes, but in this case, it's fine to place them in a separate theme. However, if any of the themes were to make explicit use of any of the methods in the Audible class, you would need to provide a minimal specification of those methods in the relevant themes, in anticipation of being composed with the **audible** theme. This minimal specification maintains the completeness of each theme and allows them to be understood in isolation from other themes.

Because we have specified merge integration (as denoted by arrows at each end of the composition relationship), all the themes will simply be merged together and any redundancy removed. For instance, there is a Menu class in each of the themes, with the exception of the **audible** theme. The **menu** theme itself includes only the behavior from R2 (scroll() and select_item()) from the **menu** individual-theme view in Figure 8–4.

The postponed R1 requirement (*the menu consists of several options...*) is not designed as being "owned" by a particular theme. Instead, each theme has its own Menu class that will be merged to the main Menu class (found in the **menu** theme) on composition.

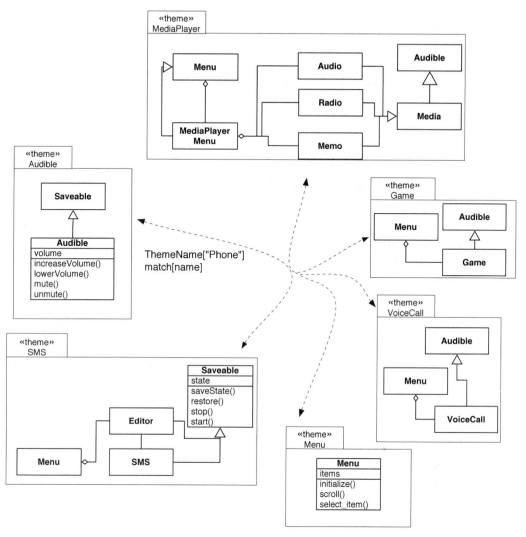

Figure 8–5 *Concept-sharing themes and their merge specifications.*

The **phone** theme is the product of the merge, as specified by the `ThemeName["Phone"]` tag.

You'll probably spot that these themes together would not make a working phone. At this point, that's fine. The requirements that we were given for the phone were not comprehensive enough to allow us to make all the design decisions we needed to in order to arrive at a fully functioning phone. In this case study, we just work with these requirements and assume that the rest of the requirements for actually getting things up and running are forthcoming. They can be added in later. They may motivate changes to these themes or may require new themes of their own. For more discussion on what to do with new requirements, refer to the "Incorporating New Requirements" section in Chapter 4.

Designing the Crosscutting Themes

In this example, we moved from designing our concept-sharing, or base, themes to designing the crosscutting theme, **preempt**. This is not a rigid order. It might be that working with the crosscutting themes prior to designing the base themes is more appropriate or convenient. In most cases, going back and forth a little probably makes sense.

We associated R5 and R6 with the **preempt** theme. Figure 8–6 shows its individual theme view. The only elements fully owned by the **preempt** theme are **mute, audio-save, audio-pause**, and **audio-resume**. The rest are all likely templates from the perspective of this theme. We can once again look at these requirements and consider whether they behaviorally crosscut the base themes. If they do, we can be confident that this theme is appropriate as an aspect. Upon inspection, you can see that if the behavior described in this theme were replaced in the base, there would be duplicated preemption handling in all of the grayed themes.

As you can see in Figure 8–7, each requirement has been captured in its own sequence diagram. The sequence diagram on the left deals with the simple case of muting a sound if a notification is coming through. The design introduces two classes: `HighPriority` and `Preempted`. The sequence diagram on the right deals with pausing activities during a voice call. Of course, the notification and the voice call are represented as templates here, as simply `sound()` and as the `start()` of a `HighPriority` behavior. In the left-hand sequence diagram, the `sound()` method triggers the behavior. `HighPriority.sound()` is bound to both `VoiceCall.ring()` and `SMS.alert()`.

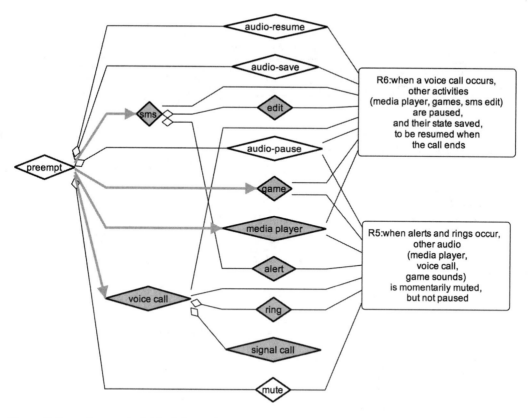

Figure 8–6   *Preempt individual-theme view.*

Several design choices are carried out in the `Preempt` theme design. Notice that the `mute`, `restore`, `pause`, `save`, and `resume` behaviors are all template parameters. This reveals the assumption that the base themes will all have their own such behavior to which these parameters can be bound. This choice was made because of a belief that these methods would be used more widely than just for this theme. For example, muting and pausing are both functions that the media player (and in fact all `Audible` classes) needs regardless of audio preemption. However, if these methods were used *only* by this theme, it would be a better design strategy to specify their behavior within the **preempt** theme rather than place them in the base just as hooks.

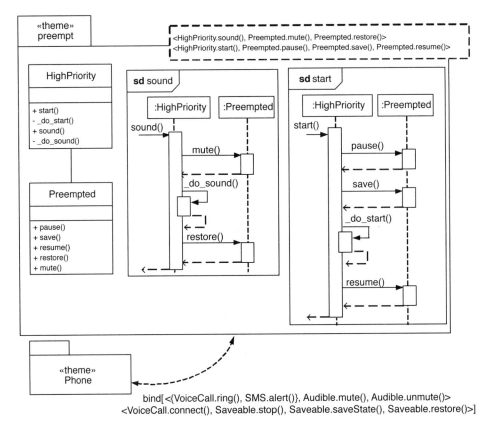

Figure 8–7   *Preempt design bound to the base phone theme.*

Referring back to Figure 8–6 you can see, once again, the grouping of **ring** as a subtheme of **voice call** and **alert** as a subtheme of **sms**. We noted earlier that we might have also chosen to group **ring** and **alert** under the **preempt** theme. Such a grouping would have altered the design of both the base and this theme. Had we chosen to perform this grouping, the **preempt** theme view would have looked like Figure 8–8, in which the **signal sms**, **signal call**, **alert**, and **ring** themes are all local to **preempt**. The **sms** and **voice call** themes would not have needed `ring()` or `alert()` methods, since notification behavior (specified in R3 and R4) would have been handled by the **preempt** theme. The left-hand sequence diagram in the **preempt** Theme/UML design in Figure 8–7 would be only slightly changed to invoke the ring sound. R5 now becomes an internally triggered requirement, since the alerts and rings would be coming from within the **preempt** theme.

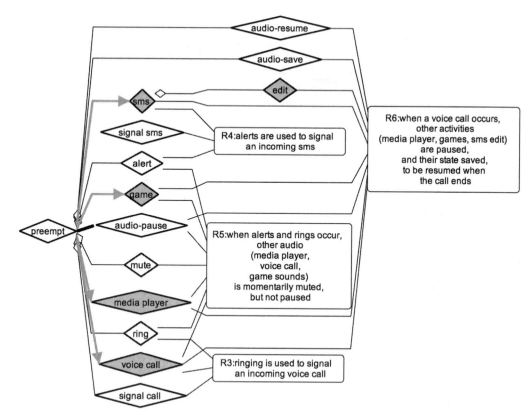

audio-resume

audio-save

edit

sms

signal sms

R4:alerts are used to signal
an incoming sms

R6:when a voice call occurs,
other activities
(media player, games, sms edit)
are paused,
and their state saved,
to be resumed when
the call ends

alert

game

preempt

audio-pause

R5:when alerts and rings occur,
other audio
(media player,
voice call,
game sounds)
is momentarily muted,
but not paused

mute

media player

ring

voice call

R3:ringing is used to signal
an incoming voice call

signal call

Figure 8–8   *Preempt individual view, had we chosen to group ring and alert with preempt.*

Figure 8–9 shows the design for option 2 (grouping **alert** and **ring** under **preempt**). You can see that the ringing and beeping is explicitly invoked from within this theme, rather than using a template parameter as was done in the design shown in Figure 8–7. Two separate sequence diagrams provide the functionality described in R3, R4, and R5: One responds to incoming voice calls (sd `Ring.incoming`), and one responds to incoming SMSs (sd `Beep.incoming`). The third sequence diagram (sd `start`) is the same as the sd `start` from Figure 8–7. It remains unchanged since the behavior of the response to an actual voice call connection was not altered by the regrouping.

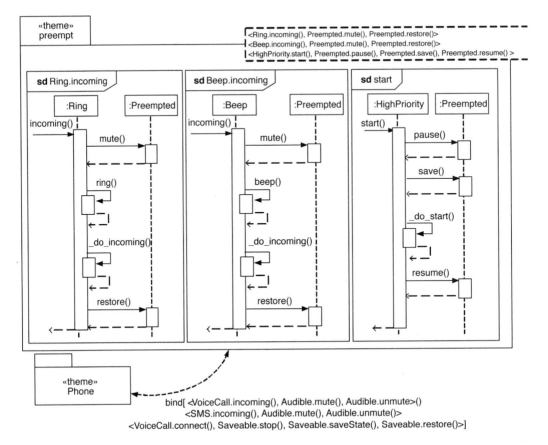

Figure 8–9   *Preempt design for Option 2.*

At this point, we may rethink our earlier choice and decide that we should have chosen the second option. We might even choose a third option and encapsulate all ringing and alerts in one **audio** theme, or a fourth, and make separate **ring** and **beep** themes. It's likely that when you reach design, you will find that some of your early choices were less than ideal. It is fine to make new choices at design and reflect those choices by reassociating or regrouping themes at the Theme/Doc level. By propagating those changes backwards, you both enhance system traceability from design back to requirements and get a sense of how your new choices affect the other theme relationships in your system.

Summary

In this chapter, we went over designing a scaled-down set of phone features. This case study illustrated that design choices can motivate reworking of decisions made in the earlier analysis phases of the Theme process. In the next chapter, we present another case study: the use of the Theme approach for capturing software-licensing concerns.

9

Case Study 2: Usage Licensing

Generally speaking, software licensing involves allowing or disallowing software usage based on a certain usage rights model. In this case study, we look at an implementation of software licensing in which usage rights are enforced according to models specific to particular applications.

In this example, developers upload their applications onto a server. Users (or purchasers) can then download the application and choose a usage model they would like to employ. Usage models might include a single payment for a piece of software or a license to use only certain features of an application. Purchasers then download the application together with the usage model, and the code appropriate for enforcing the model they have chosen. Once they begin to use the application, the enforcement code checks the usage rights at the correct intervals.

Figure 9–1 shows the initial use case for the system. The vendor uploads and registers the application, along with whichever usage models are appropriate for the application's deployment. The purchaser can then select an application and a usage model. Downloading the application prompts the composition of the application with the model chosen by the purchaser.

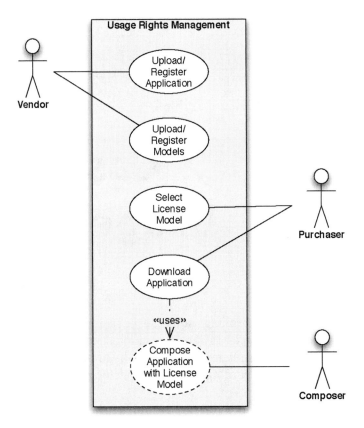

Figure 9–1   *Registration, upload, and download use case.*

You may have noticed that in Figure 9-1, the "Compose Application with License Model" action is shown as dashed. The dashed line highlights the fact that this approach suggests dynamic composition of themes; it is a user of the system, not the designer of the system, who decides what should be composed and who triggers the composition (by downloading the application and model).

Figure 9–2 shows the use case in which the purchaser actually launches the application. As you can see, the application makes use of enforcement code resident on the client, as downloaded with the application.

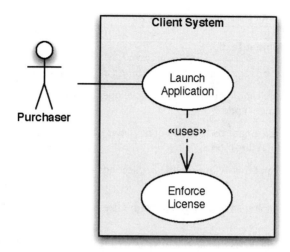

Figure 9–2   *Application-usage and license-model enforcement use case.*

This chapter goes over the requirements for the application licensing system and works through refining a set of themes (both crosscutting and base). It also gives high-level detail on how to move from some of the Theme/UML designs described to implementation in AspectJ.

Requirements

The set of requirements for the system is listed in Table 9–1. These requirements give more detail on the functionality of the system described above.

Table 9–1 *Requirements for the Software Licensing Application*

R No.	Requirement Text
R1	Application developers must register applications with the server.
R2	Application registering results in the assignment of a unique number generated to identify all clients.
R3	After application registration, developers and vendors can register applications for distribution, including registration of application details, system requirements, and usage rights models for a particular application.

Table 9–1 *Requirements for the Software Licensing Application (cont.)*

R No.	Requirement Text
R4	Application registering includes entering authentication information and contact details.
R5	After application registration, the developer uploads the application and the usage rights enforcement code.
R6	The enforcement code allows or disallows usage of an application according to a particular usage rights model.
R7	A user can browse through the applications and download applications and particular licenses.
R8	Downloading an application packages the application with the chosen usage rights model.
R9	The usage rights management system (server) must be used to verify and enforce usage rights according to specific models.
R10	Whenever an application is launched, the usage rights should be checked according to the relevant model.
R11	Several usage rights models may be enforced: unlimited-usage named-user license time-limited feature-based subscription-based pay-per-use audit-based concurrent node-locked
R12	Unlimited-usage: With this model, the server retains evidence of a single payment by the client, which, when found, allows usage.
R13	Named-user license: Clients provide their identification, and their registration is checked.
R14	Under a named-user license, if a client is registered for use, usage is allowed.
R15	Time-limited: The client retains a log of when the license started and its expiry date.
R16	Once the time limit is reached, usage is disallowed.
R17	Feature-based: When a feature is invoked, the client checks usage rights from the server.
R18	In feature-based, usage is allowed based on identity.

Table 9–1 *Requirements for the Software Licensing Application (cont.)*

R No.	Requirement Text
R19	Subscription-based: The user pays a monthly fee and checks at application launch whether the fee has been received.
R20	Pay-per-use or audit-based: Each time an application is launched, the client is billed.
R21	Node-locked: Usage is allowed based on node-identification such as IP address.
R22	In an audit-based model, users must send the logs of the previous application usage to the server for billing.
R23	Concurrent usage: A certain number of nodes or users are allowed to access the application at a time.
R24	In the concurrent model, users can satisfy the usage rights for the application only if the number of users who have concurrent usage rights at any one time does not exceed the maximum number of granted rights.
R25	The audit-based model, pay-per-use model, and concurrent usage model require server contact to determine usage allowance.
R26	For pay-per-use, audit-based, and feature-based models, usage data is logged at application launch and, additionally, according to the usage model.
R27	For the audit-based model, the logged usage data is sent to the server once a month for customer billing purposes.
R28	The time-limited model can be extended by purchasing a new license with a new expiry date.

Refining the Set of Themes

As usual, we go through the requirements and select key terms that are our potential themes. We identify all the pieces of behavior that we can.

We can also use the behavior depicted in the use case as behaviors in our list of potential themes. Here, the use cases can give us hints as to which pieces of behavior (such as downloading and certain kinds of registration) might be important and which represent separable functionality. It is not necessarily the case, though, that each action-bubble in a use case will become a theme down the road, but the high-level thinking that went into specifying the use case can be drawn upon here. In other circumstances, and depending on the use case, you might decide the entire thing deserves to be a theme. That's fine. Obviously, the granularity of a use case is not fixed, and neither is the breadth of responsibility of a theme, so the knowledge that went into the use case can be more helpful here than trying to form any rigid mapping.

We also include each of the licensing models as a separate potential theme. This choice is made because, from a read of the requirements, it seems as though separate processing is needed to evaluate different licensing models.

We arrive at the following set of themes:

allow (or disallow)	**download**	**pay-per-use**
application registra-tion (or register appli-cations, application registering)	**enforce**	**send (or sent)**
	extend	**server contact**
	feature-based	**subscription-based**
	identify	**time limited**
audit-based	**launch**	**unlimited-usage**
bill	**log**	**upload**
browse	**named-user license**	**usage registration (or registered for use)**
concurrent	**node-locked**	

As you can see, we incorporated the step of locating synonyms in the requirements into the initial identification process. The synonyms we have identified are listed in parentheses.

These themes result in the theme-relationship view shown in Figure 9–3. We must now group and refine the set of themes.

Remove Minor Themes

As you might have guessed, there is a **log** theme in the proposed set. But let's take a closer look at the requirements that mention the **log** theme, just to ensure that we really have crosscutting behavior. Figure 9–4 shows the four requirements that mention logging. Each one is significantly different,

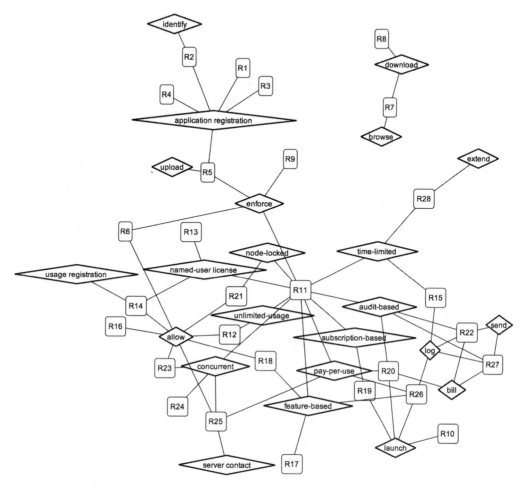

Figure 9–3   *Licensing system, initial relationship view.*

though they each refer, conceptually, to logging. One response to this variety in behavior might be to include all four kinds of logging in one logging theme. Another response might be to remove the **log** theme altogether and place the appropriate functionality into the other themes that require it. For instance, if we wind up with a **pay-per-use** theme, it will handle its own logging at application launch. This second alternative makes better sense when thinking from an aspect-oriented perspective. The logging functionality may seem as if it should be crosscutting, but it in fact isn't. Remember that

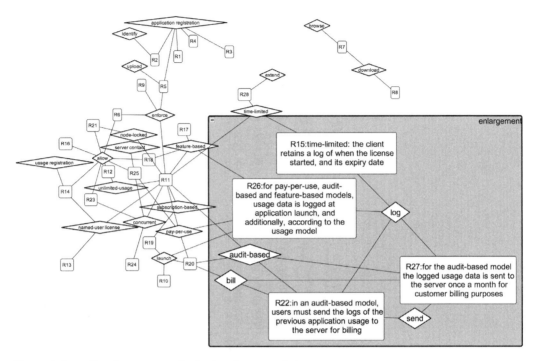

Figure 9–4 *Requirements mentioning logging expanded.*

the final step in determining whether a potential aspect is an aspect is checking whether the theme's functionality is repeated in multiple situations. If functionality is special to one situation in a base theme (as in these four special cases of logging), it should remain in that location in the base theme. So, according to that reasoning, we remove the **log** theme. Of course, logging functionality is still implemented where appropriate; it just isn't enclosed in a theme of its own.

The **send** theme is another theme that is likely not really significant. The potential **send** theme is mentioned with relation to sending logs and billing information to the server (R22: *In an audit-based model, users must send the logs of the previous application usage to the server for billing;* and R27: *For the audit-based model, the logged usage data is sent to the server once a month for customer billing purposes*). Usage data is sent to the server only in the context of the audit-based licensing model. For this reason, we decide that **send**, too, should be removed.

Since this is a partial list of requirements, it is likely that more functionality related to **send** will be needed. You may recall from the Crystal Game example, that communication-level themes arose at design that were not explicitly mentioned in the requirements. The same thing may happen in this situation, or indeed, more requirements may be added that describe this functionality. We can add a new send theme to cover that functionality when it is identified.

Grouping Themes

The **extend** theme is mentioned in only one location in the requirements. The amount of credit a client has under the time-limited model can be extended if the client purchases more. Since extension is (currently) allowed in only one model, we can group the **extend** theme with the **time-limited** model. If, in later evolutions of the system, more models are revealed to require similar extension behavior, we can extract the **extend** theme out into its own theme again. You may recall from Chapter 6 that if you were to specify new functionality that is to take the place of old functionality, the override composition relationship can be used. In this case, if we broke out a whole new **extend** theme, we could either move the extend functionality to that theme or override the license extension behavior in the **audit-based** theme.

Two fairly obvious groups are **upload/identify/application registration**, (present in requirements R1–R5) and **download/browse** (present in requirements R7 and R8). Uploading and identification only happen at the time of application registration, so these make a nice natural group of functionality. Downloading and browsing also mesh well together.

The final grouping made here is **allow/enforce**. These two terms represent two sides of the same coin: allowing a client to exercise usage rights is the same as enforcing the usage rights. If you look at the requirement shared by the two proposed themes (R6: *The enforcement code allows or disallows usage of an application according to a particular usage rights model*), it is clear that the term *allow* actually refers to license enforcement. Because the senses of these words are so similar, it seems logical to group them.

Once these themes are grouped, we arrive at the relationship view shown in Figure 9–5.

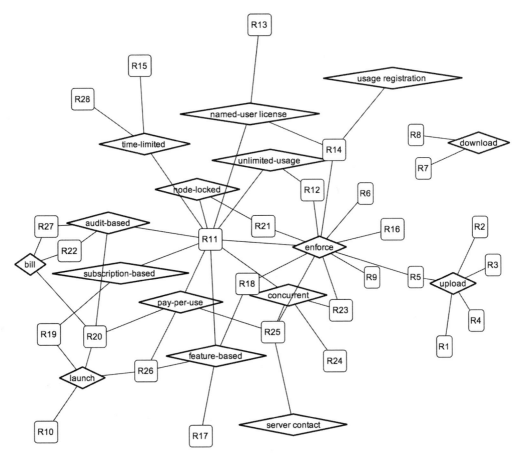

Figure 9–5   *Relationship view with removed and grouped themes.*

Dividing Behavioral Responsibilities

We now have many themes, each of which makes sense as an independent-ly understandable feature of the system. We essentially have one theme for each license model, a theme for billing, a theme for downloading, two for registration (vendor and purchaser), one for enforcement, and one for serv-er contact. As you can see, there are many shared requirements, which means we're not yet clear which theme should be responsible for which behavior. The next step is to address the relationships between these themes to determine how functionality should be parceled out.

To begin thinking about the shared requirements, it might be helpful to expand them in the relationship view. Figure 9–6 shows the same relationship view as in Figure 9–5, but with some of the shared requirements expanded.

We now go through each shared requirement and see which themes should take responsibility for them.

Requirements to Split

R20 and R26 are shared requirements that can be rewritten to remove theme overlap. R20 (*Pay-per-use or audit-based: Each time an application is launched, the client is billed*), for instance, can be changed into R29: *In pay-per-use, each time an application is launched, the client is billed*, and similarly, R30: *In audit-based, each time an application is launched, the client is billed.*

R25 (*The audit-based model, pay-per-use model, and concurrent usage model require server contact to determine usage allowance*) is a shared requirement between three licensing models and between the **server contact** theme. The fact that this requirement doesn't mention anything specific about how the server should be contacted suggests that **server contact** should be removed for now. When new requirements are elicited that make clear the kind of special behavior required for server contact, it will be straightforward to add in a **server contact** crosscutting theme that pre-empts regular server contact behavior and performs its own function. To handle the sharing of R25, it's necessary to split it into three requirements, in the same way as we split R20 and R26.

Requirements to Postpone

R5 (*After application registration, the developer uploads the application and the usage rights enforcement code*) links the **enforce** theme and the **application registration** theme. It explains that the application registration must happen before the usage rights enforcement code is downloaded.

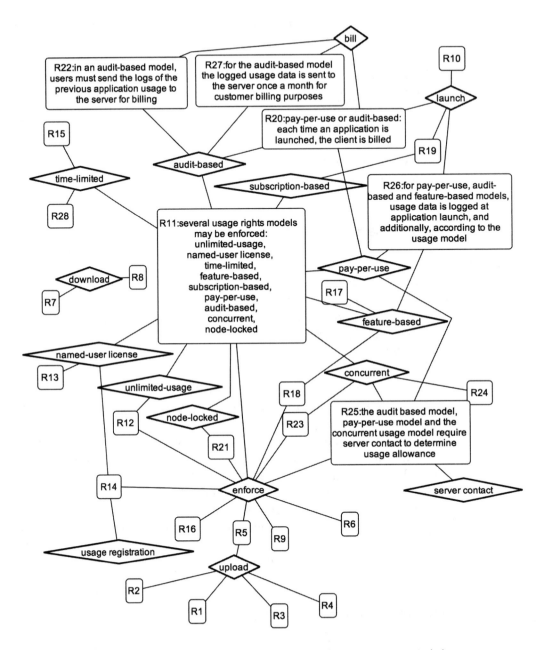

Figure 9–6   *Relationship view for the system, with some shared requirements expanded.*

This will likely be handled by a check for proof of registration when a developer tries to upload the application. Since this requirement cannot be split, and since it refers to an implied ordering rather than a triggering relationship between the themes, it is postponed.

R14 (*Under a named-user license, if a client is registered for use, usage is allowed.*) is shared between **user registration** and **named-user license**. This requirement also refers to user registration in quite broad terms and does not refer to its functionality directly, but to a check of whether usage registration has occurred. The best option for this requirement is to postpone decisions about the functionality, as we did with R5. While it is true that the requirement describes a kind of precedence (that a named-user license checks that usage registration has been done), it is not the case that license checks necessarily happen before usage registration has been performed. A purchaser might attempt to use a license, but without having registered. In order to determine whether or not a user is registered, the **license checking** theme will likely access registration logs shared by the two themes.

Requirements Shared by the Enforce Theme

The most prominent shared requirement is R11, which lists all the usage rights models that can be enforced. Though this is a straightforward listing, it reveals something quite important about the functionality to be provided by this system. Many different models are to be put in place, but the fact of their enforcement is common to all of them. Ultimately, once the license model is checked, usage rights are either granted or not granted. This suggests that enforcement is actually a behavior triggered by each of the individual models. Enforcement as an aspect is also supported by the dominance-means-association heuristic of associating a requirement with the theme that most dominates it. While R11 lists many themes, it is clearly the concept of enforcement that is dominant. Because R11 cannot be split, **enforce** dominates the requirement, and **enforce** is triggered by the license models, we associate R11 with the **enforce** theme. That association means that the **enforce** theme is an aspect of all the other licensing model themes.

But, the relationship between **enforce** and the licensing model themes is not that simple. Each license model theme has other requirements that discuss the concept of enforcement, but from its own perspective. Requirements such as R12 (*Unlimited-usage: With this model, the server retains evidence of a single payment by the client, which, when found, allows usage.*) describe very specifically what it takes to get usage access under particular models. R12 is dominated by the description of the **unlimited-usage** license model, even though the **enforce** theme behavior (**allow**) is triggered. R12 fails the third aspect-identification test: the dominant theme must also be the triggered theme. This means that R12 does *not* reveal an aspect relationship between **enforce** and **unlimited-usage**. As it stands, the **enforce** theme (which at the moment encompasses **allow**) both crosscuts (from R11) and does *not* crosscut (from R12) the licensing model themes. This is a contradiction that we must resolve to determine how to move forward to design. One way to handle this contradiction is by removing the **enforce** theme altogether. However, the enforcement behavior *is* crosscutting, so we want to keep it in an aspect theme. Also, our earlier reasoning already ruled out removing the **enforce** theme and letting each licensing model enforce itself. We need to carefully consider how to handle the relationship between the **enforce** theme and the individual licensing model themes.

In this case, we can use intuition to see that these license model requirements do not describe in any detail what it *means* to deny usage (how to control access); they only describe situations in which denial is appropriate (how to detect allowance). It makes sense that usage denial (control) should be in the domain of the **enforce** theme, whereas determining access (detection) should stay with the license model themes.

Recall that we made an early decision to group **enforce** and **allow**, stating that these are two sides of the same coin. We can see now that the distinction between **allow** and **enforce** is, in fact, the very difference between the concept of the detecting rights (determining allowance) and actually imposing control or denying usage rights (enforcing). We can simplify our reasoning considerably if we backtrack to remove the **allow** theme and let it be handled by each license model theme individually.

Figure 9–7 shows the far more straightforward relationship between the **enforce** theme and the individual license model themes. Associating R11 with the **enforce** theme results in the crosscutting view shown in Figure 9-8.

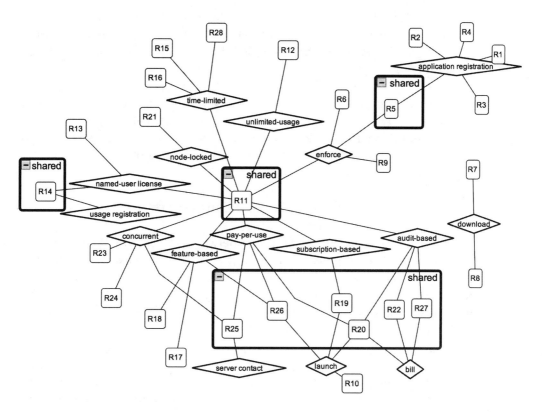

Figure 9–7   *New relationship view with the allow theme removed.*

Requirements Shared by the Bill Theme

R20, R22, and R27 are all requirements shared with the **bill** theme. The boundaries between what should be billing functionality and what should be license evaluation functionality are very blurred. If we really consider these three requirements, we can see that billing is not described in any depth. Really, there are some requirements missing: the ones that describe actual billing functionality. For instance, perhaps e-commerce functionality is needed to bill customers. Or perhaps an e-mail is sent to them. None of this is described. Though these requirements mention billing and tell us that we need some kind of billing functionality, the requirements here are certainly more associated with each individual licensing model theme than with the concept of billing. We need to backtrack and remove the **bill** theme as it's described here. Removing the **bill** theme takes care of the sharing of R22 and R27.

Later in our development phase, however, we would need to provide answers to all those questions about how billing is really carried out. Those new requirements would then be added to the set, and a new **bill** theme would be introduced to accommodate them as appropriate.

Requirements Shared by the Launch Theme

The final shared requirements are between some of the license models and the **launch** theme. R19 (*Subscription-based: The user pays a monthly fee and checks at application launch whether the fee has been received*) is one of those requirements. The others are R29, R30, R31, R32, and R33. Those requirements are the result of splitting R20 (*Pay-per-use or audit-based: Each time an application is launched, the client is billed*) into R29 and R30, and splitting R26 (*For pay-per-use, audit-based, and feature-based models, usage data is logged at application launch and, additionally, according to the usage model*) into R31, R32, and R33. We consider these requirements in a bundle for brevity. R29, for instance, reads, *In pay-per-use, each time an application is launched, the client is billed*. This requirement has already been split as far as it can be. There is no way to decouple billing (which is now in the domain of each of the licensing models, and not a theme in its own right) from application launch. The theme is dominated by the concept of billing and hence by the particular license model. The billing is triggered by the application launch. In this case, we have identified that the billing behavior (hence the **pay-per-use** theme) is an aspect of the **launch** theme. This determination is made because a theme that is both dominant and triggered by the other themes in a requirement crosscuts those other themes.

Figure 9–8 shows the resultant crosscutting hierarchy for the licensing system. As you can see, all of the licensing models are crosscut by the enforcement theme. Some of the licensing models crosscut the launch theme.

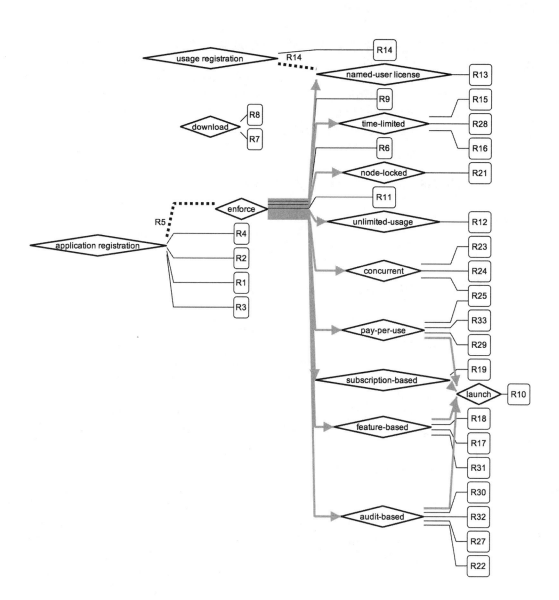

Figure 9–8   *Crosscutting view.*

Designing the Themes

Now that we have an overall concept of how the themes of the system should fit together, we can move forward to designing them using Theme/UML. You may recall that there are essentially two portions to this system: the registration/upload/download portion (as described in the use case depicted in Figure 9–1 and the application-usage and license-enforcement portion (described in Figure 9–2).

Registration/Download Themes

There are three themes that cover the functionality for application and usage registration and download. We will now discuss each theme and then address how they are merged together.

Application Registration

Application registration is described in the first five requirements of the set. This theme is fairly straightforward, though it contains a significant amount of functionality. It provides all the registration functionality for vendors, collects authentication information, and prompts and handles the upload of applications and licensing models to the server. Here, however, we won't provide a design for this theme, since it doesn't reflect anything interesting from an aspect-oriented perspective.

Usage Registration

In the set of requirements for this case study, there are no requirements central to the concept of usage registration. Earlier, we decided to remove the **bill** and **server contact** themes for this same reason. We could have made the same choice with the **usage registration** theme, but in this case we choose to keep it in and design it using placeholders for when more details about its functionality are elicited. Once these details are determined, they can be reflected in the requirements set, and the Theme/Doc diagrams shown in the previous section can be regenerated automatically to reflect the additions. The option of using placeholder designs for **bill** and **server contact** was also available to us. As Figure 9–9 shows, we've added a theme that contains the most basic concepts of a registration theme.

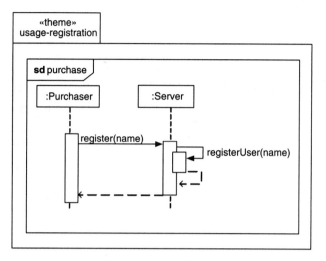

Figure 9–9   *Usage registration design.*

Download

This theme provides functionality for downloading the application. It also sparks the composition of the **application launch** and **licensing** themes. The **download** theme allows a user to select an application and a usage model (for instance, a document editor program on a 30-day trial license), and then download the application, which would be compiled together with enforcement code for that type of license. This kind of functionality requires a dynamic composition model and appropriate implementation language support, since the composition specification is made not by the initial developer, but by a running system. Theme/UML has no specific notation for dynamically determining binding. Instead, as Figure 9–10 illustrates, we use the standard UML approach and annotate the **download** theme with a note that indicates that at the point of download, the binding for the application and license model is determined and performed. This note is a reminder that weaving the selected license model with the requested application must take place at runtime. Later (Figures 9–15 and 9–16), we present examples of an application combined with different licensing models.

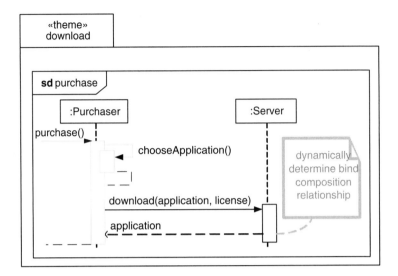

Figure 9–10   *Download theme, showing invocation of the dynamic determination of the bind specification for the application and license model.*

Composing Application Registration, Usage Registration, and Download

No special ordering relationships are needed to compose this group of themes. Using the `match[name]` attachment to the composition relationship to compose all three is sufficient.

Licensing Themes

In the requirements provided for this case study, eight licensing models are described. Interestingly, only four of them explicitly mention at which point the license should be checked (**feature-based**, **subscription-based**, **pay-per-use**, and **audit-based**). As you can see by looking at the crosscutting Theme/Doc view (Figure 9–8), these four explicitly note that the license should be checked at launch time. Individual requirements specify whether the launch should be a feature-launch or the launch of the entire application. While designing the internal details of the four other licensing themes comes a little later, it is straightforward to assume that these four will also crosscut the launch theme and so will have template parameters that bind to application or feature launch. A sketch of this is shown in Figure 9–11. Examples of the actual composition relationships with bind[] specifications are shown for the **feature-based** licensing model (Figure 9–15) and for the **time-limited** licensing model (Figure 9–16).

Now that we come to design the licensing themes, it is imperative that we determine when the other four licenses should be checked. Inspecting the requirements associated with those licenses, an implicit assumption that they are checked at launch time is evident. This represents another instance at which we can backtrack to take functionality into account that wasn't explicitly mentioned in the requirements. It is fairly straightforward to add

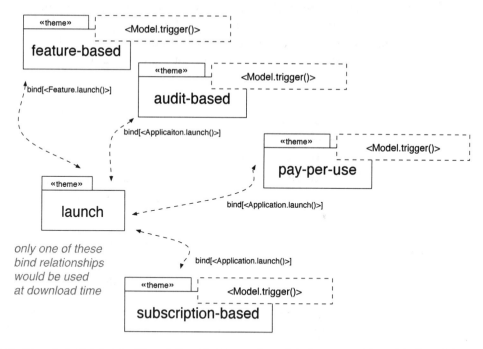

Figure 9–11   *An initial sketch of the relationship between four of the license models and the launch base theme. Only one of the bind relationships would be chosen upon the download request from the purchaser.*

the requirements that describe when the other licenses are checked and to regenerate the diagrams. This regeneration would reflect that each of the other licensing model themes crosscuts the launch theme. Their overall template and binding design are the same as those depicted in Figure 9–11.

Each model actually performs its own checking and keeps track of all the information necessary to determine whether usage should be allowed. Any logging that's needed happens within the particular model. We will see an example of a model design in Figures 9–15 and 9–16. The overall binding and template structure so far is shown in Figure 9–12.

The launch theme shown in Figure 9–11 and Figure 9–12 handles the application and feature startup. Figure 9–13 shows the structural design for the launch theme.

Next, we put in place the license-enforcement functionality. The individual model themes check whether the license is valid or invalid, but what happens once that determination is made belongs to the yet undesigned **enforce** theme. As discussed earlier, enforcement could have been built into each licensing model. For instance, looking at Figure 9–12, you can see that the

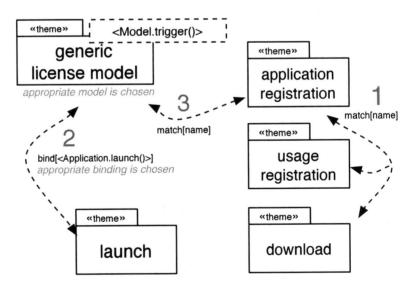

Figure 9–12   *Overall design for the registration and license model themes.*

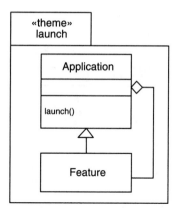

Figure 9–13   *Structural design for the launch theme.*

generic license model theme is triggered by the `Application.launch()` method. Since Theme/UML leaves the actual invocation of a trigger method up to the aspect theme, it would be straightforward to simply never call the real `Application.launch()` method from within the triggered **model** theme. This would effectively deny usage based on the check that occurred in the model. However, this separation is handy, since at some future point, you may want to alter the way in which enforcement occurs without having to change every underlying licensing model. You may, for example, want to issue a warning message rather than simply denying service. Changing that warning method behavior is more convenient if it is encapsulated in the enforcement theme.

The **enforce** theme crosscuts the license themes. Its role is to intercept the license checking, grab the result of the check (whether the license is valid or invalid), and then deny usage if the check is not valid. The **enforce** theme can be designed as depicted in Figure 9–14. Notice that the current denial of service is simply a system exit (the application is killed). If you want something more elegant to happen, that functionality could be inserted in addition to the call to `exit()`. Notice also that there is no "continue" behavior described in the **enforce** theme. The underlying license model theme (which we look at next) is what allows the application to continue start-up if no enforcement action was taken. The rest of the behavior of the model theme is continued after the final return from the **enforce** theme.

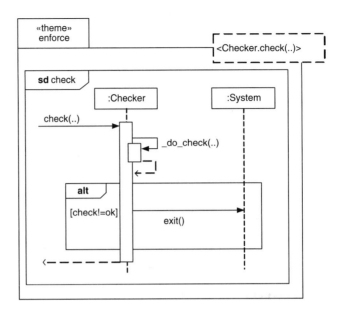

Figure 9–14   *Design of the enforce theme.*

Figure 9–15 depicts the **feature-based** license model-checking functionality and also the tailored binding specification for the bundled application. Both binding specifications (1 and 2, as marked in the figure) are generated automatically, and composition is performed automatically. The way in which this is carried out depends on the capabilities of the language you choose. We do not delve into dynamic aspect-language details in this book, however.

You can see that the **feature-based** license actually has two sequence diagrams, one for catching the start of features (at which point the license is checked) and another for triggering logging functionality (which takes place only at application start-up). Had logging occurred at the same time as the license checking, the logging functionality would have been included in the checking sequence diagram. You may recall that it is not allowed in Theme/UML to have two sequence diagrams within a theme both triggered by the same behavior.

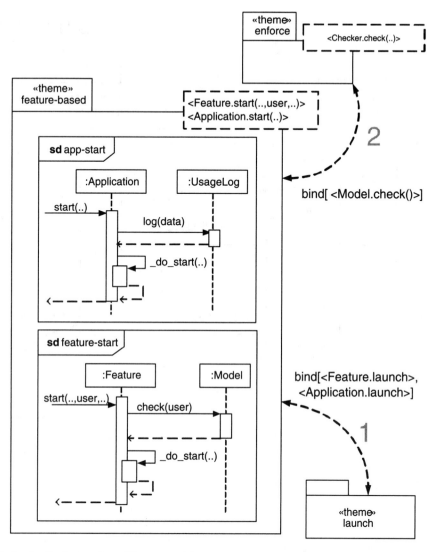

Figure 9–15   *Design for the feature-based license model.*

Figure 9–16 shows another example of a license model bound to the **enforce** theme and the base **launch** theme. In this case, the trigger for enforcement is the start of time-logging.

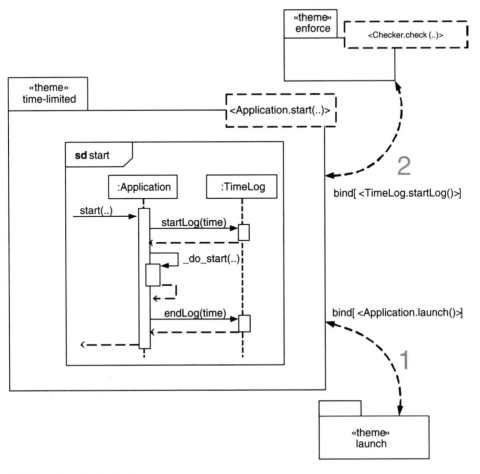

Figure 9–16   *Time-limited design.*

Looking at Code

We now take a quick look at some AspectJ placeholder code for the application and license model part of our system. This code is presented just to give a concrete sense of how this design might be carried out. The approach used to map the themes to implementation is slightly different from that described in Chapter 7. In that chapter, abstract aspects were used to capture the separation between the template methods (which became abstract pointcuts) and the bind specifications (which became concrete pointcuts).

Here, for convenience, we use concrete aspects and concrete pointcuts to mix the semantics of the Theme/UML templates and binding specifications. Of course, we lose the separation that the abstract pointcut approach gives us. First, we describe the base class, and then the AspectJ aspects used to implement the **generic licensing model** theme and the **enforce** theme.

Listing 9–1 shows some placeholder AspectJ code for the base application. It defines a simple class, `Application`, that contains one method, `start()`.

Listing 9–1 *Application Theme as Core AspectJ Code*

```
public class Application {
  public static void main(String [] args) {
    Application a = new Application();
    a.start ();
  }
  public void start(){
    System.out.println("Request Start");
  }
}
```

Listing 9–2 provides an outline for a **generic license model** theme as it would appear in AspectJ as an aspect. Here, we have defined a concrete pointcut (`checkModel()`) that specifies application start-up as the join-point of interest. The `checkModel()` before advice occurs on execution of the `Application.start()` method. The **model** theme contains one method, `check()`, that performs all the necessary checking for the validity of the usage license. It returns true or false, depending on the results of this check. Another option would have been to place the license-usage checking inside the `checkMethod()` advice. We discuss the implications of each option when we go over the next aspect, `Enforce`.

Listing 9-2 *Generic License Model Theme as an AspectJ Aspect*

```
public aspect Model {
  pointcut checkModel(): execution
                        (* Application.start (..));
  before(): checkModel(){
    System.out.println("checking...");
    check();
  }
  public boolean check(){
    //perform all license usage checking
    return resultOfChecking;
  }
}
```

The **enforce** theme is described in Listing 9–3 as an AspectJ aspect. It contains one `after` `returning` advice on its `enforce()` pointcut. The enforce pointcut is bound to the execution of the `Model.check()` method, which is defined in the `Model` aspect shown in Listing 9–2. Had we chosen to place the license-usage checking directly inside the `checkModel()` before advice, we would have had to use a different construct, the pointcut declaration, to define the pointcut:

```
pointcut enforce: adviceexecution() && within(Model);
```

`adviceexecution()` is a construct that selects all advice execution joinpoints. The `within(Model)` specification denotes that the advice that is being executed should be within the `Model` aspect (it selects all execution within the named class or aspect). The above enforce pointcut designator selects all the joinpoints that are the execution of advice within the `Model` aspect. This construct is useful to us only if there is just one advice in the aspect. At the time of writing, there is no way to specify *which* advice execution joinpoint to select based on its pointcut name.[1] In this case, that is not a problem, since `Model` has only one advice. But in general, we would choose to place aspect functionality that we want to crosscut into a method rather than straight into the advice.

---

[1] It is likely that in the future, `adviceexecution` will be able to identify specific advice through use of annotations. Still, the approach suggested here (using a method to capture advice behavior) is probably preferred.

In the `Enforce` aspect, an `after returning` advice is used. The result returned by the `Model.check(..)` method is captured, and action can be taken depending whether the result is true or false. If the check fails (returns an invalid result), then a system call to `exit()` is made to stop execution of the application. Otherwise, application start-up is allowed to continue.

Listing 9–3 *Generic Enforce Theme as an AspectJ Aspect*

```
public aspect Enforce {
  pointcut enforce(): execution (boolean Model.check(..));
  after() returning(boolean valid) : enforce(){
    if(!valid) {
      System.out.println("Your License Has Expired");
      System.exit(1);
    }
    else{
      System.out.println("You have a valid license");
    }
    return valid;
}}
```

Summary

This chapter presented a case study on using the Theme approach for a software-usage licensing system. As we did in the previous chapter, we used an abbreviated Theme/Doc approach in which no individual theme views were used. That choice was made because the requirements were few enough that we could keep in mind what the structure of the themes should be without needing additional reminders or clues.

We then walked through designing the two-part system. The first part covered the functionality set out by the first use case (refer to Figure 9–1) and comprised three base themes (**usage registration**, **application registration**, and **download**), which were composed together. The second part addressed the second use case (refer to Figure 9–2) in which purchasers use the application they downloaded. Usage was allowed depending on the license model selected at the time of downloading. Three themes would be involved in any composition of this part of the system: the

enforce theme, the **launch** theme (which runs the application), and the chosen license model theme. The **enforce** theme was designed to crosscut the license model theme, which in turn crosscuts the **launch** theme.

Finally, we went over some code examples of how to implement the second use case in AspectJ. Rather than using abstract aspects, as discussed in Chapter 7, we chose to fuse the implementation of the bind relationship with the template parameters found in the Theme/UML model.

The Crystal Game

The sample system used throughout this book is a location-aware game called the Crystal Game. It takes place in a setting fitted with the proper sensors for capturing location information about the players. The setting has virtual crystals sprinkled around it. The object of the game is to obtain as many virtual crystals as possible before the time period of the game is up. Players with handheld devices roam around the game area. Their devices inform them when they have found crystals, which have been hidden around the game-play area. They also are informed when they have encountered another player or a nonplayer (computer-generated) character (NPC).

This appendix presents all of the requirements for the Crystal Game. Each requirement is numbered to simplify identification. Most of these requirements describe very specific behavior. Some are relatively ambiguous. Ultimately, we must refine all of the requirements and resolve all of their ambiguities. Most of the requirements presented here have already had their ambiguities resolved and have been refined as far as is needed. Some have been left ambiguous so that we can use them in the book as examples of how to identify ambiguous requirements and refine them.

Requirements for the Crystal Game

Game Setup

R1:   The user interface of the game should show a layout of the game boundary and game locations.

R2:   Location is defined by four points, forming a rectangle, and is outdoors.

R3:   The game boundaries are defined by four points.

R4:   Not all points within the game boundaries are inside game locations.

Player and Nonplayer Character Types

R5:   There are three basic player types: wizard, warrior, and sage.

R6:   Each player type has its own user interface and user options.

R7:   Every nonplayer character in the game is also one of these three types.

Starting the Game

R8:   Players can either initiate a new game or join an existing game.

Creating a New Game

R9:   Players select a game by name to join game group.

R10:   One player is chosen to create a new game.

R11:   To create a new game, a player chooses *Begin New* from the Options menu.

R12:   The player is then prompted to enter a port number for the new game.

R13:   The range of port numbers that are permitted is 3000 to 5000.

R14:   Multiple games may be created in the same location at the same time and not interfere with one another.

R15:   The player is also prompted to choose a time limit and a name for the game.

R16:   The host player's location at the time the game is created becomes the throne room.

R17:   The new game randomly distributes crystals throughout the game area.

R18:   When the game environment is initially populated with crystals, a random number of random locations are populated with a random number of crystals up to 10.

R19:   Each other player is sent to a randomly chosen location.

R20:   Players have a set amount of time to reach the location to which they are sent.

R21:   If players do not reach their initial location within the specified time, they lose 1 energy point.

R22:   Magical items are cloaks, swords, keys, and rings, and are randomly distributed around the location.

R23:   Not more than one NPC is sent to any one location.

R24:   NPCs are randomly sent to locations.

Joining an Existing Game

R25:   To join a game, a player must be in contact with a player who is already a member of the game.

R26:   The new player should choose *Join Existing* from the Options menu.

R27:   They will then be prompted to enter the machine name or IP address of the other player's device.

R28:   The other player's device then sends the game state to the new player, allowing him or her to join.

R29:   When the player joins the game, he or she is asked to choose a player type.

Playing the Game

Object of the Game

R30:   The object of the game is to collect as many crystals as possible and return them to the throne room before the time limit expires and the game ends.

R31:   Crystals can be collected by discovering them in a location in the world, interacting with characters, or dueling other players for them.

Exploring the World

R32:   Players explore the world by walking around the game-play area.

R33:   They are unconstrained in their motion except that they cannot leave the game-play area.

R34:   When players leave the game-play area or select *leave-game* from the Options menu, they automatically lose the game and drop all the crystals they carry.

R35:   Dropped crystals are rescattered throughout the game area.

R36:   If a player's game device fails, as may happen in a power failure, the player can rejoin the game with the same number of crystals and the same game state as long as he or she restarts before the end of the game.

Entering Locations

R37:   Players lose energy faster while in a location: they lose two units per five-minute period.

Obtaining Crystals

R38:   If a player enters a location that has no players or characters in it, the player may pick up any crystals or magical items they see.

R39:   Otherwise, crystals can be obtained from characters or players according to the rules below.

R40:   Players gain 10 units of energy when the game begins.

R41:   As they proceed throughout the game, their energy dissipates by one unit for each five-minute period.

R42:   Energy is gained by two units when they find a crystal upon entering a location.

User Interface

R43:   The display on the device is split into three areas: information, world-map, and local-map.

R44:   All game information is shown to the player via his or her handheld device in the information area.

R45:   The amount of time remaining is shown in the information area of the device.

R46:   The player's energy level is shown in the information area of the device.

R47:   Game elements (crystals, NPCs, magical items, player representations) are all shown on the handheld device as colored dots with labels.

R48:   A count of crystals collected is shown in the information area.

R49:   Any magical items in possession are shown by colored dots in the information area.

R50:   The player can tap on the dots to see the options available.

R51:   The world-map is shown at all times.

R52:   The world-map shows a green dot at the player's own location on the map and a yellow dot at the location of crystals in the game.

R53:   Depending on the player's type, different kinds of information are shown on his or her world-map.

R54:   Sages are shown the locations of magical items as blue dots.

R55:   Wizards are shown locations of NPCs as purple dots.

R56:   Warriors are shown locations of players as red dots.

R57:   Once a player enters a location, a local-map is displayed on his or her hand-held device.

R58:   The local-map shows a detailed view of the crystals and other magical items in the location.

R59:   Otherwise, the local- map is shown as blank.

R60:   The local-map also shows more detail about players and NPCs in the location.

Interaction Between Players

R61:   When two players meet upon entering a location, they perform a duel of rock, paper, scissors.

R62:   Each player wagers a crystal on the outcome of the duel.

R63:   If one player has no crystals they will wager the promise of the first crystal they find on the duel outcome, or they may wager two magical items in their possession.

R64:   A player may wager two crystals to force another player to wager a particular magical item in their possession.

R65:   If a player wagers two crystals for a magic item, then the other player is entitled to ask for a magic item instead.

R66:   Each player sees the other player's information in his or her own device's information area.

Interaction with Nonplayer Characters

R67:   When a player encounters a character, the character poses a challenge to that player.

R68:   The type of challenge depends on the character's type.

R69:   However, if a player meets a character of his or her same type, the character grants the player any crystals that it carries.

R70:   Players may be involved in only one duel at a time.

R71:   If there are both another player and an NPC in a location when a player arrives, the other player takes precedence over the NPC, and a duel occurs, followed by the challenge from the NPC.

R72:   Duel losers pay their debts immediately, or, if they cannot, their debts are automatically repaid when they become able.

Wizard

R73:   Wizards are magical beings.

R74:   When a player meets a wizard, the wizard sends the player to look for magical items hidden around the location.

R75:   Magical items may have already been picked up by a player; if so, that player must be located and challenged.

R76:   Players in possession of a target magical item are identified on the world-map.

R77:   Completing an errand successfully provides four units of energy to the player.

Warrior

R78:   Warriors respect physical prowess.

R79:   To win their crystal, they ask the player to run to a particular location and return within a certain time period.

R80:   When a player completes a physical test challenge successfully, they gain three units of energy and win a crystal.

Sage

R81:   Sages honor knowledge.

R82:   The sage asks a player a riddle, which, if answered correctly, is rewarded with a crystal.

Finishing the Game

R83:   Players must return to the throne room before the time limit expires and the game ends.

R84:   Failure to do so means that the player loses.

R85:   Of the players that do return in time, the one with the most crystals wins.

R86:   If more than one player has the same number of crystals, the one with more energy wins.

R87:   If more than one player has the same number of crystals and energy, then they must duel to decide which wins.

Additional Requirements

Some requirements are added through the course of Chapter 4's analysis process. They are included as follows:

R88: Players that are wizards should have magical icons and terms displayed in their user interface.

R89: When wizard characters meet players, they should speak to them using magical language.

R90: If a wizard type player meets a wizard character, the wizard gives them any crystals the wizard carries.

R91: If a sage type player meets a sage character, the sage gives them any crystals the sage carries.

R92: If a warrior type player meets a warrior character, the warrior gives them any crystals the warrior carries.

R93: Players can join an existing game.

R94: Players can start a new game.

Bibliography

Booch, Grady, James Rumbaugh, and Ivar Jacobson. *The Unified Modeling Language.* The Object Technology Series, Addison-Wesley, 1998.

Coady, Yvonne, and Gregor Kiczales. *Back to the Future: A Retroactive Study of Aspect Evolution in Operating System Code.* In the proceedings of the International Conference on Aspect-Oriented Software Development (AOSD), 2003.

Coleman, Derek, Patrick Arnold, Stephanie Bodoff, Chris Dollin, Helena Gilchrist, Fiona Hayes, and Paul Jeremes. *Object-Oriented Development: The Fusion Method.* Prentice Hall, 1994.

The Concise Oxford Dictionary. Clarendon Press, Oxford.

Cook, Steve, and John Daniels. *Designing Object Systems: Object-Oriented Modeling with Syntropy.* Prentice-Hall, 1994.

Dardenne, Anne, Axel van Lamsweerde, and Stephen Fickas. Goal-Directed Requirements Acquisition. *Science of Computer Programming*, 20:3–50, April 1993.

Dijkstra, Edsger. "On the Role of Scientific Thought," *EWD* 477, August 30, 1974. Neuen, The Netherlands.

Easterbrook, Steve. *Elicitation of Requirements from Multiple Perspectives.* Ph.D. thesis, Department of Computing, Imperial College, London. 1991.

Gamma, Erich, Richard Helm, Ralph Johnson, and John Vlissides. *Design Patterns: Elements of Object-Oriented Software*. Addison-Wesley, 1994.

Griss, Martin, John Favaro, and Massimo d'Alessandro. *Integrating Feature Modeling with the RESB*. In the proceedings of the International Conference on Software Reuse (ICSR), 1998.

Harrison, William H., Harold L. Ossher, and Peri L. Tarr. *Asymmetrically* vs. *Symmetrically Organized Paradigms for Software Composition*. IBM Research Division, Thomas J Watson Research Center, RC22685 (W0212-147), December 30, 2002.

Jackson, Michael, and Pamela Zave. "Distributed Feature Composition: A Virtual Architecture for Telecommunications Services," *IEEE TSE Special Issue on Feature Interaction*, 24(10):831–847, October 1998.

Jacobson, Ivar, Grady Booch, and James Rumbaugh. *The Unified Software Development Process*. Addison-Wesley, 1999.

Kiczales, Gregor, John Lamping, Anurag Mendhekar, Chris Maeda, Cristina Lopes, Jean-Marc Loingtier, and John Irwin. *Aspect-Oriented Programming*. In the proceedings of the European Conference on Object-Oriented Programming (ECOOP), 1997.

Mowbray, Thomas, and Ron Zahavi. *The Essential CORBA: Systems Integration Using Distributed Objects*. Object Management Group, John Wiley & Sons, 1995.

Nuseibeh, Bashar, Jeff Kramer, and Anthony Finkelstein. "A Framework for Expressing the Relationships Between Multiple Views in Requirements Specification," *IEEE Transactions on Software Engineering*, 20(10):760–773, October 1994.

Reenskaug, Trygve, Per Wold, and Odd Arild Lehne. *Working with Objects. The OOram Software Engineering Method*. Manning Publications, 1995.

Siegel, Jon. *CORBA Fundamentals and Programming*. Object Management Group, John Wiley & Sons, 1996.

Tarr, Peri, Harold Ossher, William Harrison, and Stanley M. Sutton, Jr. *N Degrees of Separation: Multi-Dimensional Separation of Concerns*. In the proceedings of the International Conference on Software Engineering (ICSE), 1999.

Wirfs-Brock, Rebecca, Brian Wilkerson, and Lauren Wiener. *Designing Object-Oriented Software*. Prentice-Hall, 1990.

Index

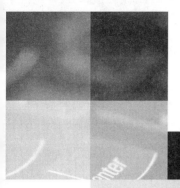

Steps Involved in Applying Theme/UML to Theme Design

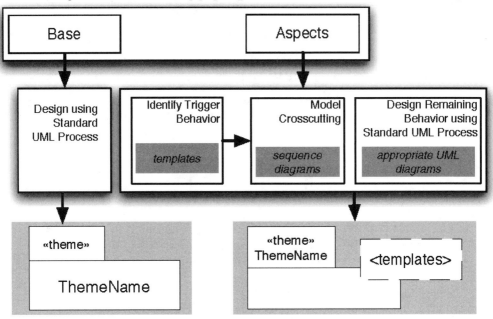

Steps Involved in Applying Theme/UML to Theme Composition

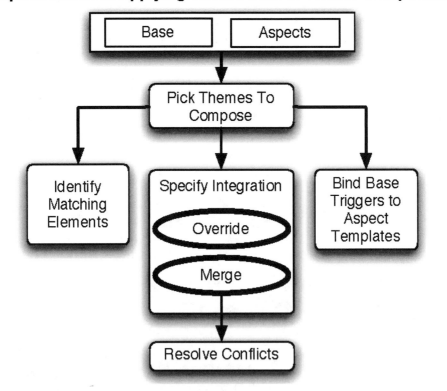